I0708542

CREATOR'S SONG
Ancient Voices Speak

CREATOR'S SONG
Ancient Voices Speak

Eva Black Tail Swan

Big Country Publishing

Creator's Song *Ancient Voices Speak*
Copyright© 2012, by Eva Black Tail Swan
Library of Congress Control Number: 2012939286
ISBN: 978-1-938487-04-0

Cover Artwork by: Jeff Hunter
Interior Basket Drawing by: Veronica A. Nowak
Cover Design: Kyle Petrove
Interior Book Design: Kyle Petrove
Back Cover Photo: M. Cory Gordon

All rights reserved. No part of this publication may be reproduced, stored in a retrieval system, or transmitted, in any form or by any means electronic, mechanical, photocopying, recording, or otherwise without prior written permission from the publisher.

The author and publisher of the book do not make any claim or guarantee for any physical, mental, emotional, spiritual, or financial result. All products, services and information provided by the author are for general education and entertainment purposes only. The information provided herein is in no way a substitute for medical or other professional advice. In the event you use any of the information contained in this book for yourself, the author and publisher assume no responsibility for your actions. Big Country Publishing, LLC accepts no responsibility or liability for any content, bibliographic references, artwork, or works cited contained in this book.

Published by
Big Country Publishing, LLC
7691 Shaffer Parkway, Suite C
Littleton, CO 80127
USA
www.bigcountrypublishing.com

Printed in the United States of America
International printing in the U.K. and Australia

For my father
and to the memory
of my father

*I dedicate this book
to the memory of my father.*

*Thank you for always being there
and for sharing the gift of your wisdom
and experience so generously,
so unconditionally.*

*Your voice can be heard in many of the
messages written on these pages,
and it speaks within my heart
each and every day.*

Thank you, Dad,

*for teaching me how to live a good life
and to know our Creator.*

GRATITUDE

My deep and sincere gratitude to my friend Michele for recognizing the power of these daily messages and for believing in me and my work. Through your advice and encouragement I stepped out of my little cave and into the warm bright Sun. I whispered the words Creator sang to me each morning upon the Wind for all the world to hear, and *Creator's Song* was born.

My deep and sincere gratitude to my friend Marti for taking on the project of reading through *three hundred and sixty five pages* of daily messages (which were written in the wee hours of the morning), and correcting all of my grammar, spelling, and typing errors. Your insight, wisdom, and recommendations were a lifeline for me as I went through each and every message and prepared them for this book.

My deep and sincere gratitude to everyone who signed up to receive *Creator's Song* as a daily message. For believing in me, for your support, for responding to the messages that touched your hearts and brought you relief, healing, understanding, growth, and expansion. You are always there, right in the front row, each and every morning as I begin ceremony. I see your faces and feel your spirits… and though I can always feel the spirits of *"all people"* each day in ceremony… it is you who walk with me… and sometimes even guide me… to the place I am to set ceremony… and to the message I am to receive. Thank you all for being a part of my morning ceremonies.

My deep and sincere gratitude to Creator. Thank you for trusting me with this most precious gift and for teaching me how to hear your song. Thank you for the gift of life… for every lesson, every joy, every breath…what an amazing journey!

My deep and sincere gratitude to you, the readers, for this book was written for you. Each morning as I set ceremony and sing the prayer songs for all people, you are the people for whom I pray. Each morning as I hear the *song* of our Creator, I know that you are the people for whom our Creator sings.

FORWARD

Eva and I were introduced by a mutual friend over two years ago, and I was immediately impressed with her warmth and humility, and instantly knew that we would become friends. Over lunch we planned a workshop that the two of us would later present. I learned that she lived about 80 miles east of Denver on a ranch with her husband, whom she referred to as "the cowboy," and a herd of buffalo. I also learned that although she had other influences, her Cherokee heritage formed the base of her spirituality, one that honored the ancestors and the Spirit-that-moves-in-all-things, yet did not judge or exclude other spiritual or religious paths.

We went on to do a very successful workshop in Estes Park, Colorado, in the heart of the Rocky Mountains. I remember Eva being nervous at first, confessing that although she offered ceremonies for groups at her ranch, doing a workshop like this was new to her. For her part of the presentation she was so open, guileless, and honest that the group was immediately charmed by her, and particularly enjoyed her storytelling. Needless to say I was delighted to share in this adventure with her and came to appreciate the remarkable depth that this woman possesses.

I began receiving the daily inspirational pieces called Creator's Song from Eva by email and admired the simple wisdom that was put forth in these writings. As I got to know her I learned that she felt she always had a connection to God, but during a period of illness in 1974, she began daily prayer for herself, her family and friends, her community, and for the Earth. She has continued this sacred ceremony every morning since then, receiving messages from Spirit that she since has started conveying to others and writing these out in the form of *The Creator's Song*.

Though in the past she has enacted this ceremony in whatever setting she found herself, these days she gets up very early every morning and walks the land on her ranch. She heeds the inner promptings of Spirit and receives messages via particular Earth elements that speak to her during these morning walks, whether the wind, the standing ones, the ancestors, or other beings. She is beyond committed to this assignment; she is devoted, and has amply demonstrated this.

In this book you'll find carefully chosen selections of these communications. Read them one at a time and savor them, meditate on them, perhaps as a daily morning ritual. Another use is when you're looking for guidance, pick up the book, open it at random, and read the message. Take your time to absorb the message, just as Nature takes her time, and you'll discover other layers of meaning. I'm sure you'll find years of inspiration and enjoyment from these readings and will find yourself seeing, hearing, and feeling the world in which we live in an entirely fresh way each and every day.

—Dr. Steven Farmer
Author of *Earth Magic, Animal Spirit Guides and Sacred Ceremony*

INTRODUCTION

A person recently asked me why I go ***out*** to ceremony every morning and create the ceremony out on the prairie, rather than call the energy of ceremony to me and stay in the in the warmth and comfort of my home. "After all", she said. "You certainly have the power to do so."

"Yes that is true" I answered. "We all have the power to call to us the energy of whatever it is we need, and most of the time that is good and right and appropriate. But when it comes to those things of God and Spirit, we have gotten far too comfortable with calling God to us rather than reaching up and out to our Divine Creator."

It seems to me that in moments of trauma or despair, in times of emergency, in times of trouble, or when dealing with the unexpected, we all just instinctively know how to call out to the Highest of all things for assistance, and this is good and right and exactly what we should be doing.

But to make (or find) time each day or each week, to go (with intention) to a place, or to gather in some way, for the simple and singular purpose of becoming sacred and ***being*** with God (Creator, the Ultimate Power… the ***Unnamable One***), has gotten pushed back in the order of priorities for many of us.

That is not to say that it is a church or organized religion that we must find and attend, and that is not to say that a church or organized religion is not the place either. For each of us have (or will find) our perfect place, and this place will be right and perfect no matter what (even if for some, that place is the quiet place within…the place of meditation or journey).

The point is not ***where*** we go, but rather ***that*** we go. That we consciously make the effort to go to the place of God…daily (or weekly)…with the pure and simple intention of just being there. For each time we make this effort, we are lifted from the mundane to the spiritual. We are immersed in the purity and perfection of all that *is* the High Place. We begin to understand what it is to simply *Be* in the presence of God (our Creator), and our inner-sacred begins to awaken and expand.

So when it is difficult for us to actually go to a place, then we can (and should) create a space and time...*a ceremony*...in the place where we are, but instead of calling our Creator to us, we should make it our practice to reach out to (and for) our Creator.

And you may wonder, "What is the difference?" Well, it is the difference of giving and receiving...of showing honor and respect and gratitude...versus expecting blessings and graces and of being entitled...

... it is the difference of going to visit your friend... rather than expecting your friend to (always) come to you... it is knowing how essential it is to have balance in our lives... and about making the choice to remove ourselves from the toxic, crazy, frenzied (and often, negative) energy of the physical world to spend time in the place of purity and perfection and grace.

For when we immerse ourselves in the purity and perfection... *the grace*... of our highest and original spirit, we *become* our highest and original spirit, we become authentic and strong and peaceful and light.

Ceremony is one of the best things that we can do to bring about goodness and peace to the world, for it helps us to become the very best of ourselves. And when we strive to become the very best of ourselves, we find peace and grace *within* ourselves. As we live our lives in this way we inspire others to do the same.

When I sat down to choose the Creator's Song messages for this first book, I realized that if you read them as a book, they begin to tell a story.... my story. For within the words of each daily message, I could somehow feel my own growth and expansion.

I also found that as I read each message I became immersed in the sacredness and energy... the ceremony... of each particular morning. I found myself on the prairie among the Old Ones and Animals who joined me in ceremony each day, and I felt the spirits of all who came in spirit to attend. So if you allow yourself to, I believe that you too will be able to experience the sacredness and energy of each morning ceremony.

__The Creator's Song messages I chose for this first book are from June 2010 through May 2011.__ I removed the actual dates on each page but I did keep them all in order. You will notice that each day brings a new message, lesson, teaching, ceremony, journey, or experience. You may also notice that some teachings seem to be repeated in more than one message as they become woven into the tapestry of this amazing gift.

Repetition is a valuable tool that was used by most *__indigenous peoples.__* It is sacred and powerful... like the beat of a drum...like the beat of your heart. The Elders of my tradition would tell us that whenever something is repeated, it is asking you to take a closer look or to listen with your spirit so to truly hear.

Whether you decide to read this as a book...or open it to a random page daily and let it speak a personal message for you, let the simplicity of the words and the power of their meaning flow through you... and feel them deep within your heart and spirit...as they set you out upon your own journey of growth and expansion.

... ni ga na ye gv na...

... v i sv i...

... safe journey...

–Eva Black Tail Swan

MESSAGE FROM EVA

I feel it is important to mention here… at the beginning… that when I go to ceremony each morning, it is a ceremony for all people… and everything I experience during my daily ceremony… I share with all people.

Whether it is Rain, Wind, or Snow, heat from Father Sun, the cold of Winter, the love of Grandmother Moon, or any of the Medicine Beings who come to join in my daily ceremony… I open the space of ceremony for all and any who need or desire to be present.

I invite your spirit to come here, and I ask (I intend) for all that is created during ceremony to go swiftly to whoever is in need (wherever and whomever they may be). You only need be open to accept… if it is your desire to do so…

… and so, for example… even if it is not snowing where you are… if it is the Medicine of Snow that you need…you will experience Snow.

Eva Black Tail Swan

A Note to the Reader

The process of publishing a book has been an amazing journey for me. Christina Winslow at Big Country Publishing was so generous to share her wisdom and expertise (as well as her patience and understanding) with me along the way.

Creator's Song: Ancient Voices Speak is a compilation of messages that I receive during my daily morning ceremonies. Each morning I am given a message for all people from one of many Old Ones, Elements, Animal Spirits, Grandmothers, Grandfathers, Plants, Trees, Stones, (and the like).

Translating these messages is something that many people have inquired about and that I have not yet found a way to explain. But what I have discovered though the process of publishing these messages into a book, is that each messenger (if you will) has a different way of speaking, a different way of accentuating the important points of their message, and that each voice flows with its own individual rhythm.

Many people have subscribed to receive these messages daily (as I receive them). I have received comments from many of my ***Creator's Song Community*** who always mention how each message is unique and individual and how each day the message seems to speak to them in a very personal way.

During the editing process for this book we noticed that if you read the messages one after the other there are many inconsistencies in such things as words that are capitalized, italicized, phrases in parentheses, and rules of proper grammar. So the question then became whether to adjust each message in order to follow the proper rules of grammar or to keep them exactly as they were received, in order to give the reader the experience of reading each message just as it was received.

Christina and I talked in length about this and decided that for a book such as this it is important to keep each message just as it was received and to write this "note to reader" to explain the inconsistencies.

Thank you for your interest in my work and for forgiving the imperfections in proper grammar so that the messages brought forth in this book can be presented with the same sacredness and energy in which they were received.

Eva Black Tail Swan

do na da go hv i

Eva Black Tail Swan

TABLE OF CONTENTS

...and so it begins...

... as I close my eyes... the song of a newborn day plays within my heart... Mother Earth begins... with the beating of her heart she calls to her children... and as each one steps forward... their own song blends together with the others... until they sing as one in rhythm and harmony with their Mother... and this song plays within me like a symphony... deeply moving within my heart...,

... and Grandfather Wind comes now... into this place where I stand... completing the circle... for Wind is the **breath of God...,**

... and the words come now... as a whisper on the Wind... but they are not spoken... they come through feeling and emotion... a sense of knowing that is felt deep within one who is blessed with an invitation to attend such a ceremony...,

... and the message comes now... as a song within my heart... and it is a song like no other song... for this song is the **voice of God***... this song carries the message sent for all to hear... this song is...*

... CREATOR'S SONG ...

JUNE
2010

I sleep deep throughout the night… as if in a faraway place… and in the last moments of twilight-(blissful)-sleep… just before I wake… I feel the presence of wisdom and mystery rising up within me… of that which is hidden… and of that which is secret…

… and I hear a calling from within… and I feel a seeking to come out… and I see it is the Old Shaman who has come on this day… and everything falls into place now… as we walk the paths and trails of this land together…

"… dear children… find your silence and trust your stillness… for the only way to know the secret medicines that live within you… is to allow them to speak to you…,

… you must cease your ongoing chatter (of both mind and mouth)… and listen with your heart and spirit… listen with your feeling and intuition… listen open and eager to know… listen in the place of dreams… in that powerful moment of in-between… just before you wake…,

… for the secret medicines that live deep within… are as many as they are powerful… and they are the true treasures you seek… and they know you have forgotten them (there within)… and they whisper for you to remember now… to remember who you are…,

… so calm your voice and still your mind… and breathe out all your heavy breaths… so to breathe now, shallow and light… for the whispers of your inner-sacred… have weakened and grown weary… and you must find that space of twilight sleep… and ask them to speak up… and give them a place of quiet and still… and listen with all your might…,

… then feel instead of listen… feel instead of think… feel your secret medicines awaken and become…,

… for as you breathe together now… (as one, as whole, in sync)… you will feel your truth awaken… as your secret treasures rise up… and you will feel yourself complete…"

… a s qua di s di… and so it is good

I am greeted by a soft spoken spirit on this day. A quiet Shaman Spirit who tells me of the need to expand our heart energy. We sit for a long while in complete silence (completely still), before we begin the prayer songs for all people…

… and as we sing the prayer songs together… our voices blend … and our hearts expand into one…

"… within the very depth of you … an infant has begun to form… and with each beat of your heart… this new life grows and expands…,

… it is you that is forming… you (yourself) who grows within… a deeper wisdom… a truer knowing… a lighter touch… a stronger will… a higher, more expanded version of you… is waiting to become…,

… like a shell wrapped around its precious seed/nut… you are wrapped around this new you within… holding and protecting that which is softer and more delicate… waiting to

be sure of its survival out in the world…,

… so you still yourself… and sit for a time… and you listen to your heart… and you feel each beat and find its song… and breathe in deep and breathe out strong… and you feel your heart and love expand…,

… for with each beat and deep, deep breath… you stretch and grow within… your wisdom grows and your love deepens… and you discover (then)… that which has been growing within… is ready to emerge…

… and you offer now into the world… (through the greatness of your heart)… a promise to be healed and mended… and a chance to be at peace again… a way to live with a softer voice and a lighter touch… ***a way to live as one…***"

… a s qua di s si… and so it is good

From within a place of deep purple, I awaken… I leave the sacredness of a space so high and pure… and return to this familiar place I know as home, as Earth.

I sit for a while now… before I gather my ceremony bundle… I sit for a time to consider where I have just awakened from… and how I have found my way into such extraordinary places lately… *and why.*

The Old Shaman (who has been with me for more days than I can count at the moment), steps forward now… and reminds me that it is time to begin ceremony for today… we walk out onto the prairie together… and as we set ceremony… I see that we are in the center of a field of purple flowers…

… the power and energy of this space is tangible, palpable, intense… though it is also soft and calming, pure and cleansing… and nothing negative or harmful seems to be allowed within it…or is it that nothing *physical* in allowed within… for I can see it is our spirits which are most present here…

… we sing the prayer songs for all people now… the Old Shaman and me… and as we sing, the prairie sings too… and Grandfather Wind blows strong against us… and the sacredness of this space grows and expands…

"… allow the pure and clean and positive within you to expand now… allow all that is lower, negative, and worrisome to be pushed out… see it as a grey smoky mist that disintegrates instantly in the light… and be for a time, in a state of purity and grace…,

… now… in this moment of purity and grace… take notice of your mind and thoughts… and know what it truly is that lives within you… for it is no longer about what the physical world has lead you to believe about your-self… but who you truly are that is important now…,

… you are upon a time of spiritual awakening… and you must become familiar with your highest *Self*… in order to access the unlimited power of this pure and healing space and time… and you must call upon the sacred-ness of this place… from your own pure and healing place within…,

… and in order to see beyond and above… you must step out of all that weighs and holds you down and back… and allow yourself to rise and flow with the pure and healing energy that will lift you up and up…,

… and within this sacred place… you will know your own inner-sacred… instantly… and you will know where all your medicine is kept… and you will make the transformation then… as your inner-sacred moves up and through and out… and you will feel yourself become whole and true and complete…"

… a s qua di s si… and so it is good

The Old Shaman wakes me on this day with the song of a Drum. I hear the soft heartbeat sing in rhythm with my own heart as I begin to stir. I feel the vibration dance across my skin as I return from the dream-place. I pause for a moment as I contemplate whether to sink back into the place of dream and journey… or to wake and follow the guidance of the Old Shaman…

… one strong, loud, thump of the drum tells me to wake and follow… and so I rise, gather my ceremony bundle, and follow the Old Shaman out onto the prairie…

"… listen now… to the rhythm of life… listen with the whole of your body… listen with your spirit, heart, physicality, and mind… allow yourself to be consumed in the vibration of life… as it beats and flows and sings around you…,

… find your own rhythm and vibration within this song… and feel your own rhythm and vibration reach out to touch the very heart of this song… feel the oneness… feel the wholeness… feel each and every living thing and being as you feel that one heart beating…,

… this is how Shaman connects to all things… this is how Shaman feels the dreams of all people… this is why Shaman dreams for all people… all life… and all things…,

… for the patterns and vibrations and rhythms of all people, all life, and all things… move through the song of the drum… and they speak to the Shaman deeply and completely… and the Shaman listens with the whole of their being… and they know without thought or voice… what they are called to do…,

… and then naturally… without question, thought or voice… their entire being (spirit, heart, body, and mind) aligns with all that is… and the Shaman **becomes** the dream…"

… a s qua di s di… and so it is good

As I walk out into the morning, here on the Mountain, I sit for a time with the old Grandfather and Grandmother Stones. They offer wisdom and love to us (for us) as I sit with them each for a time, but it is the Standing Ones who bring me the message for this day.

I walk out to each of the young (newly planted) Tree People, and visit for a time, before I set ceremony in the space where we will hold our class and ceremonies on this day…

… and as I sing the prayer songs for all people, I hear the voice of the Old Shaman speak (through the presence of an Elder Standing One)…

"… connect to and with your roots… seek your ancestors and accept the strength they offer you… for the knowledge and understanding they hold for you…. will bring you strength to expand and live more fully…,

… there is a blessing within each experience… seek this blessing and honor it… for it will become the root of the wisdom you gain throughout your **Earth Journey**…,

… know the Standing Ones as the caretakers of Mother Earth… and be (then) as a Standing One… sink your roots deep into your Mother and nourish her with your love… and be nourished by her love in return…,

… and as you move about within this physical life of yours… remember that there will be times you must dig deep and deeper to get to the root of certain issues… and remember to honor each of these times as the blessings they are… and you will be filled (then)… with the wisdom each has come to give…"

… a s qua di s di… and so it is good

It is the Keeper of the Sacred Fire who wakes me on this day. I sit in ceremony and feel the *Fire* from within me begin to expand as Father Sun rises. The knowing of transformation and becoming sacred expands within me, too…

… and the Keeper of the Sacred Fire begins to speak through the warmth that rises up within me… as it begins to push its way through (and out of) me…

"… allow the Fire of your Father the Sun to move into and through you each day… stop for a moment each day… and ask this powerful Fire to burn away all that is old and un-serving from within you… for as these are burned away… they create a new and vibrant energy within… energy to fuel your forward motion… while they open the space within to receive…,

… for it is time to reduce the heaviness of the load carried within… it is time to walk lighter… it is time for your physical bodies to become more efficient… it is time to receive in every moment of your physical life… the pure and sacred light from above…,

… move now… with your Sacred Fire burning strong and constant… for negativity will not and cannot build up within your Sacred Fire… but all that is positive will live and grow and expand within it…,

… keep your Sacred Fire burning as you walk now… and you will walk directly into that which you have set out to manifest and become…"

… a s qua di s di… and so it is good

On this day as I walk out into the morning, the ground feels alive with movement. I hear the rumble of large (heavy) hooves running, and I look up to see the Spirit Horses coming toward me. I stand completely still (with eyes closed) as the Spirit Horses run right up to and then past me. I feel the strength and beauty of them within me now, as if they just ran through this place (at this very moment) only to replenish me.

I walk now, out to the place where I will hold ceremony for today. I stand in the tall prairie grass and feel the nourishment of the land rise up through me. I quiet as the air around me begins to move, and I listen as I see that one of the Spirit Horses approaches me now...

"... the message of finding time to receive and be replenished... has not been taken seriously... you must listen again now... and begin to care for yourselves and others with nurturing and compassionate love... love that nourishes the spirit, mind, body, and heart...,

... build the energy of assisting... begin the act of working together... feel the love of others (rather than their hurt, pain, anger, and disgust)... and allow others to know and feel your love (that which is pure and real)...,

... for in order to shift from the downward spiral to an upward one... all must begin to seek out the goodness in one another... and then nourish and nurture the goodness you find there within... with more of the same...,

... Mother Earth is shaking and shifting at this time... she is readjusting, and in a process of her own healing... two-legged... you are the only ones who do not know this instinctually (and then naturally act to assist)... so listen, now... look around from a different perspective... and take note of the changes that have occurred just over the course of a year...,

... pulling together... and walking in the way of healing, assisting, nurturing, and nourishing one another... is how you can take action to assist Mother Earth in her process of self-healing... she is completely capable of healing and rebuilding herself (she has done this over and over for longer than any two-legged could ever know)...

… you can assist her by walking in love and compassion for others… allowing yourself to receive love and compassion… and remembering that what you give out and receive back in… will directly influence how Mother Earth heals at this time…"

… a s qua di s di… and so it is good

In the cool of the morning it is a high energy that greets me (a beautiful purple mist). I walk along the paths and trails of this ranch as if walking through water, for the energy is so present that I am completely immersed within it. I set ceremony near where the Buffalo stand, as they have called me to them. They are silent (now) and stand closely gathered, as if already in ceremony, and so I sing out the prayer songs to begin our ceremony for today.

I watch them (our sacred Buffalo relatives) as they watch me, and I feel as though I am sitting center within their circle. I am held in the purity of all that is *Buffalo Medicine* as they move in even closer around me, and a deeper knowing of the Medicine they have to share with us (two-legged) becomes strong and certain.

We are lifted (now) together (the Buffalo and I) into the pure and sacred space of Creator. I find my way to stillness as the message from the High Place flows into my heart. Within this space of purity and light (assisted by the presence of beings so completely giving), I am given the message that we are to know on this day…

"… as you begin this day… know that the ***purple healing mist*** is always present and available to and for you… you need only acknowledge its presence… and with the intention of your mind… call it to you…,

… your heart holds the knowing of all that you need and desire… even if/ when your mind cannot name it… even if/when your voice cannot speak it… simply sit within the sacredness and purity of this space I give to you on this day… and surrender yourself completely… into the ***purple healing mist***…,

… become quiet and still, then… and trust your heart to speak… let go of your thoughts, now… and allow yourself to receive… expect nothing here… and accept everything here… for all that you seek to know and be and realize… will become strong and certain within you here…,

… for the *purple healing mist* repels and removes all that is lower and negative… allowing only that which is higher and positive to remain… and without the distraction of the physical plain… you are able to awaken more of your higher *Self*… for you access the unlimited power of the *High Place* (here within the *purple healing mist*)… and you *know* without need of thoughts or words or voice… to teach and explain…,

… vision follows then… and the ability to see beyond the mundane… clear sight that guides you past where the physical word would lead you… to the place where your spirit knows the way…"

… a s qua di s di… and so it is good

The fragrant aroma of rain on fresh-cut grass wafts through my open window and beckons me out. I rise early and make my way out the door without waking the doggies. I stand upon this prairie that I know so well, feeling as if it is all new and different.

I breathe in the morning air (as the healing elixir that it is) and feel it move all through my body, awakening and replenishing as it goes. I close my eyes and then open them again, and through the misty air (that hangs around me like a cloud)… I see the Ancestors dancing upon the hill…

"… look up two-legged… look up as you dance in your circle… look up and show your face to your Creator… look up and see what your Creator shows to you… in the stars and clouds and movement of the sky…,

… your message is to look up… reach up… aim high… and settle for no less than the highest of your aspirations… for to bring about great changes… and to create good and new and healing and peace… you must look up, reach up, stand up, show up… and know that you are strong enough to reach the heavens…,

… as you dance around the sacred circle… with your face lifted up for Creator to see… you show your passion and commitment… and all that you dance for (all that lives in your heart)… begins to move and shake and rise up and out…,

… and you stretch up then… as you follow the passions of your heart… and you become strong then, too… and you find that as you look around the place where you dance… it all looks new and different… and you know then that you have reached the High Place… and that all you have been dancing for… is certain to come about…,

… and with your face still looking up… you dance your gratitude dance… and as you turn and spin and twirl… your feet touch upon the Earth again… and you know that you have been in the **highest place**… and that you have stretched beyond all boundaries… and that you will continue to reach up as you continue to dance… and that you will not give up…"

… a s qua di s si… and so it is good

As I walk out into the morning, the smell of fresh *Prairie Sage* fills the air. The morning is damp and cool, which seems to awaken all of the grasses and plants and trees of the prairie, and they blend together now into an incredible potpourri that consumes me. I stand for a moment to breathe it all in, truly becoming one with all that surrounds me.

As I make my way out onto the open meadow where I will set ceremony for today, the smell of *Prairie Sage* begins to stand out and becomes more and more intense as I walk. I follow this guidance now, as I know I am being lead to our ceremony place for today.

I find myself in the southwest meadow of the ranch as I begin the prayer songs for all people, and the smell of *Prairie Sage* becomes stronger and stronger. I feel the earth beneath me begin to rumble a bit now, and as I look up I see a beautiful *Smoky Gray Medicine Horse* (with charcoal black hooves, main, and tail) running toward me… and the smell of *Prairie Sage* grows stronger and stronger as she nears…

"… from now until the Moon grows full again… you will (at last) let go of something that you have been working to release… you will keep the wisdom of this lesson, though… and the knowing of how each experience of your life deepens your wisdom… will become more clear and certain for you…,

… remember that as your release, you open again to receive… and that in order to receive, you must make room (by releasing that which no longer serves you)… it is important to allow yourself the emotion of sorrow, grief, and even exuberance as you release (so to make the release complete)…,

… then set your eyes ahead… for as the Moon grows full and bright… you will see the new beginning that is born from releasing the old…"

… a s qua di s di… and so it is good

The whole of the Star Nation watched over me as I drove home last night. Their brilliant light guided me along the dark country roads. I walked with them for a while once I arrived home, as I am safe and protected in their light.

It is the Cloud People who wait for me now, as I walk out onto the prairie only four hours later. They hang low over me and feel full, as though they are ready to release the tears of a burden they have carried for much too long, but they (too) tell me they are here on this day to keep me safe and protected.

I walk ceremony on this day, walking along the paths and trails of the ranch as if I am walking with a dear friend. I listen to the wisdom of this dear friend, and together we pray for all people, but it is the knowing that this dear and sacred being surrounds and protects me as we walk, that speaks loudest within my heart…

"… you felt the protection of the Star Nation… for they all stood together as one to protect and keep you safe… you feel the same protection from your Cloud Relatives… and from within the voice of the Sacred One who walks with you on this day…,

… know, two-legged… that all must come together now in this same way… all must stand as one with the purpose of protecting one another…without need of recognition, approval, instructions, or compensation… for as each sets their intention to keep safe and protect all others… they too are kept safe and protected…,

… understand, two-legged… there is no (one) great disaster to wait for and protect from… it is the shifting from protecting that which is yours (from a place of entitlement and possession)… to protecting that which is here for all (to a place of caretaking and stewardship)…,

… proceed now, two-legged… with only positive emotion… as you set out upon the path of keeping safe and protecting Mother Earth and all her children… proceed from a place of purity and generosity… release all/any anger, judgment, control, and/or demands… for these block and inhibit the very thing you wish to achieve…,

… as you move forward… let this become your nature… that which is *just so* and natural to you… (from as it should be, to that which is common, basic, natural)… for it will be the purity of your intentions (and actions) that create the greatest outcome… and your people are in need of a great outcome at this time…”

… a s qua di s di… and so it is good

I wake on this day to soft rain falling. Rain that began yesterday as fierce and threatening tornado conditions, settled down overnight, and drenches the prairie now with all that is pure and nourishing from the High Place.

I stand in the cool morning rain and feel the love of Father Sky and Mother Earth as they touch one another through the rain… Father giving… Mother receiving… here in the darkness of morning they begin their dance…

… for in the heat of the afternoon… Mother Earth will release back to Father Sky… that which she no longer needs… and Father Sky will receive her generous gift… placing it with the Cloud People… who will keep this sacred gift safe and protected… until Mother Earth and Father Sky dance again.

I walk now... slow and quiet... careful not to disturb the beauty of this sacred dance... I *stand* in ceremony on this day... whole, content, complete... as I am touched by both Earth and Sky... and I sing the prayer songs for all people silently within now... as the song of the prairie is too beautiful to disturb...

... and it is Grandmother Willow who speaks to me now... soft and quiet like a whisper... her voice moves in and between the drops of rain... and I feel as though I am lifted into the place of in-between...

"... be aware now, two-legged... there is a new rhythm of life for you to discover... a new vibration for you to sync with... a new way to achieve harmony and balance...a new energy to blend with...,

... consider this loving dance between Sky and Earth... Father abundantly giving... Mother graciously receiving... Mother generously giving back... Father wisely receiving (storing up for another time)... for this is the nature of life... it is the way all of nature lives... it is the way two-legged must find their way to living... in consideration of one another... giving abundantly to one another... receiving graciously from one another... giving back generously... and receiving again wisely...,

... replenishing one another... bending to and fro in support of one another... naturally giving when there is need... openly receiving when there is need... considering only the perfect balance and harmony of life... rather than how and when compensation will arrive...,

... for as each begins to *dance life* in this way... more will step up to join in... and soon the dance of life will become one of nourish and replenish... rather than one of take and destroy..."

... a s qua di s di... and so it is good

A ga s ga ~ u (ga) se di (the Rain Keeper) whispers to me as I sleep. I rise and walk out into the foggy misty rain that blessed this prairie all day yesterday and throughout the night. I am immersed in the presence of **a ga s ga ~ u (ga) se di,** as I stand upon the open space of this ranch and sing the prayer songs for all people. My voice sings out soft and low on this day, as I am balanced in both the High Place and the Physical world… and it is my heart that speaks now… singing the prayers of what I feel within…

"… recognize this oneness, two-legged… acknowledge this partnership… remember that you walk as a part of Great Spirit (not as separate from)… as you move about in your daily life… remember that whatever you create… is created through the partnership between yourself and your Creator…,

… make time as often as you can… to spend time in the purity of the High Place… allow yourself to be saturated by the purity and perfection there… just as you have become saturated by the heavy misty cloud of air that you stand in now…,

… for each time you spend time in the High Place (time with Creator/ God/ Great Spirit)… you begin to shift… from vibrating to and with lower energies… to vibrating to and with higher energies… you retain more of the High Place within you, then… and you share this pure and perfect energy with others then, too…,

… and know, too… that as you become more and more in balance and oneness with all that is of the High Place… you need only feel (and/or) intend your desires, goals, and dreams… and they will be received instantly and manifest quickly… for you will be one with all that is…,

… but remember… that as you become more and more balanced with the High Place… and your vibration shifts up… your goals and dreams and desires will shift and change as well… and that which you seek to bring forth and manifest… will truly be in partnership with Creator/ God/ Great Spirit…"

… a s qua s di s di… and so it is good

I stand in the early morning surrounded by the spirits of many Old Ones. I feel the wisdom of a long ago time, and honor the sacred beings who have come on this day to speak. I set ceremony in the circle of stones that mark the place where the Tee Pee once stood. I sing the prayer songs for all people, and I hear the voices of Shamans and Medicine People from every lifetime singing with me.

The heartbeat of Mother Earth becomes strong now, and the air around me becomes still... as the Old Ones come forward, one by one, and begin to speak...

"... call to your Old Ones, two-legged... call to the wisdom and teachings they have placed within you... for it is time to give to the world all that you have to offer... and for this you must draw upon all that has been discovered, learned, experienced, and put to use throughout time...,

... seek within with open eyes... and honor the wisdom of all who come forth to share it... make no distinction of man or woman, race or culture... for the wisdom they bring is the voice of God speaking... the hand of God reaching... and comes forth to benefit all...,

... look to the whole of the Star you live upon... as one place where many live... see the importance of **all and each** as valuable and necessary... and reach out to honor the wisdom, ideas, and knowing each one brings forth... for it will be through the effort of all... working together as **One**... that creates the shift in energy... which will bring about the peace and healing you seek..."

... a s qua di s di... and so it is good

As I stand in ceremony on this day, I listen to the song of the prairie. Life that is reborn after many days of gray. I can see the blue of Father Sky, even in the dark of this early hour, and the winged of the prairie surround me (already in song and dance).

I light my ceremony fire, and watch as the sacred smoke rises easily in the calm, still air. I dance on this day as I sing the prayer songs for all people, drawing up the nourishing love of our Mother the Earth with each step I take, and bringing down the purity and perfection of our Creator's love as I spin and twirl.

I stand now, completely aligned and in balance with heaven and Earth, and I move into the place of stillness as I listen for that which I am to know on this day…

… it is a wise and elder Standing One who comes to me now… and I sit in the comfort of his shade… I rest in the knowing of his guidance… and I listen to the wisdom of his years…

"… it is time to honor the wisdom that lives within you (all) two-legged… that which is hidden there within you… and is your true being… for held within a protective cocoon within you… is your true and perfect spirit… and in this time of transition… it is ready to emerge… to come forth and assist you… to make the changes you are working so hard to make…,

… and there is no secret to releasing your true sprit from within… you must only become aware of its presence within you… and call for it to awaken and rise up…,

… then align yourself with all that is of the High Place… and stand firmly rooted in your Mother, the Earth… breathe in the purity of your Creator's breath… while feeling every bit of your physical body… as it stands strong and solid and true… empty your mind (then) of mundane thoughts and any worries that lurk there in… as your spirit awakens and rises up… and the voice of your true spirit begins to speak…,

… and in this moment you will know true clarity… and you will understand with great wisdom… for you will have seen the happenings of all your life… from both physical and spiritual perspectives at once… and the path that lies before you now… will become clear and certain…"

… a s qua di s di… and so it is good

I walk among the Cloud People on this day. Ancient Spirits call out to me as I move about in (what can only be described as) the highest of the physical realm… the highest (or the last) Sky of the Earth World.

I feel the presence of Grandmothers and Grandfathers here in this place… extremely ancient beings who stand rooted in the Earth Mother… but reach all the way up into this higher realm.

I am still for a moment now, pausing to get my balance and a sense of direction, and I see that a council of Elders have gathered here. I move toward them as if being drawn rather than intentionally moving to them, and I instantly feel the power and sacredness of the space in which they stand (though there is a welcoming softness here too).

I see now that these are the Sequoia (Redwood) Standing Ones who have called to me on this day… and I acknowledge them each, individually, before I settle into ceremony and listen to what they have come forth on this day to say…

"… come now, two-legged… come and wrap your arms around our trunk… place your heart to our heart and know as we know… feel your own perspective expand and shift… as you feel the depth of Mother Earth perfectly blended with the heights of Father Sky…,

… quiet now and listen, two-legged… to all the stories of all the generations through which we have stood… see what we have seen, feel what we have felt… then sit with this wisdom… and apply it to your own life… and every situation there within…,

… and through this time with us, two-legged… find this knowing to be true… ***the only thing that restricts you from achieving your goals and dreams… is you… and that if and when you decide to set forth upon your true life journey… that is when you will truly begin to live…"***

… a s qua di s di… and so it is good

I walk the prairie on this cool morning, listening to the Lions and Bears from the Wild Cat Preserve (across the road) sing their morning song. My Owl Sister u gu gu calls out for me, and I follow her voice to the place I am to set ceremony on this day. I am immersed in the peace and harmony of this land as I light my ceremony smoke, stretching outward in spirit as I sing the prayer songs for all people.

I am drawn upward now through the rising smoke, up and out and into a space that allows me to feel the hearts of all people who live upon this Star we know as Earth. There is a magnificent web here in this space, a web that instantly awakens a knowing within me of how we each affect one another though our own feelings, thoughts, actions, and beliefs…

"… children… know that whatever you create (or fail to create) in this (your Earth) life… goes on and on to affect future lifetimes… (just as the feelings, thoughts, actions, and beliefs of your ancestors has created the world you walk in today)… and know, too… that it is by and through the awareness of who you are and who you become… that you create (often without even the knowing that you are doing so)…,

… it is time to become consciously aware of what your spirit is guiding you to know and do… to quiet yourselves for a time… to become separate from the collective consciousness for a time… so to know your true purpose… and to take the actions (make the changes) that will guide you along your true path…,

… standing as one, upon this infinite web… it is easy to feel there is nothing you can do to affect the chaos that is so out of control within your world…

but you must see and know, now… that as each finds their way to their own healing, wholeness, and truth of spirit… all are affected… by and through the Oneness of this infinite web…"

… a s qua di s di… and so it is good

It is the Grandmother Olive Standing One who greets me on this day. I see her there with her fragrant white blossoms that show even in the darkness. I see thousands of yellow Ladybugs drawing to her now, and I see the sharp thorns of her branches as I find myself moving close to her as well.

Grandmother Olive brings peace and harmony to the whole of this ranch. She brings peace and harmony to (and within) me as well. I have been missing my Father so deeply these last few weeks (so deeply it has been almost debilitating)… and Grandmother Olive has come today to comfort and ease all and any who are experiencing this (or any) kind of deep heart pain, hurt, sorrow, sadness, wound (or the like)…

"… the sweetness of my perfume will draw you near… the beauty of my flowers will catch your eye… you will move closer to me then… and as you reach to touch my flowers… my thorns will stick you (drawing blood)… and the Ladybugs who rest upon me will fly… and you, two-legged, will (at last) cry…,

… cry deeply then (all) two-legged… allow that which has been welling up within you… to flow out (like the blood that flows out from the thorn prick on your finger)… and feel completely as you cry… for the healing that follows this flow of emotion… will lift you to a higher level of understanding… to a place of harmony and balance… and to a place of true peace…,

… then sit with the Ladybugs, two-legged… and listen to them closely… for as they settle down upon you… they whisper wisdom and knowing (answers) from the High Place… they return within you the knowing of your own will to grow and expand, to learn and to live… and they will remind you of your goals and dreams, two-legged…,

… and the negativity, fear, doubt, and confusion will flow out then… like the poison flows out through the blood… and the purity of all that you are yet to do and be… becomes strong again… and you will know and feel (at last)… the balance and peace and harmony and strength that lives within you… ***and so it is good***…

… a s qua di s di… and it is good

Much of my Dreamtime seems to be spent in very high places lately, for I wake on this day feeling (again) as though I have returned from a faraway place. My head feels light and my mind, spacey.

I walk out onto the prairie and head straight for the large circle of Grandfather Stones. I sit with the Grandfathers for a long while… waiting to be certain I am grounded.

I can feel the ground beneath my feet now, as I sit upon the Grandfather of the West (hoping he will bring me back down to Earth)… but I still feel as though I am walking with the Cloud People… and so I stop fighting to control… and begin ceremony on this day… in this amazing place of in-between…

"… in order to achieve great things… you must strive for greatness… so too… if you wish to awaken your highest spiritual being… you must spend time with it, here in the High Place…,

… it is time to become aware of your aspirations… to allow yourself to aspire (to aim, desire, hope, dream, wish, and want)… it is time to spend time in ***spiritual flight***… flying high and soaring higher than you have ever allowed yourself to before…,

… for there are no boundaries or restrictions around you… only the illusion of limits and confines… limits and confines that appear very real while standing in the physical realm… but vanish instantly once you rise up into the higher knowing of your spirit…,

… take the time now… and set your intention… to walk among the Cloud People each day… (or ask to be taken there within your Dreamtime)… spend time in your highest spirit daily and often… then dream and wish and make your plans… for you will achieve your highest aspirations… once you truly believe you can…"

… a s qua di s di… and so it is good

It is the Corn Maiden who comes for me on this day. She waits at the end of my Dreamtime, with her basket full of freshly harvested corn, and calls me for to follow her back into the dream-world for a time.

As I turn to follow her, I hear her say… "remember to feel gratitude today"… and I stop for a moment to realize how important her message of gratitude is for me today (especially today)… and so as I follow Corn Maiden, I begin to sing the gratitude song… and then I begin to feel gratitude within me… and soon we are there…

… we are standing on a small hill overlooking a huge corn field… I can see the people (ancient people in ancient times) working… and I can see the Corn growing abundantly… and in the next moment I see the people (ancient people in ancient times even further back)… and I see that they are dreaming for the sustenance that will help them survive…

… and Corn Maiden begins to whisper now… and so I quiet and listen…

"… **Dreaming the Future** is a powerful tool of Medicine People… but all people can (and should) do it… most people have **Dreamed a Future** already and may not even know it… especially as children this occurs…,

… look at this beautiful field, two-legged… see the people working… see that they are the same people who dreamed this nourishment to reality…,

… remember to be grateful for all the happenings of your life, two-legged… for prayers answered and for dreams manifested… and remember, too… it is not enough to simply dream the future you desire or need… you must take action as well… and then continue to **work your field**…,

… what is it you are dreaming for the future (yours or for others yet to come)… begin now (if you have not)… speaking, feeling, and showing your gratitude… begin now (if you have not)… to take the actions necessary to manifest your dream(s)… then continue each day *working your field*… and soon… you will have created something that will last through time…"

… a s qua di s si… and so it is good

It is the voice of my Owl Sister u gu gu who wakes me on this day. I walk in the heavy mist that sits upon the prairie as I follow her. She leads me up the road and to the top of the little knoll on the North side of our ranch. The air is heavy and wet (like a thick fog), and I am soaking wet as I near the top of the knoll. I set ceremony here, and begin the prayer songs for all people as u gu gu sings from just a few feet away.

I stand as the first rays of Father Sun touch upon the prairie, and I see the misty fog sitting upon the valley below me. Looking more like smoke than fog, it seems to be breathing, and I stand in silent prayer as I look down upon this land we have been called to care for.

I turn completely around as I look at the valley below me, and find it difficult to recognize anything. I do see the top of our barn, and from there I look hard to see the Buffalo standing in the West (the smoky mist still moving as though breathing).

u gu gu has stopped singing now and I hear the Buffalo sing out their morning song (they must know I am looking for them). I look out across the land and see the tops of the Cottonwood Standing Ones peeking up from within the smoky mist. They look as though they are dancing, and I hear the sacred voices of the Old Ones from off in the distance as u gu gu flies right toward me from out of the smoky mist…

… it is a very sacred ceremony I am attending on this day… and I listen as u gu gu sings out from behind me now…

"… deep within the smoky-mist of your inner-world… you will find you own place of wisdom… from within this place of wisdom… your dreams will speak and your vision will become clear…,

… on this day (your Summer Solstice), commit to spend some time (for the next seven nights) with your Grandmother the Moon… sit with her, call her into your Dreamtime, dance beneath her, look upon her from your window… however you choose to honor her… be sure to acknowledge her… for with the assistance of your Grandmother the Moon… you will come to gain great insight into your own future…,

… this will be a magical time for you then… a time to speak out your dreams and wishes, wants and desires… a time to concentrate your prayers on the healing of all people and all lands… a time to set new intentions for the life you have been given… a time to draw together that which has been split apart…,

… the time between this, your Summer Solstice and your Fall Equinox… will move fast… and you will notice rapid growth in many ways… remember to think with clear and positive thoughts… remember to spend time in quiet stillness… remember to respect all people and all things… and remember to honor the wisdom and vision that lives within you…"

… a s qua di s di… and so it is good

It is the Old Woman who comes on this day. She rides in on a blue-dun-colored Horse (with a black main and tail) and they stand in the circle of stones that mark the space where the Tee Pee once stood. I am singing the prayer songs for all people when I see her, and so she sits upon her magnificent Horse (there in the circle of stones), waiting patiently until all the songs have been sung and all the prayers have been felt…

… as I move into stillness I feel her presence expand… I open my eyes and see that she is waving for me to come… as I move toward her she reaches out and catches my arm… she pulls me up onto the back of her Horse… and together we ride off quickly…

… into the gray-black of Father Sky, we ride… up to a quiet place, lit by the soft glow of Grandmother Moon, we stop… and here within this place of perfection and grace… the Old Woman begins to speak…

"… you do not need me to bring you to this place, young one… but you do need me to remind you of the importance of finding your way here (daily)… for it is time to remember (and time to remind others of) the importance of building a strong center… and of nourishing and replenishing that strong center, yourself, and others daily as well…,

… no matter what the next part of your journey may hold for you (each and every one of you)… you must know now (truly know and take seriously)… the importance of maintaining a strong center and of minding your health and well-being at all times…,

… it is the wisest of the wise who know how to (and how important it is to) create and build the supply before the demand occurs… and it is the wisest of the wise who know, too… that by using all of the experiences of one's lifetime to create a strong center… one also draws nourishment and strength to replenish and build upon that which is already here and ready to grow and expand…,

… draw upon all of the experiences of your life now… use them to remind you of your own strength, wisdom, resilience, and tenacity… for in these you already possess a reservoir of nourishment to replenish yourself with… and as you bring all of these together within yourself… you will naturally become strong and centered (and ready for anything)…"

… a s qua di s di… and so it is good

I wake to a feeling of sacredness around me. I walk out to find that sacredness surrounding me still. I stand in ceremony and feel this sacredness expand. I sing the prayer songs for all people, and hear the sacred voices of their spirits sing out within my own voice...

"... within each being... there is a rare gift that makes them (each) unique... you, yourself possess a rare gift within that makes you who you are... sit with this for a time now... and contemplate your knowing of oneness...,

... then set your thoughts to see... that just as each living being is related (to and with one another)... each is also rare, special, individual, and unique...,

... as you sit with this knowing... begin to acknowledge your own rare gifts... realize just exactly how and why you are unique and individual... then begin to see the special and rare gifts that make others who they are... and then honor and respect them (each)... for that which is their own... just as you would like to be honored and respected... for that which is your own...,

... once you come to this knowing... know it deeply within... know it on all levels and in every way... for as you see, know, acknowledge, honor, and respect the rare and unique gift that each and all people carry within... you begin to recognize one another as your family (your kin) in a deeper way (spirit to spirit)...,

... and your true essence begins to emerge then... and rare gifts from the High Place begin to arrive (for you each)... and you will notice the sacredness within you more completely... and you will know that it is real... and you will see the sacredness in all that surrounds you as well...

... and through these (most unique) rarities of one another... you will truly *know* Oneness..."

... a s qua di s di... and so it is good

As Grandfather Wind blows hard across the prairie, I hear the sound of Grandmother Ocean (her waves breaking against the shore). The sense of masculine and feminine standing together in balance rises up within me, and I can feel the emotions in my heart begin to stir.

There is a freshness in the air now (something like just after a rain or emerging from a pool on an extremely hot day) … *it is time for cleansing your emotional energy* … I hear a voice say (as I move from prayer song into stillness), and I instantly find myself in another dimension… dancing on the Wind and touching down upon the Water…

"… whether your emotions run deep within you or are right there just beneath the surface… your emotions affect your physical health, movement, and state of being… it is time now to cleanse your emotional energy… for energy builds and builds when emotions are left too long without attention… and this energy can and will cause disease, illness, or disruption in your sense of well-being…

… allowing yourself to cry is a perfect way to begin the cleansing of emotional energy… screaming and ranting is also good… the important thing is not to let your emotional energy build to the point where you cannot control how, when, and to whom you release it (upon another, at a breaking point for instance)…,

… go within if you can now… and seek specifically to address your emotional self… do not just open the door and peek in… but go completely in and sit with your emotional self for a while… ask questions… sit in silence and listen for answers… feel what it is to be in emotional balance… and feel how you are *emotionally* at this time…,

… if you find that you are over charged and out of balance emotionally… call upon your Grandfather the Wind or your Grandmother the Ocean to assist you… ask them to assist you in bringing forth the tears you must cry or the rant you need to scream out…,

… then go into a safe and protected place nearby… or out to an open space you know… and cleanse your emotional energy… cry or scream… sob or rant… but release what has built up within… so that you may see and think and physically be… clear and healthy, and emotionally balanced again…"

… a s qua di s di… and so it is good

I stand beneath the soft-orange glow of Grandmother Moon on this warm still morning. The feminine energy fills this valley, and I feel as though a dear friend has embraced me… standing by my side with a strong compassionate arm stretched across my shoulder… telling me (without words) that I am loved and all will be okay.

I watch as Grandmother Moon makes her way through the black of Father Sky… gracefully, in perfect movement with the song of the prairie, she sinks into the horizon and finally disappears… and I whisper "thank you" for the opportunity to witness her dance.

I move now, keeping the same pace and rhythm with the song of the prairie, somehow dancing as I walk. I make my way to the place where I will set ceremony on this day, and as I sing the prayer songs for all people, I feel the presence of my dear friend beside me again… and again… I feel as though all is good and I am okay…

"… children… sit within this space and set your intention on the relation-ships in your life… consider your relationship to and with each (friend, sibling, partner, spouse, child, parent, co-worker, and the like)… and consider their relationship with you…,

… shake off all of the past (the history)… and any feelings of resentment, jealousy, misunderstanding, and such… for it is time to realize the gift you offer one another… and to be generous in what you provide to one another… as well as to be gracious in receiving from one another…,

… it is time to strengthen all the relationships in your life… and to find strength in knowing that you have support around you… it is time to step up in all of the relationships in your life… and to be the strength and support for others as well…,

… weave yourselves together in the way a basket is woven… hold and support one another as a group, a tribe, a nation, a people (one people), *a basket*… rest easy in the knowing that others will hold you (and keep the basket strong) if you fray or become weary… keep yourself healthy, strong, nourished, and replenished, and ready to support and hold any who find they need to pull back and rest…,

… for this is the dance of life, children… the holding of one another in trust and support… the keeping of one another close within your hearts… the stepping (side by side) in perfect rhythm around the sacred drum… (who beats the same heart-beat as each and every *one*)…,

… and this is how to reach your full potential, too… by drawing together as one… in respect and honor of the strength and abilities of each… rather than breaking apart in the name of your differences…"

… a s qua di s di… and so it is good

Grandmother Moon lighted my drive home last night, and stayed with me as I slept. I wake on this day to the sound of sacred drums, and the vision of a drum stands center of my mind's eye (and stays there even after I open my eyes).

As I gather my ceremony bundle and make my way out onto the prairie, I am accompanied by the beating of the sacred drums, and the image of this drum remains steady and solid in both my mind's eye as well as my real (awake) sight.

At first she (the drum) looks like our Grandmother the Moon as she will be tonight, full and round with varying shades that show her beauty. But this drum has something to tell us, and she wastes no time in making this known to me…

"… whether I represent your personal beat of life… or the heartbeat of all living things… I come on this day to remind you of the power of your song…,

… do you know your song?… do you know how to find it?… have you allowed your song to be heard by others?… or do you sing your song only to God?…,

… become empty now… allow all that shapes and colors you to fade back… listen only to the song of your inner-drum… and then listen so to recognize that which is purely and simply you…,

… be empty as your song sings to you… allow it to fill you… and then share its gift with others… allowing yourself to empty (so to be filled again)…

… this is healing for others as well as for yourself, two-legged… this is the power of your song… the power of you…,

… walk in step with this rhythm now, two-legged… fill with the perfection of your own song… and allow it to spill out for all to hear… move in this healing way, two-legged… and healing will come about… (for you, for others, for all things, places and beings)…"

… a s qua di s di… and so it is good

Whoopi (our last Buffalo-cow to calf this year) showed signs of birthing yesterday morning as I walked the ranch after ceremony. The Cowboy and I kept a close eye on her all day. I walked out to say a prayer around 3:00 pm, and she had still not birthed her calf. I watched as two Ravens stayed close to her (somehow protecting her, assisting her), and they told me they would care for Whoopi and not to worry (though I kept my eye on her anyway).

I went out just after midnight, and found Whoopi still trying to birth her calf. I spoke prayers out loud and offered sacred smoke, and then the two Ravens flew up to let me know they were still there. My physical presence is not needed here now, so I went in to tell the Cowboy how things were going.

"It's a long time birthing," I said, and we each spoke our concerns and said our own private prayers… entrusting Whoopi and her calf to God now…

The Cowboy came with me out to ceremony this morning... and we went directly out to see Whoopi... she was nestled on the west side of a small hill and we could only see her head... I heard soft flute music playing and saw no sign of the two Ravens...

... Whoopi stood up when we were about a hundred yards from her, and we saw our first glimpse of her calf... wobbly and waggling its tail... still a bit wet... we figured it had just been born... we gave Whoopi a good look-over and saw her calf begin to nurse... so we breathed out our sighs of relief and let them be...

"... whatever it is you are called to begin or create at this time... it is now time to move forward with it... shake of all of your old and limiting thoughts and ideas... and step forward with a new attitude and fresh determination...,

... do not become distracted or discouraged... but rather, allow nothing to stop you... for it is time to tend to the seeds already planted... and assist in birthing the new...,

... Mother Earth is becoming fertile again... and we are called forward now... to assist her in birthing the new..."

... a s qua di s di... and so it is good

I wake from many dreams on this day. Some people would ask me what I ate for dinner... but Grandmother would tell me to call them each back, and find the story they tell...

... and so I spent the morning with Grandmother, sorting through my dreams and stringing them together... piecing their story into an order... and finding the message they bring for me personally... as well as the message they bring for us today...

"... however fast the world seems to be turning at this time... you have the power to slow your pace whenever necessary... without making any further commitment or absolute choice... you can step out of any situation for a time and rest from it...,

… remember the energy that builds when you are immersed within (and part of) a happening… remember that this energy can take on a character, personality, and attitude all its own… you can be influenced greatly by this energy while immersed within it… so step out for a time and get a clear perspective…,

… the situation will wait for you… divine timing will allow all to unfold in right time and space… and you will be more ready and able to follow and accept the divine timing and to receive the messages from the Universe… when you are standing strong and clear and refreshed… with no influence from the heat of a situation…"

… a s qua di s di… and so it is good

As I walk the prairie on this day, I find myself standing near our newborn-buffalo-calf, and I notice, too, all of the new birth upon the prairie. I set my ceremony within looking distance of Whoopi and her calf, and I sing the prayer songs for all people as I watch the newborn wander around and play…

… a fresh new air stirs up around me as I move into stillness… and a voice that is soft and gentle and sweet… begins to speak…

"… feel the new life around you… feel the curiosity and wonder… begin to be excited (about anything, about everything) again… for there is a new spirit-guide awakening within you now…,

… any and all who have called out for assistance… any and all who have grown discouraged (dismayed, disheartened, saddened, or worried) about life as it is now… allow yourself to awaken to this new-spirit within you…,

… breathe in the cleansing of this new-spirit… breathe it all the way through you… and breathe out its freshness in every thought you think and every word you speak… for in order for there to be a shift (a change, transition, transformation)… there must be a new energy to draw it forth…

… then, as you begin to know the new-spirit that has emerged within you… allow it to speak… listen with respect… for this new-spirit-guide within you… is a wise old teacher… one who has assisted in the rebirthing of life (people, nation, and the world) many times…,

… with the soft and gentle voice of the new… the oldest and wisest of all knowings emerge… and from out of the chaos… comes the dawn of a new time of peace…"

… a s qua di s di… and so it is good

The Cowboy and I spent a good part of the evening (last night) watching the Buffalo. We had gone out to check the fences and test the moisture of our hay meadow (it is ready to be cut and bailed), and ended up spending the remainder of the evening captivated by the new baby (Buffalo).

The evening was hot, but Grandfather Wind brought much appreciated relief, and the prairie began to move again as Father Sun sank out of sight in the Western Sky.

The prairie grass is tall (to my waist and in some places higher), and Mother Earth seems to sigh with delight as Grandfather Wind combs it (her hair) on this cool morning. I set ceremony at my altar on this day, and sing the prayer songs for all people softly as I listen to Mother Earth and Grandfather Wind whisper to one another (through the voice they make, wind upon grass).

I move into stillness on this day with a feeling of intensity that is balanced perfectly with peace, calm, and contentment… and I hear the message we are to know on this day, in the voice of both Grandfather Wind and Mother Earth as they sing it out in unison…

"… step up and walk in your own truth… recognize your own Medicine… and be proud of who you are… do not hold back because you are different… but instead share who you are with the world… while respecting others for who they are… for together you (all) make up the whole…,

… it is time for the quiet voices to be heard… for the silent thoughts and dreams, the wisdoms and knowing… of those who have been too meek to speak, to be shared… for it is a time now for all to join together… and assist one another in strengthening and healing that which has been weakened and even broken…,

… trust is what has been lost… and trust is what must be found… and so think on this for a time… what is it that makes one trust… what is it that takes that trust away… find these and begin there… for to rebuild that which has been weakened and broken… you must begin with trust…,

… then trust that which lives within you (each)… to be a part of the **whole** healing… and realize all that you are… as you assist in this task… and you will **all** stand strong and tall then… each on your own… ready and able to respect and bend… while maintaining the truth of your **Self** as you do…"

… a s qua di s di… and so it is good

JULY
2010

On this day the prairie is calm. I stand at my alter singing the prayer songs for all people as the energy of Father Sun stirs in the East. The rising of Father Sun always brings about the notion of awakening within me, and as I look up I see Grandmother Moon sitting high above me. Time is the word that comes into my mind now... Time, and every aspect of it, washes through my thoughts as I sit in silence before moving into stillness...

"... the question of time... is one we hear spoken in the prayers of many... *when will it be my time... how much time before this is over... how much time before that will begin... what can I do with such little time... how much time do I have... how can I get back the time I have wasted... what have I done with the time I have been given... it is too much time for me to wait... too little time to be together... there isn't enough time (in a day, a week, a month, a year, a lifetime)...,*

... the importance of time is measured by each individual and situation in a personal way... and time is then used by each in the same personal way... to young ones, time has no meaning... while the elders make note of every minute... and in this place of time, of now (here in the present time of your lives)... too much is (has to be somehow) crammed into small spaces of time...,

... longevity (then) becomes the notion in the corners of the mind... longevity, and the notion of mortality (and the mark one will leave behind)... and the issue of time becomes (then)... like a dark shadow that looms above... and the use of time becomes more and more distorted...,

... re-examine the notion of doing nothing, two-legged... sit with the idea that part of caring for yourself, is giving yourself time to *"be"*... spend time in the place of nothingness (doing nothing)... and allow the questions you have about time to be revealed and answered within this place...,

… plant your seeds and tend to them… but then allow them to grow as they will… give yourself time in the same way you would give your garden time to mature and grow… see yourself and your life in this way… and balance your time with work and play and rest and *"being"*… and you will find (then) the time you spend just *"being"*… is the most important time of all…"

… a s qua di s di… and so it is good

It is ka ma ma (Butterfly) who wakes me on this day. I hear the soft fluttering of her delicate wings, and feel just a whisper of the gentle breeze she makes as I journey back from the Dreamtime. I am still for a moment, listening for her voice. She calls me to stand in the dawn and bring forth the *Medicine of Transformation.*

The prairie is cool and damp as I walk out, and the whole of the Star Nation stands waiting for my ceremony. I set ceremony in the East and sit in silent prayer as Father Sun rises. I open myself to the power of transformation as the new day begins, and I offer this power to all people as I sing the prayer songs for all (for each) on this day…

"… whatever needs to be transformed within your life… begins with that which is held within your mind… for whatever it is you believe and think on most… will be that which becomes your experience…,

… look to that which is your greatest desire… and look (then) to how long you have desired it… look to your daily routine, habits, conversations (with others and with yourself)… and look too, to your thoughts and inner dialogue when you are alone and silent… for hidden within each of these is a root… that once found… can easily assist you in discerning that which keeps you from your own personal transformation…,

… all change begins with thought… it is simply the most powerful of thoughts that will govern your actions and decide your choices… routines, habits, and patterns are powerful… as they require no thought… for they are set and familiar… and so the task becomes to set new thoughts that bring about new routines, habits, and patterns…,

… transformation is consciously deciding to change… and then making change… sometimes, just one thing (one change) at a time…,

… to make a change you must use your mind… think… plan… commit… so to shift the power from that which has always been… to that which is now to be… to make a change you must find the root of that which keeps you from changing… and understand it… know it completely… and through this process… it loses its power…,

… there is no way you can go about in the same old way and transform as well… just as there is no way the Caterpillar can fly… in order to be a Butterfly… the Caterpillar must first transform (do the work)… just as in order for you to change and transform… (to achieve, become, acquire, and/ or possess that which you desire)… you must also do the work…,

… the Medicine of transformation is here now… equally available for all who wish to use it… you have only to open your mind… and let the old out, so the new can come in…"

… a s qua di s di… and so it is good

Life on the prairie is as wonderful as it is difficult. Yesterday we noticed our mama Buffalo (Whoopi) was not doing so well. I spent most of the day out in the pasture trying to encourage her to eat, but only managed to get her to drink water.

The Cowboy found her even more lethargic only a few hours later and pulled the baby out. He spent several hours trying to figure out how to get her to drink from a bottle, and got more of the calf-formula on himself than into the calf.

I got home about 11:45 pm and we sat up feeding the calf from about midnight until almost two-o'clock this morning. When I went out this morning at 4:00 am, I found our mama, Whoopi, had died, but our baby (who we have set up in the barn) was standing up drinking from the water bucket (we have great hope and trust that she will be okay).

Ceremony this morning was in honor of my sweet Whoopi (I attended the ceremony given by her Buffalo family). I picked Whoopi myself when she was just a few months old, and she has been with me for almost fourteen years. She was the "Boss" of the heard from the beginning, and was the best mother of them all. She provided us with extraordinary calves each year, and many times raised the calves of other "mamas" who weren't quite into it.

Many of the messages (from the Buffalo) I have received over the years came through Whoopi, and I loved her dearly.

When I walked out this morning, all of the other Buffalo were gathered around Whoopi, her son from two years ago, "Truth", was right by her side… I stood quietly in honor of the ceremony being given in Whoopi's honor… and stepped forward only when Whoopi's sister Rosi moved to offer me a space…

… u gu gu, my Owl Sister, sang out her song as the winged of the prairie (including the two Ravens) sang along… and I felt the presence of many four-legged of the prairie nearby as Coyote and Wolf began to sing too… the Lions and Bears from across the road spoke out their prayers as well… and Cougar (who came in spirit) sat upon the knoll bringing strength and power to their ceremony… (and a porcupine even attended)…

… the message for today comes in the *Medicine* of the many four-legged and winged who attended this morning's ceremony… each has specific *Medicine* to offer… and each will speak to each of us, personally… if we will only listen… so listen now… to the messages that come on this day… and offer your support (if you will) through positive thoughts and prayers for Whoopi's daughter to survive…,

… thank you, Whoopi, for your many gifts over the years… you live on in the very earth of this prairie… in each breath it breathes… and in the song of every morning… the setting of every Sun… and in the messages you have brought to us over the years…

.. a s qua di s di… and so it is good

I t is the message of renewal that speaks on this day. I am shown the renewal of life in many ways as I travel the long path back from the Dreamtime…

… new birth and reseeding… life going and life coming… the circle of life appears in every way… and my understanding of life deepens…

… the words that accompany the images that guide me awake on this day… are clear and precise…

"… inner-spirit provides strength… and this, dear children, is renewal… allow the peace and stability of this knowing… to nourish you in every way…,

… as you contemplate that which you will leave for future generations… think also upon what it is you carry-on from someone of the past…,

… you are each the renewal of something (or someone)… so provide your-selves some time to sit with this new understanding of renewal…,

… consider how you will honor the process of renewal (that which you bring forth)… in your most personal and individual way… then consider how you will assist those who bring about renewal through you… so that they may do so with honor, respect, integrity, and devotion to and for the future that is still waiting to become…"

… a s qua di s di… and so it is good

There is no walking the prairie on this day. The rain has stopped, but the saturated earth is not ready to be walked upon yet. I sit with the "baby-buff" in her warm dry stall and sing the prayer songs for all people... (we do ceremony together on this day)...

"... gratitude is the message for today... gratitude is the gift for you (each) to share on this day... take some time (sometime today and every day) to feel and express gratitude...,

... consider every aspect of your life... consider every person and being in your life... all experiences (great and small, positive and negative)... each lesson and each hardship... each prayer answered and each blessing... and each time you thought a prayer was not heard or answered...,

... just feel gratitude all the way through your entire being... until you are saturated with it to your very soul... until your spirit expands and your heart swells... truly and sincerely (intentionally) **become** gratitude... and stay in this place of pure and total gratitude for as long as you can...,

... make it your intention to remember this place... **this feeling**... for you to return to quickly (instantly)... with only a thought or intention to do so...,

... for the power of gratitude is what you (each) need at this time... to heal and expand... to know and understand... to bring about clarity in what has come to be... as well as in what is yet to become...,

... it is time to move beyond feeling gratitude (selectively as you are accustomed to)... to **knowing** gratitude in every and all ways... through and through..."

... a s qua di s di... and so it is good

I went to see the Old Shaman in the Dreamtime last night. I saw him standing on the little hill that hides his small cave-like home. He was waving for me to come there, and so I traveled across a hidden bridge that leads down a narrow path and into a deep forest that takes me to him.

The forest was dark and cold and I walked for a long while, searching for the small path of stones that lead up to the Old Shamans door. I followed his voice (which came as the wind)… *"Close your eyes, child… for you can only find the path with your spirit…"*

It has been many years since I have traveled to see the Old Shaman. I am never sure if he calls for me or if I call for him. I only know that great changes occur whenever I go to spend time with this **wise one**, and that once I return, I am shown that everything I experience in my time with him, all began many days before.

All time spent with the Old Shaman is a magical time with many mysteries… some that take years for me to understand and accept (take in)… and everything about the experience of going to see the Old Shaman has meaning. He (the Old Shaman) told me once that he can only be seen by the highest of our physical *Self*… and that we have to travel deep within ourselves and find the pathway that connects us with our highest *Self* in order to even know him.

… "You pay attention then…" he says… "You remember everything… where was I standing… what was I wearing… did I speak… how long it took to find the bridge… how long it took to step upon it… how long it took to cross it?"…

"… in your struggle to make the changes you have set about to make… look to see who it is that is blocking your progress… look with the highest of your spirit… and see revealed in this being… it is you, yourself standing there in your way…,

… it is a natural human characteristic… to want to take everything with you when you move… but as you have learned throughout your earth-life… this is neither possible or practical…,

… changes must be made in order to change… old must be let go of and discarded… and new must be taken in and accepted… otherwise there is no change…,

… so it is up to you now, young ones… do you move to another location with all of your possessions in tow… and find a way to stuff and fit all of this into your new space… or do you expand into the new space… look it over for a while… and decide then… what it is you will need and use…"

… a s qua di s di… and so it is good

The prairie is very still on this day. It is soggy-wet from the storm, and so very black. The Cloud People are hovering close, and it is always darker when they are here.

There is only one small glow of light coming from Kiowa, and it seems to be pulling me to set ceremony there in the West. I feel a sacred presence around me as I sing the prayer songs for all people, and there seems to be a window of some kind just there in front of me. It is an opening of some kind that I know I am to look into…

"… find a quiet moment each day… and offer love to another… not just to those near and close to you… but to those you have never even met… look out in any direction as if there were nothing in between… then let your spirit travel as far out as it will… and feel love for whomever it is that stands before you there…,

… be in this place then… for as long as you can… and get a knowing of what everyday life is there… what are the wants and needs of these people… what are their dreams, what are their desires…,

… open your heart to send out whatever you can… and allow yourself to receive as well… send out what it is you, yourself need at this time… for you have the same needs as another (somewhere, anywhere, everywhere)… then write down your knowing of the place you have been… write (if you can) what you felt while you were there…,

... and tomorrow do this again in another direction... travel to another place... know a different people... and each day continue with this prayer... of sending love to people and places you have never met...,

... and soon you will begin to see the change... as all people share in this one Universal thing... this thing that requires no words (no translation)... for love is understood in the same way by all...,

... and know, too... in this powerful and personal way... that it is by offering to another through your own love... that one begins to know another as they know themselves... and that when you know another as you know yourself... you (finally) begin to know all people as your relatives..."

... a s qua di s di... and so it is good

It is another wet, soggy morning on the prairie. I go immediately to feed the baby-buffalo and begin preparing myself (spirit wise) for ceremony as I sit with her. As I gather my ceremony bundle, I can hear her rustling around in her stall, and choose to set ceremony inside on this day. As I sit in the warmth of this 12 foot x12 foot stall, with this sweet little baby resting next to me, I sing the prayer songs for all people and feel the spirit of the entire Buffalo Nation rise up within me...

"... call to your animal spirits, two-legged... call to the characteristics and medicine of those you call your *Totems*... rest from the drama of two-legged life for a time... and be in the simplicity of one who guides your most basic instincts...,

... are you wolf or bear... hawk or eagle... do you need the medicine of deer or elk, ant or butterfly... maybe snake is the medicine you need at this time... you may not even know... it is best for you to sit for a time now... quiet and still... and allow yourself to become empty... then ask for the *medicine* you need at this time to rise up within... to come forth and show itself to you...,

... release any thoughts of knowing your *Totem* at this time... for you may block another who wishes to come through... honor and respect all of the animals... the four-legged, winged, crawlies, and swimming ones...

for each carries powerful *medicine*… and each is ready and willing at all times… to share what they possess with you…,

… take note of all and any who come to assist you… notice the smallest as well as the greatest who cross your path… did you hear the frog croaking… did you see the moth… do the winged hover around your dwelling… or maybe it is the cat or the dog that speaks to you on this day…,

… maybe your *Totem* for this time will come in the way of a story you hear or an image you see… through a dream or a song… or simply by coming into your mind… listen then, two-legged… listen for what is trying to be told to you…,

… then sit for a time and release your two-legged self… allow the teaching of your *Totem* to flow within you… honor this wisdom, then… and use what is being shared with you… even if it is simply to let go of built-up stress… or to sleep deeply for a time…,

… remember your animal spirits, two-legged… remember that you carry their *medicine* within you… and call upon this *medicine* when you get lost in your life… or whenever you need assistance no other can provide…"

… a s qua di s di… and so it is good

On this morning, I walk the many paths of this ranch before I set ceremony in the Grandfather Stone Prayer Circle. I walk the Labyrinth with specific intention just before I enter the Grandfather's Circle, and I sit in the North (the place of the Old Ones, Father Wind, Wisdom, and Knowledge).

In the North on the Medicine Wheel (as I know it) there is a place of contentment - a place where you can look upon your life and know it as a whole. Where all of what we (as human, two-legged) label as bad and good, wrong and right, should-of and shouldn't-have, and so on and on… is not seen in the way we wear it… but instead is looked lovingly upon as the whole of who we are… and a brilliant shimmering light projects from within its middle (heart)… and that is the truth of who we are…

The Elders say that here in this place, we see ourselves as God sees us… and we become content (truly content, for the first time in our lives) with who we are.

I sit in the North of this Grandfather Medicine Wheel, with all of the *Medicine* the Labyrinth so generously offered, and search for a place of contentment. I call for Grandfather Wind to come, but the prairie remains still. I let go of my pounding thoughts and I stretch myself as far up as I can. I expand out to touch the whole of the world, and I root myself deep into the cool wet earth… and from here… I call for the Grandfathers (who sit in circle around me) to speak…

"… dear child (children)… close your eyes and quiet your mind… breathe in the perfection of you… breathe out all that is illusion… and look again at what surrounds you…,

… brush away that which is negative (anything you know as bad, wrong, ugly, hateful, etc.)… and search for the good… see past the illusion… to that which is truth… and know the world as a whole… rather than as parts and pieces… and see it all as it is seen from above… as it is known in the North…,

… trust in the good and worry not over the bad… but use all of who you are to expand the positive… and the negative will diminish, naturally…,

… it is easy to see the blessing in every stumble after time has gone by… to see the positive only after the negative has been felt… but you can set your intention to know and trust in the perfection of each experience as they occur… to recognize the positive quickly (instantly)… so the negative is given no time to take root…"

… a s qua di s di… and so it is good

On this day, I set ceremony in the circle of stones that mark the place where the Tee Pee once stood. I feel a fire burning in the center, and I feel the Tee Pee wrap around me like a blanket. I hear the *Old Woman* chanting soft and low, and I sit quietly as she sings her Medicine Song. I find myself sitting at the South corner of her sacred fire, and the *Old Woman* sits directly across from me in the North.

We speak no words, but get right to our work. It seems we have been called upon in a healing way (a Medicine way), and the Village we sit in ceremony for, has circled around our lodge. I can hear them chanting and singing. I can hear the soft heartbeat song of their drums. I can feel their love as well as their fear... and I can feel the prayers of their hearts...

... and I see a beautiful earthen bowl sitting close to the fire... as I turn my head to look... and all becomes quiet now... as the *Old Woman* begins to speak...

"... it is not a healing for the Star you know as Earth, child... it is a healing for the people who live upon her... your Mother the Earth is more than capable of healing herself... and she knows the healing needed by her children... is the task at hand...,

... together with the animal and plant kingdoms... she has called upon the **Medicine Peoples** (of every place upon her)... to reach within... to the most sacred part of their being... and bring forth the **medicine** that is their very own... to bring it as an offering... and to place it in this **sacred bowl**... which is placed here today for this healing...,

... and each will walk strong and tall... as they bring forth their offering... whatever that offering may be... for it is the coming together with the same intention... that ignites the fire and creates the ceremony... which brings forth the healing... and honors the request that has been made of us...,

... so come together now, children... reach deep into your sacred place... and bring out the **Medicine** that is your own... share your gift with others... and offer it into this **earthen bowl**... this **Medicine Bowl** for all people...,

… and be assured, children… that you each have a gift to offer… for your gift is in the thoughts you think and the words you say… your gift is in the way you look upon and act toward one another (as well as the Earth and all thing and beings)… your *medicine* is in the way you live your lives… and in the consideration you give to those who will come after you…,

… for you are the ancestors of the future generations… and everything you do (or do not do) will influence the world they will live in… and it is time for each of you to keep this knowing clear and present… and to live your lives with the future in mind…"

… a s qua di s di… and so it is good

I feel the Medicine of Coyote on this day. It is morning, but it feels like night. Father Sky is black, and then he goes blacker. I see the Star Nation close and bright above me, and then they are gone. I gather my ceremony bundle and walk to the center of the ranch, so to find grounding, balance, and direction.

I hear the wild yipping of the Coyotes all around me. I feel them as they run past. It becomes quiet now as I sit and listen… as one lone Coyote approaches me…

"… take a look within and around you… check to see what is real and what is not… evaluate your physical experience… then determine, what from within you has helped to create it…,

… remember how good you are at fooling yourself… how easy it is to justify your actions… how important it is to be right… how necessary the explanation… and how desperate you are to have someone hear it (believe it)…,

… now… look again… is the one you are fooling, *you?*…,

… spend some time with this question… for the Medicine I bring will teach you about yourself… I can help you to know if the *Truth* you hold so desperately… is real or illusion… if it is working to your benefit… or to your demise…,

… as you journey forward… be sure you look with clear eyes that see only truth… for it could appear that you are moving… when you are actually standing still…."

… a s qua di s di… and so it is good

Coyote returns on this day (or maybe he never left). There seems to be more he wants to say… more work to do… more hidden within… more truth to reveal…

"… ah, yes… when you begin to work with my Medicine… there will be many layers to peel away… much to sort through… and great wisdom waiting to be discovered…,

… I remain as your guide… because I am persistent, patient, and focused… but my greatest gift… for you who seek on the deepest levels of your being… is to remind you about balance…,

… work a while, and play a while… be sensitive to and aware of… the energy that is building as you concentrate on your goal… and when it gets too intense… back off and release… play a while… relax…,

… for without this release and balance… everything becomes more difficult… your vision becomes clouded… and you lose sight of your true goal… you may end up digging a deep hole in one place… when what you are looking for is in a completely different location…,

… two-legged are masters of illusion… the art of fooling oneself has been developed and perfected over generations… it is very likely in your DNA… recognize this, two-legged… do not fool yourselves into thinking… that the inner-work you seek to (need to) do now… can be done in one day…,

… I will stick with you… if you will stick with *it*… I will assist you to remain focused… push you to maintain persistence… and remind you of the importance of being patient…,

… and…,

… I will let you know when it is time to take a break… (reminding you that you are not giving up)… I will yap and circle around you until you notice me… I will take you out to play or run… I will sit with you while you rest or sleep… whatever you need to do to release the build-up of energy… I will be there to help you…,

… and somewhere in this process of digging deep within… you will find your balance… you will realize the importance of balance in all things… and you will have discovered a way to keep balance in your life… (and this lesson is a true wisdom you carry within)…"

… a s qua di s di… and so it is good

The fragrance of fresh-cut hay meadows and cool morning air fill my senses as I walk out on this day. I stand upon the knoll on this day, and with eyes closed, I beckon the Universe to hear me. I present my request, sing the gratitude song, and set ceremony for all people here where I stand

I sing the prayer songs for all people, and call upon the powers of the Universe to assist any and all who are in need (and ready) to make use of this incredible gift (and I sing gratitude again).

It is Snake who joins me in ceremony now… Snake who wishes to speak

"… allow your deepest wishes and desires… to join together with the energy of the Universe… set your mind to move on that which you have been pondering… and then get up and move…

… for everything is coming together… doors are opening (windows too)… the heaviness is lifting now (fear and worry and doubt)… leaving a lighter air to walk about in (belief and faith and trust)…,

… walk out (sometime today)… and shed that heavy skin… for it is Summer… a time of rapid change and growth… move and walk and even dance around… and feel the resistance has lifted…,

… allow yourself to shift and change and transform… in every happening you experience… for each experience of your life… has the power to transform you… if you will allow it to…"

… a s qua di s di… and so it is good

I walk the prairie on this day in search of what I am truly seeking. I walk the paths and trails that lead to each sacred place on this ranch. I walk the Labyrinth (counting the times I step out and begin again). I walk a figure-eight pattern around the outer edge of the Labyrinth and each of the six stone circles (which includes the Tee Pee circle), and count the passes I make in front of my altar space. I sit (finally) upon the center stump in front of my altar and wait for ceremony to begin…

… it is an Old Spirit who begins to speak now… an Old Spirit who feels young and new…

"… as you search for the answers, and the guidance to lead you forward… call upon on the Old One who lives within… search without expectation, but completely open and accepting… and find that it is you who answers the call of the **seeker within**…

… be renewed at every ending… see the finality of each beginning… know the circle that you live within… and realize that it is ever turning…,

… know that once you have expanded (learned, grown, accepted, and discovered)… there is permanence in that expansion… and from there you simply strengthen and renew…,

… call to the Old One who lives within… the "Seeker" who calls to you… draw toward one another until you meet… and then set about to know each other completely…,

… for it is a time of renewal now… a time to realize how far you have come… and to see how far you can go…,

… it is time to acknowledge that you are the wisdom within yourself… and that when you call out… it will be you who answers back…"

… a s qua di s di… and so it is good

I t is Crow who wakes me on this day. Her distinct call breaks into the silence of my sleep, and tells me of a message I am to share…

"… it is a strong center you will need now… as there is much to be done… and the path ahead is full of illusion… (it will show you truths in many shapes and forms)… stay centered and grounded… and keep your intention on the knowing of truth…,

… rely on your inner-knowing… trust in your ability to sense truth… (to feel it… to discern it… to know it)… and call upon your spirit-messenger within… to assist you in finding truth within the illusion…,

… call upon the light of your Grandmother the Moon as well… for her light is soft enough to cause no alarm… yet bright enough to allow you to see clearly… and with her as you your beacon as well as your guide… illusion will dissolve before your eyes… leaving only truth for you to see…"

… a s qua di s di… and so it is good

T he prairie has been blessed with much rain this season and it brings the Frogs up close to the barn. They sit in council just in front of the door I must go through to feed our Buffalo-baby.

I am very respectful as I step over these peculiar looking Elders. I never impose upon their ceremony or disrupt their silence. But last night, as I was locking up (after the midnight buffalo-feeding), I heard them whisper for me to join them, and so I did.

They spoke to me of remembering *"the gift we are given through the waters that fall from the Sky Place"* … reminding us to make use of *"the sacred cleansing waters*" … and then they told me of how the waters that fall from the Sky Place… assist us to uncover that which we have hidden within…

"… the most sacred part of any being… resides deep within them… (at their very center)… called by many names… this heart (or soul)… represents the very life of a being…,

… there once was a time when this (most sacred) part of a being… was kept out and open… for all to see and know and experience… but it has come to be the most hidden and protected part of all beings now… (so hidden and protected that you, yourselves, don't even know how to experience it most of the time)…,

… we (our council) have been watching the falling waters wash away the crusted mud from around that Old Grandfather Stone… and this is our message for you today, two-legged…,

… let the falling waters remind you… that the sweetest most sacred and personal part of you… your heart and soul (your very spirit, essence, being)… has much to offer you (and the world, too)…,

… let the cleansing waters that fall from the Sky Place… wash away that hard-crusted shell you have encased yourself in… and allow you to meet and know your true **Self** at last…,

… let these waters become your healing… as they soothe and smooth you… and allow yourself to be (for a time) **completely** in spirit… so to reacquaint yourself with the purity and perfection of you… before you begin to cover and shield and protect this most sacred part of you (again)…,

… be cleansed and healed… by the purity of your own spirit… and leave an opening this time… so you can spend time in your own perfection whenever you want (or need) to…"

… a s qua di s di… and so it is good

On this mid-Summer morning, I walk out to warm air and the promise of a hot day. I can feel the growth on the prairie (I can almost hear it), as I go over my watering plan for today. I am nourished by Mother Earth as I walk to my ceremony place, and it is *The Three Sisters* who join me for ceremony on this day…

(The Three Sisters… Corn, Squash, and Beans… were the sustenance of life for our Native Ancestors… known to many as our Life Force… they teach many lessons about living long and well…)

"… as you nourish the land and provide for its growth… remember that you require nourishment as well…,

… listen to your body, two-legged… and nourish it well… supply yourself with pure clear water as often as possible… for water will naturally cleanse you within and without… this you know…,

…but listen (now) to this… it is the nourishment of your spirit, mind, and heart that bring us to you on this day… remember to nourish and tend to every aspect of your being…,

… your fields require tending, watering, and rest… your body requires nourishment, exercise, and rest… so too do your spirit, emotions, and mind…,

… in this season, there is an abundance of that which is given through Mother Earth… much of this is cared for in such a way… that it can be stored and used throughout the Winter…,

… consider this, two-legged… as you nourish and tend to your own spirit, heart, body, and mind… for we see far too much taking and using… and not enough nourishing and storing… too much working… not enough resting…"

… a s qua di s di… and so it is good

I sleep deep and sound throughout the night. I feel as though I have been held in a very sacred place… bathed in soft, pure, peaceful… *tranquil* light.

It is a voice that guides me now… a voice that speaks no words… but guides me somehow out onto the prairie. I look for the source of this voice… which seems to come from within a presence that surrounds me… a presence that I can almost see… almost touch… cannot quite make out in any physical way… but can certainly feel and sense…

"… be aware, child (children)… for you are about to experience a shift in vibration… if you are aware… and if you look… trusting that you will see… you will see the light that circles around you at all times… the light that is your light… the light that is your highest being… your highest *Self*…,

… be in this (your perfect) light, child (children)… immerse yourself in it… come to know it completely… for this light, is the purest part of you… your highest vibration… your relationship with the High Place… and all that is of the Divine…,

… remember this light… remember how it feels and how you feel within it… and call to it… when you find yourself experiencing challenging times… allow yourself to rise up into your own perfect light… knowing that you will gently drift back (again) when it is time…,

… for each time you rise and fall… you will stay a little longer in the High Place… and you will not fall as far back when you return… and through this process… you will become your higher *Self*… and then one day you will see… that there is an even higher *Self* for you to rise up to… and then you will begin again…"

… a s qua di s di… and so it is good

Eagle has been around me for the past few days. She has been quite elusive… keeping herself just enough in the shadows to not be seen… while flying just close enough to the light to be sensed and felt.

I walk out on this day to see Eagle sitting at my altar (her mate sitting a few hundred yards behind her on the fence post). I felt the energy of this sacred messenger the instant I stepped into her view and stopped immediately…

… I walk forward seven steps now… and set ceremony within this circle of Eagle's energy…

… all of the Medicine of Eagle flows through me now… first lighting and expanding my spirit… then my heart… and my physical body begins to feel light and clean now… as my mind begins to process all that Eagle has to say…

"… it is time for you to allow Grandfather Wind to blow upon you… for the waters that cleanse and heal… have left you wet and muddy… unable to fly…,

… you have not fully released that which has been cleansed from you… and so you remain mired within it… unwilling to let it go completely…,

… know this, two-legged… I (Eagle) represent your spirit… I am here because your spirit is calling for you to shake off that which holds you down and back… and fly above it all… fly high and higher… and allow yourself to be illuminated by the light of the High Place…,

… you have been standing in shadow so long now… that you have become too accustomed to it… step out now… into the light… and allow the sacred breath of Grandfather Wind to blow upon you…,

… then, as your wings are dried… your mind will be cleansed of all that is shadow… and as you call for the light to enter every aspect of your being (through the breath of Grandfather Wind)… you will take flight… and your spirit, heart, body, and mind will be cleansed of the shadow that holds them down…

… you will take flight then, two-legged… and you will soar into the illumination of you…"

… a s qua di s di… and so it is good

Bear came to me in the night. Together we danced the sacred ***Bear Dance*** (which is a ceremony that calls to all that we hold within). Bear stayed with me throughout the night (then) and gave me many dreams… the first being a knowing of today, in which I was shown a cooler day, rain, and the importance of sleep… the last being the message I am to share with you on this day…

"… there is great strength and wisdom held within the most hidden part of your mind… there is great fear and agony held within this place as well… for all of the experiences of your life have been recorded here… those which were explained and understood… as well as those which are still worrisome and upsetting…,

… for many two-legged, I represent a time to go within… a time to seek within… a need to go within in search of a specific answer… or the knowing that something held within the most hidden part of the mind, is causing havoc in their life somehow…,

… in all cases… call to me (Bear) when you need answers and/or explanation… call for me to accompany you into your dreams… for I can guide you through the/your Dreamtime… and (if you ask me to) I will assist you to sort through that which is still a smoky mystery… I will help you connect this deep and hidden part of your mind… with the part that can discern answers, meaning, and explanation…,

… I (Bear) am strength to many… your mind is strong as well… know that just as I can push down a tree (with my strength, cunning, and tenacity)… so too can your mind stop you in your tracks (with equal strength, cunning, and tenacity)…,

… go within now, two-legged… with the specific intention to seek out that which is unexplained… to find that which is misunderstood… to clear away the smoke which distorts the clarity…,

… then set out upon your path again… with the strength of Bear (and the strength of your mind) intact… and find then, two-legged… more grace and ease as you move forward…"

… a s qua di s di… and so it is good

It is the Black Bird who calls out to me in the early morning… "Come, follow me," she says… and so I follow her to the place where the Black Birds gather. I sit with the Black Bird for a time, waiting for the one who will guide me in.

I am greeted by the Magpie now, and I follow her through this enchanting place… in search of the one who has called me here.

I see Crow now… she flies above the Magpie and me… as we travel through the land of Black Birds… her voice is startling at first… and then becomes almost magical… we begin a conversation that I completely understand… even though I do not understand the sounds coming from my mouth… or how I am able to make them.

There is silence now… and I see that I stand alone at the entrance of a bridge of some kind… Magpie and Crow seem to have pushed me forward, hanging back to be sure I step upon the bridge… "It is Raven who waits for you"… they say… "But you must find your way to her on your own from here… you must cross the bridge and she will be there…"

I step upon the bridge now… and find myself moving quickly across it… I see Raven there on the other side… and hurry to meet her…

"… do you know that it is trust that brought you here… somewhere in the deepest places of your being… you trust… and do you know that all two-legged walk in two distinct worlds… your waking physical world… and the world of dreams (where you are now)… and it is time (now) for you to bring these two together…,

… there is a space between your inner-world and your outer-world… but that space is becoming less now… and it is time to create a bridge between these two… (which can be easily done now… for they are already drawing together)…,

… there is mystery in both the inner-world and the outer-world… and your vision is impaired when you stand in one place or the other… it is as if you are looking through only one eye in either place… but if you can find a way to balance the two… to stand center between them… (upon a bridge that connects them)… you will see with two eyes open… and you will see all there is to see…,

… and you will see, too… that when you desire without trust… your heart is closed and your hands are clenched… but when you desire open and trusting and ready to receive… you stand waiting with heart, hands, and arms open wide… and the deepest places within you will move…,

… and you will understand then, two-legged… why you must create the bridge that merges the two worlds… for this is how to bring forth… all that you desire…"

… a s qua di s di… and so it is good

The Rain Keeper, a ga s ga ~ u (ga) se di has been hovering over our ranch for several weeks. I have felt him in the early hours of morning, and seen his reflection in the sheets of rain that pour down in the dark hours of night.

He waits for me on this day… I felt him in the damp morning air… I heard his voice call out to me as I was preparing the milk bottle for our Buffalo-baby… and as I sat feeding our *sweet buffalo girl* he called out her name… "Heart"… is what he calls her… and I saw her look up and around at that moment… as if acknowledging *it is so*…

… water is heart and heart is emotion (I think to myself)… and then I quiet and settle into ceremony as a ga s ga ~ u (ga) se di begins to speak…

"… it is time to clear out old emotions and feelings now, two-legged… to settle within yourselves that which creates the inner-storms… to repair and replace that which has been ravaged by these storms… and to feel the relief of being refreshed and renewed…,

… as the heavy rains pour down upon your lands… see that much soil is washed away… and many treasures rise up… treasures for you to find and keep…,

… allow my rains to assist you in this same way *within*… allow my rains to wash away the old… to wash away that which you have used to cover your true emotions… so to reveal, at last, *your truth*… no matter the result or consequence…,

… for truth is always the treasure… it is pure and honest and real… it will assist you in reaching that which you strive to reach… sometimes by taking away that which is no longer of use… and sometimes by taking away that which actually causes pain and strife…,

… see then the perfection and joy of finding your own truth within… of *being* as you feel… of *feeling* as you *are*… of knowing (without doubt) what to repair, what to replace, and what to let go…,

… for much *dis-ease* and *dis-order* can (and will) manifest… when you are out of balance in the place within…"

… a s qua di s di… and so it is good

As I was driving out yesterday, I saw an unusual Rainbow. It was wide and short, like a ribbon (or a scarf), and it stretched out across the face of Father Sky. There was no arch to it at all… it just hung there with the Cloud People… until Grandfather Wind gave it a little push… and it moved into the shape of a Hawk.

The storm that followed was big and loud and intense. It shut down the power, and held up the people, and brought down even more water from the Sky Place than anyone could believe.

... and I just kept remembering that unusual Rainbow...

When I got in my car to drive home, the storm was over and it was after 10:00 pm... and the notion of seeing a Rainbow never even crossed my mind... but there... in the misty air that hung like fog... with the assistance of my headlights... was that same ribbon-like Rainbow... and it stayed there... right in front of me the whole way home.

I wake on this day remembering the promise that the Rainbow symbolizes for many of us. And as I sit in ceremony, singing the prayer songs for all people, I hear the message brought forth by... *Rainbow Hawk...*

"... it is the complete oneness of all things and all people... that will restore the harmony sought by all... know that as Father Sun shines upon you... he shines upon all (people, things, beings)... and that **each** is seen as (known to be) a seed from the High Place...,

... allow yourself to be nourished and to grow... assist others by nourishing them and providing them a space to grow... for you (all people, things, beings) are a Rainbow to us in the High Place... you are a ribbon of colors that all blend together... different but same... and as you move and flow in this way... you assure us of the same promise that Rainbow makes to you...,

... so draw together now... be your own color in the same Rainbow... bring back peace and harmony to your land... and find the joy and happiness that waits to be born... and that waits for you to know it..."

... a s qua di s di... and so it is good

I am not surprised to see Grandmother Willow as I walk out on this day, for she has a strong connection to and with the element of Water (and we have had much rain lately).

I walk the soggy paths for a while (breathing in the pungent fragrance of wet earth and prairie grass), until I finally make my way to the stone prayer circles (where I settle and set ceremony for today).

Grandmother Willow stands close to me here, quiet and patient, she waits for me to move into stillness before she speaks...

"… two-legged… in this year of transition, transformation, and change… learn how to work with the healing waters that fall from above… understand the smooth flow and the soft and gentle fall… as well as the fierce storms… notice the stagnate standing pools… and then consider the running creeks and babbling brooks… the streams and rivers that flow and bend and move forward… always moving forward…,

… think of the lakes that hold (as they are cool and fresh and deep)… and the oceans that move in and draw out… ebbing and flowing in partnership with the Universe… and think of your own selves, two-legged… of how you are made of water… and of the tears that well up within you and fall down… reminding you of the importance of emotion…,

… then find these examples in the many relationships you are part of…,

… there has been too much separation (in regard to relationships) over the past decade… moving from personal, verbal, and physical contact… the other (sterile, disconnected, and impersonal) means of associating to and with one another… all of which impair your ability to sense and feel… to be compassionate to one another… and to use your gift of insight and inner-knowing…,

… it is the relationships in your lives that you must tend to now… (always and without fail)… find a way to be *with* one another again… to re-connect with one another and to make life (and living) personal again… for the healing that is needed now… is in your hands… and all that it will take to bring about this healing… is just one step… this step… stepping forward into personal relationships…,

… for this one step will lead to another and then another… and soon there will be balance and connection and caring and community again… and this will bring healing…"

… a s qua di s di… and so it is good

The Cloud People speak on this day. They began gathering a few days ago, creating a soft, white, pillow-like blanket across Father Sky (which sank lower and lower as more began to gather, and their empty *airy* bodies filled with moisture, turning them gray and then black).

They cover the prairie (now) like the skins that cover a sweat (*o si* - sweat lodge), and whisper among themselves. I heard them as I fell asleep last night and again as I awoke this morning.

I follow their guidance as I walk out onto the prairie… and their whispers become song… and their song becomes ceremony…,

… and I settle… right where I stand… as their ceremony has begun…

"… the **sacred fire** that commands the **sweat**… is what you need at this time… for the **sacred fire** combines with the **sacred water** and creates steam… hot, pure, powerful, healing steam… that pushes out all that is dark and negative and un-serving… making room for the light to come in and expand and take root…,

… it is the doubt that has rooted in your thoughts and mind and holds you back… and it will be the pushing out of these… that will allow the faith and trust to return… and as your faith and trust return… your thoughts will change… and your mind will work *for* you then… rather than against you…,

… and it will be (then) as though your wishes have all been granted…"

… a s qua di s di… and so it is good

There is a magical place here on the ranch, one that can only be seen under the light of Grandmother Moon when she is full and sitting high in Father Sky. It is a place where the *nun ne hi* (fairy folk - little people) gather, similar to a summer powwow or a reunion-type celebration.

There is an *old woman* who always attends these fairy gatherings, she seems to be a gypsy (or the like), and she very definitely carries *medicine*. But she stays just on the outer edge of the obvious circle the *nun ne hi* create for their gathering.

I can hear the *nun ne hi* singing from deep within the Dreamtime, but it is the herbs and oils the *old woman* is burning that wake me and guide me out. I know just where to look as I step into the light of Grandmother Moon (for the smoke from the old woman's fire shows me), and I move quickly as I make my way to this enchanted gathering.

I stand with the *old woman* now, who quickly douses me with smoke from her herb-pot, and together we honor the ceremony brought forth by the *nun ne hi* on this day...

"... we are magical beings to you, two-legged?... elusive and mysterious?... we know... we can see the captivation in your eyes... it is okay... you can look upon us in this way... but know that we represent a magical place within you... one that you must seek out now, and find... for it is time for you to see from the place only we can take you... it is time for you to see with eyes only we can provide...,

... it is the tiny details that you miss, two-legged... when you look from such a high place (standing there on your long-two-legs)... come now... allow yourselves to become small like us... and see what we can show you from where we stand...,

... under the brilliant light of Grandmother Moon... where all is lit and illuminated... see those things that have been just beyond the reach of your sight... closer now to you (as we are)... and with eyes that see beyond... see that which has always been beyond... see all that you have missed...,

... for you know the answers are always there, deep within... but do you look far enough, two-legged ?... do you look deep enough?... do you look until you find?... and do you look beyond there as well?...,

… seek now from our perspective… and see all that is still there for you to find… go further now than ever before, two-legged… for you know now… there is always more for you to find and see and know…"

… a s qua di s di… and so it is good

As I stand beneath the beautiful soft-white fullness of Grandmother Moon, I look up to see an empty shield. There she stands (our dear Grandmother), high in the azure blue of Father Sky, completely round and full… and the knowing of being empty fills me… and the empty shield awakens within me… and I am content…

"… close your eyes, children… direct your focus on your own feelings of contentment… search for what it is that makes you feel content (or why you don't)… set aside the loss of loved ones for a time now… look beyond any and all **things** that you have acquired and lay claim to… all material things that you insist are yours, valuable, necessary… all that you have convinced yourselves you cannot live without…,

… for it is time to go within now… and allow the empty shield to show you about your own character, personality, and generosity from a different perspective… for true contentment comes from within, children… and how you behave… your character, personality, your basic way of being, how you act toward others, and how you live your lives… all tell the story of what is going on within you…,

… in order to draw and attract… whatever it is that you wish for, need, and desire… you must have cleared away all the clutter from within… there must be room for your desires to move in… once you have drawn them to you… otherwise they will just pass on by…,

… but this teaching is not about what to keep and what to purge… it is not about what **material things** you possess that make you valuable and important and feeling content… it is not about how to fool the Universe into thinking you have room for more possessions (when you really don't)… it is about what you believe is the true value of **you**… and how to know **true** contentment…,

… this teaching is about you… stripped completely bare of all physical and material things… (even your notes and certificates of accomplishment)… and about knowing that you are valuable and worthy… just because you *are*…,

… so go to this place, children… allow your spirit to lift you as your possessions and achievements all fall away… and feel true contentment as you simply *be* the purest version of *you*… and feel what it is to be *empty* in this place, children… to give-away all notions of the mind that do not serve a world of peace and harmony…

… and see your empty shield before you now, children… see that all of your wants and needs and wishes and desires have shifted and changed… and feel how full you are, now… how being empty fills you… and know this is true contentment… and know this (too), children… whatever you draw to you now… will show up and stay… and there is plenty of room within you now… for all that you call forth…"

… a s qua di s di… and so it is good

The morning is bright and warm. I stand at my altar (in the presence of all the Stone People who join me on this day) singing gratitude to Creator and the Universe for my very existence.

I pause for a moment before I set ceremony, to be in the quiet stillness of the prairie… and my spirit begins to journey… to become one with all that is here… I travel the curves and bends of Mother Earth… I feel the tickle of prairie grass as Grandfather Wind gently blows across it… it is as if I have become the earth…

… I feel bare and exposed… as I lay out for all who walk upon me… to live upon me, to build upon me… and I feel joy in the knowing of what I provide to and for all living things and beings… and I understand the greatest teaching of all now… a teaching brought forth by generations of our ancestors… for I feel a protection that is solid… and deep within me…

… and in this moment, I know now… truly know… that protection comes from within…

"... dear children... become supple... and allow yourselves to adapt and bend with the ever turning, ever flowing movement of life...release whatever rigidity keeps you from taking on a new (and higher) perspective... and allow yourselves to soften and bend... to look from a new place... and to see through another's eyes...,

... understand, too... that having a solid core... does not mean that you must be rigid and unbending... but rather that you are solid enough to be strong... and flexible enough to move and flow and bend... so to manage with grace... any experience, situation, and/or circumstance that may arise...,

... and this is your protection, children... for as you are strong and flexible within... you are able to hold yourself together without... you see all that is going on around you with clear eyes... you move and flow **with** life as it moves... rather than resisting or pushing against the natural movement...,

... and you flow, then... you are prepared for anything and everything... and you see in all directions at once... rather than just the direction you happen to be looking at the time..."

... a s qua di s di... and so it is good

There is a sacredness in the air around me on this day. I walk the prairie with certain and precise steps... placing each foot softly upon the land... taking each step in honor and respect of our Mother the Earth...

... it is a walking prayer of gratitude I make on this day... and a feeling of abundance rises up around me...

... I stop now... sing my gratitude song one more time... and set ceremony under the brilliant light of Grandmother Moon...

"... it is a time to realize your true potential... to sit with the knowing of the gifts you offer to the world... and to recognize your worth and value...,

… there is a gift within you each… and each of these are sacred, unique, and valuable to the well-being and healing of the world you live in… and it will be through the realizing of your inherent gifts (and the sharing of them, too)… that true healing will begin…,

… step back for a time… sit in stillness… close your outer-(two)-eyes… and see with your inner-(one)-eye… see in perfect focus… the whole of what you have to offer… and that which you have to gain (or lose)…,

… see what you have shared of yourself… from that special and unique gift that is only you… see if there is more to be shared… more that can make a difference… more that has the power to inspire another…,

… for it is a time now… when the earth is giving (abundantly) of that which has been planted… and it is a time now for all to recognize this process… to know that in order to take of the harvest… you must have planted the seeds… you must have participated in some way…,

… so gather now… with the intention of sharing and giving… for the greater good of all… rather than for the good of only one… know your value, know your worth… and know the importance of each and every *one*…,

… walk your prayers of gratitude on this day, children… and make each step you take… every day… in honor and respect of that which is sacred and abundant within each and every *one*…"

… a s qua di s di… and so it is good

The morning is cool and damp as I walk out on this day. I set ceremony in the circle of stones that mark the place where the Tee Pee once stood. I smell the herbs and wood of the sacred fire that warms this space, and I feel the presence of the **Old Woman** as she prepares to assist me in ceremony.

Together we sing the prayer songs for all people, and I feel the smallness of this space expand. I feel the heavy skins that **are** the structure of the Tee Pee as they wrap around us… and I feel the spirits of many two-legged begin to enter…

"… yes, children… come in, come in… come in and sit by this sacred fire we have set just for you… come in and sing the song of your heart… come in and sit with us for a while as we pray…,

… close your eyes… as your thoughts go in for a time… find the energy that is yours… and sway with it as it moves… allow the warmth of this fire and the power of your heart… to blend together as you rest… feel your own sacredness expand… as you listen for the voice from the High Place to speak…,

… for this is a ceremony just for you… to help you locate that which is sacred within… to assist you in remembering how special and valuable you are (and always have been)… and to remind you that you are capable of discerning for yourself that which is right and wrong, good and bad (and all things in-between)…

… this is a ceremony where you can be in the presence of your Creator… (just the two of you, together)… and regain your own personal power… where you can let go of that which has been imposed upon you (by others, as well as by yourself)… and see how old behavior patterns, fears, and relationships… even old secrets and promises made in moments of pressure, fear, anger, distress, and during intense and emotional times… can rob you of your own value, worth, voice, and personal power…,

… allow this sacred fire to burn away the illusion now… and see for yourself… that which is real and yours and true… for you are a sacred being… and your voice is strong and pure… and you are valuable, worthy, and important…,

… and it is time now for you to see and know (too)… what we in the High Place see and know (already)… it is time now for you to be the sacred being that you are… and to live as a person of value and strength… who walks in their own personal power… rather than one who believes they are inferior… and lives accordingly so…"

… a s qua di s di… and so it is good

There is an expanding awareness of feminine energy all across this Star we know as Earth. The need for feminine loving, caring, nourishment, and nurturing, is felt by everyone these days (in some way or another).

Here in my little part of the world, we have been experiencing much rain (also in many other parts of the United States and other countries as well). Water is *emotion* and Water is *woman*, too. Water is the feminine aspect of the elements, which can often symbolize cleansing, but always represents emotion, heart, relationships (even if it is the relationship you have with yourself), water is about what and how we feel. Water also brings about an expansion of our feelings, and sometimes an oversensitivity to our feelings… it can bring our feelings up to the surface (so to speak).

As I sit in ceremony on this day, I am filled with emotion. I feel the pressure of the heavy-water-filled-sky pushing in on me… I feel the water I am made of swelling up within me… I want to cry… or do I need to?… I want someone to take care of me (just for today)… or do I need this kind of Mothering?…

… it is the Old Woman who comes to me now… and my tears begin to fall instantly… as I realize she has come in answer to my own personal call…

"… it is time to stop and honor your feelings… to respect the emotions that you feel inside… and to allow yourself the time and space to acknowledge, feel, and release…,

… it is time to give of yourself, too… to share your feelings (the happy as well as the sad)… and to offer support to one another in the way of true compassion… to show that you understand the need to feel, understand, and then release those feelings that have been pushed down inside…,

… look to one another now… share the gift of emotion (that only two-legged possess) with others… notice that you are all **like and same** in this way… begin to open and trust through emotion and heart… and follow the flow that is created then… for it will be by and through your hearts… that you come together as one…"

… a s qua di s di… and so it is good

AUGUST
2010

Opossum has been hiding about lately. Keeping just on the outer edge of my inner (and outer) vision... allowing me to know she is there... but not showing herself to me fully... she keeps me mindful of her *medicine*... and waiting for her message...

... until today, that is... I walk out on this morning to find Opossum waiting for me... and she wastes no time in telling me why she is here...

"... in the process of finding one's own inner-truth... there comes a time when one realizes the multitude of illusions they have wrapped themselves in... in order to survive in the world around them...,

... much of how one adapts to and manages through day to day life... (the illusions one will spin around themselves)... are necessary forms of survival, protection, conformity, and such... ways of getting along, of honoring others, of keeping peace, and so on...,

... but it is important to look in on this aspect of oneself from time to time... for it is all too easy to **become** the illusion one is trying to present... and to get lost in such illusion as well...,

... the world around you is asking more and more of you these days... and you are trying to **"fit in"** more and more these days as well... the idea of how you appear to others (and fit in with the world around you) is important... and it is sometimes necessary for one to present them self in a way that is contrary to (or does not match) how they feel inside...,

... it is because of this that many are getting lost in their own illusions... and are in need of finding themselves again... (of finding their truth)...,

... remember now... being out of balance and under too much stress for too long creates disease... remember, too... that spending too much time trying to keep up the illusion... keeps you out of balance and imposes an incredible amount of stress upon you...,

... and it is perfectly okay for you to take time to retreat from time to time... it is, in fact, a very healthy practice to get into... so take this gift that I offer you now... and spend some time with yourself... take the time to get to know yourself again… to find out just how wonderful you are… and to remember the **real** you who lives within…,

… set aside some time as often as possible… to just be with yourself… to rediscover your own truth… and to rediscover who you really are… what you really like… what you really dislike… take time each day to honor yourself… and you will automatically honor others… and others will begin to honor you back then too…"

… a s qua di s di… and so it is good

Each day (for about four or five weeks now) as I drive the twelve miles of dirt road that take me from the ranch to the highway, I am accompanied by to wo da ~ gv ni ge i "Black Hawk" (a very large and beautiful black Hawk who has greeted me every day since we moved here to this valley).

He usually waits for me on a fence post near the animal rescue across the road, and flies along with me all the way to Highway 86. Yesterday he followed me and the Cowboy for quite a while as we drove out of town to a family gathering.

Hawk Medicine is many, and it is always up to the individual (as well as the individual circumstance or experience) that the message of any *animal* is revealed… but one thing you can be sure of with Hawk… is that whenever Hawk appears… he is bringing you a message… *it is time to pay attention… heads up… keep a sharp eye… keep your eyes open… and so on…*

Hawk flew with me throughout the Dreamtime last night, and waited for me to come out this morning. I set ceremony near his favorite fence post there in the North, and after all the prayer songs were sung, Hawk flew up and circled above me… telling me the message we are to know on this day…

"… be inspired now… set new goals and follow them through… for it is a time of achieving… and much shifting is upon you…,

… in this space of time… much can be released… but much can be gained as well… renewing the old and beginning anew… are equally important as

you move forward now... for there is balance and wisdom in bringing in
the new to refresh the old...,

... look forward... while remaining mindful of what is behind you... see
the whole (big) picture... and stay flexible, creative, and mentally clear
(sharp, aware)... for it is a time of achieving now... and much shifting
is upon you ..."

... a s qua di s di... and so it is good

And so it is to *wo da ~ gv ni ge i* my friend the Black Hawk who
greets me on this day (again)... he guides me into the North, on
this cool and wet morning... and into the place of the *Standing Ones*...
where a circle waits for me in a flat, open space...

... I stand in the center of this sacred circle... and feel the presence of
an *Old One* watching.... I set ceremony... and sing the prayer songs for
all people... with the assistance of this village of *Standing Ones* who are
circled around me...

... the space where I am sitting begins to expand... as I feel the vibration
of earth shifting... and the *Old One* who wishes to speak on this day...
steps out from behind the veil that separates our physical reality from
that of the High Place...

... it is the *Keeper of the Stories*... one of the oldest *Twisted Hairs* (as
some tribes would call him) I have ever met... he sits with me now... in
the sacredness of my ceremony circle... and I honestly believe I feel the
village of *Standing Ones* move in closer... so as to hear what the *Old One*
has to say...

"... there is much being said, these days, about what the land is telling you...
but I am here to tell you... that the land is trying to teach you to listen for
yourself... it is time for you (each) to know how to hear what the Earth is
saying... and to read all the messages that surround you daily as well...,

... you (each) are the Story Keepers of the future generations... and you
(each) must develop the gift within you... so to record and recall the

happenings of your time… do not be content to rely on your technology to do this for you… but take the responsibility upon yourselves to keep the stories within you…,

… you do not have to know and record *all* of the happenings of your time… for you (each) will keep the stories of those things that are significant to you and to your own experiences… then you (each) will share the stories you have kept within you… and a deep trust will birth among all people again…,

… your friend the Black Hawk has significance (too) on this day, young ones… for he reminds you that there are many messages waiting to be received at this time… his color tells of your unlimited power and potential…and not to be persuaded by the bleak and dismal ideas that some would have you believe…,

… Black Hawk tells you, too… that you must stand in the place of **Black**… where there is no other influence to distract you… where all possibilities live… where it is only you and your Creator… in order to truly receive the information that is calling out to be heard…"

… a s qua di s di… and so it is good

I am greeted by the whole of the Star Nation as I walk out on this day… it has been too long since I have spent time with my Star Relatives… and so I walk ceremony today… singing the prayer songs for all people… and listening as my Star Relatives sing their prayer songs back to us…

… there are no words in the voices of the Star People… they speak through sound… through tones that are not necessarily heard by human ears… but are always received (felt and understood) within the heart…

"… listen, brothers and sisters… quiet your minds and rest your bodies… listen with your hearts… for the songs we sing to you on this day are about love… and the grace with which you give love (to yourself and to others)…,

… first be reminded of the true meaning of love… not our (or anyone's) definition of love… but your own understanding of love… and how it is (and has been) expressed to you by others… and how you (have and do) express your love to others…,

… how do you receive love?… and how do you give it?…,

… love is the most powerful healing tool you can ever possess… and it can be the most destructive and damaging tool as well…,

… and so as you work your way through this year of deep and personal reflection (work, challenge, shift, change, transformation, and such)… you must find time… to look at the *Love* in your life…,

… from childhood to now… look at what love means to you… look at your first experience with love… was it given (or bartered with)… conditional (or unconditional)… used (or misused)…,

… and how do you give love to others… and do your offer love *to* yourself… do you feel love *for* yourself… do you allow yourself to receive love… or do you feel unworthy of love (of being loved)…,

… look now, brothers and sisters… look deep within, look high above… find the most simple, pure, and true meaning of love… for it has become distorted, misused, and misunderstood for far too long…,

… begin to know love again… as the most pure and perfect emotion… and know it as the most pure and perfect gift… know love as the most important gift to give and to receive… and come know (then) the healing power of love… then set about to love… and see what you can heal…"

… a s qua di s di… and so it is good

I wake on this day to the smell of Sweet Almond Oil and the sense that my Grandmother is near. I hear her voice in the stillness of this dark and cool morning, and follow as she sings her Medicine Song.

*Sweet Almond Oil is my Grandmother's **signature** (if you will) **Medicine,** for she used it (in one way or another) in all of her Medicine Work. I too have become known for my use of Sweet Almond Oil, as I use it in most all of my Medicine Work, as well.*

I find myself standing atop the small knoll that is just to the Northwest of my altar. I can feel my Grandmother in this place, just as I can feel her *Medicine* in the air. I set ceremony and begin to sing the prayer songs for all people, as Grandmother sings her *Medicine Song*… filling the space around me…

"… the work of mending that which has been broken… is a delicate thing, sweet child… it must be understood that time is to be given and respected… for there is a process to follow and an individual to consider…,

… each are made of the same blood and bones and flesh… but each are wounded in different ways… and must be treated accordingly…,

… just as a garden of many vegetables planted at the same time… will mature in their own time… the healing that has begun for all people… will come to fruition for each in **their** own time…,

… it is a delicate process, sweet child… and each will find their way to their own healing… it is just for you to continue to provide the sweetness for each to recognize and follow… and to be the example that assures… with faith and trust and determination… anything can be achieved…"

… a s qua di s di… and so it is good

There is a feeling of protection in the air as I walk out on this day. Not a warning of danger or the sense that protection from danger is needed…

… but rather like a warm blanket placed upon the sleeping child… the supportive arm of a dear friend placed around one's shoulder… a parent sitting up waiting to be sure you arrive home safely…

… it is the feeling of looking out for one another… others looking out for you… and you watching out for others… being genuinely and sincerely protective of the goodness in and of all things and beings… rather than being protected from anything bad or destructive

... there is a certain comfort in feeling this kind of safety... of feeling that everyone is looking out for the best interest of one another... and the lack of any need to be constantly on the lookout for someone trying to take advantage of you, sabotage you, hurt or harm or steal from you... is so overwhelmingly comforting... it is almost indescribable...

... Wow!... What happened?... (to us as a people)... you really don't realize the stress and pressure (and worry and fear) we live with... moment to moment... every day... until you are given the contrast by having these things taken away for a time...

As I sat in ceremony on this day, held within the protection of this wonderful loving cloak... I was given the knowing of our message for today... it was not spoken... but rather offered through a feeling...

... it was the feeling of being loved and nurtured, and cared for in such a way... that you feel completely safe and protected... knowing (really knowing) that you are being looked out for... that your best interest is always considered... and that whatever happens is for the best...

... the message I came away with on this day... is that we all need to examine how we look after one another... not from a place of control... or with any other motive or agenda... but simply to be sure we are all being cared for and nurtured... that all people are (and live) safe and protected... and that this is how it should be...

... a s qua di s di... and so it is good

Crow brought the message (to me during the night) that Eagle is coming. I woke on this day to be greeted by the Eagle pair that inhabit this valley, and I saw Crow fly off into the shadows to keep watch. I stand silent and still for a time (now) before I walk out to set ceremony, to be sure I do not disturb the "Winged" who have come to join us on this day.

There is no mistaking the energy that is present when Eagle is near. You may be able to miss the subtle energies of any other winged, but you would never miss Eagle's.

It feels as though the prairie has been lifted up and moved into a high and sacred place. It feels as though all of the critters (and life) on the prairie have stopped what they are doing to sit with me in ceremony... to wait for the message Eagle brings.

It feels as though Creator is looking right at us... looking upon just this one little spot of the world...

"... two-legged... take a moment to examine the rules of conduct that you live by... the laws and rules set down by the ones who claim to know...,

... now, look in on your own personal principals and rules of ethic...,

... look to that one request made to you by your Creator... ***"walk in good relation with all things (beings, people)... for these are your relatives"...,***

... do you see a difference?... do you see the highest of these?... do you see the lowest?... do you know where your own personal behavior, actions, beliefs, and integrity lie?...,

... it is time to redefine your own personal character... to sharpen the lines of right and wrong within yourselves... and to stand above what the laws and rules of the physical world govern... for the ***spirit world*** holds you to a much higher standard...,

... reassess and reset the rules and laws that you live by... and stand on the higher ground... for when you stand in this higher place... you will see the truth of all things... and you will live your life as Creator intended..."

... a s qua di s di... and so it is good

And so the Eagles return to me on this day... flying out of the darkness of my Dreamtime with such speed and force... that I am taken into the Sky Place (carried) upon the wind they create...

... flying with my brother and sister Eagle... I move quickly through the cobalt blue of the lower sky... and into the deepest blue-black of the outer sky...

… and we glide and circle now… just exploring this vast and infinite space… and the silence is incredible… as our wings make no sound… and the beating of our hearts… is all that we can sense…

… we are in the Sky Place… the place where Shamans and Medicine People journey to, when they go seeking… and we feel them here… we hear their thoughts and questions… and we feel their power…

… and the words come now… from a voice that seems to be above and beyond where we have gotten to on this day… from out of the void… the words come now…

"… this is your place of power… this is your place of truth… this is your place of direction… this is your place of enlightenment…,

… allow your spirits to be lifted up… allow your spirits to be released… allow your spirits to soar… into this sacred and High Place…,

… be among the sacred ones… who journey and pray on your behalf… and make your own prayers here… ask your own questions… and seek out that which confounds you…,

… for the truths that you search for are here in this place… and the power that is here is your own… the answers speak out before the question can be asked… and the desires of your heart are already known…"

… a s qua di s di… and so it is good

It is Raven who greets me on this day. I hear her call to me as I wake. She calls out ***eight, nine, ten***… and I rise then and move quickly. A large council of Cloud People has gathered here in our little valley, creating the sense that I am walking deep within an enormous cave.

Raven joins me as I walk the paths and trails of this ranch, and we walk as though we have never been here before. Our voices seem louder today, and they echo a bit, and we seem to be guided by a magical force of some kind. I can hear the nun ne hi (little people, fairy folk) whispering as we walk past certain places, and this cave (of a sort) in which we are walking seems to be getting smaller.

The knowing of our own sacredness expands now, and it feels as though we are sitting within an *o si* (sweat lodge) as we set ceremony for this day. I can feel the heat from the sacred stones, and I hear the Old One calling for the door to close…

… it is just me and Raven now… sitting in this place that seems only big enough for two… I hear the rain falling, but do not feel it… I feel the movement of the Fire Keeper, but do not hear him… I hear the Old One who *pours* for the *o si* (sweat), but do not see him… and I slip away now… into the sacred place of deep within…

"… is the place within you dark, child?… open your eyes and see… for it will be through your own eyes… that light awakens the dark… and shows you there is nothing to fear…,

… for the darkness is simply the unknown… and sometimes that which you have put away for a later time… but, whichever it is for you… it is time to light the darkness within… and get on with it…,

… for that which you seek… can only be found when you go looking for it… and all that you desire can only become so… when you believe it is so (and then open your eyes to see it)… you must acknowledge all possibilities… and then open yourself (completely) to receive…,

… but the physical world is too heavy with doubt now… so heavy that even Raven could not find the air to take flight within it… so you must find your way to the place within… for the place within will guide you up and up… the place within will take you up and out and to the highest place…,

… and from this highest place… you will bring forth the vision of your wants and dreams and desires… and in this highest place… you will see all of these take shape and become so… and then… from within your own highest place… you will bring all of these back into your physical world… and you will see and know then… that they really are real…"

… and the Raven calls out… eight, nine, ten…

… a s qua di s di… and so it is good

I sit with the Old Woman on this day. Father Sky is black on this morning, and all of my Star Relatives have gathered above us. Raven is here again, but just for a moment. She hops along the upper ridge of my ceremony area and then flies up quickly... blending into the black of Father Sky as she goes...

"... a Bridge has been created now (says the Old Woman)... lay back and look up... follow the path of your sister Raven... and find your way to the Bridge she has made for you...,

... but sit for a time before you step upon the Bridge... for this Bridge leads you to the place of solution... bring to mind that which has been puzzling you... that which keeps you unsettled... and continues to take more of your (thinking) time than it should...,

... allow your mind to empty and your thoughts to clear... set down your bundle and your burdens before walking upon the Bridge... and go only when you are free of expectation...,

... for once you arrive at the very center of the Bridge, it will crest... then you will be able to stand in the present and see both past and future... this is important, child... for the solution you seek requires you to know of the past while looking into the future...,

... to use the wisdom of that which knowing and honoring your history offers... as well as to foresee that which may come to be through your action and decision...,

... you will close your eyes then, child... and receive all that you can from the place where you stand... ***past, present, and future***... and when you have received all there is to receive... you will open your eyes and make your way down the Bridge...,

... and take care then, child... for it will be important for you to know when you get to the bottom of the Bridge... did you go completely across?... or did you go back down the same way that you began?..."

... a s qua di s di... and so it is good

And so it is the Old Man who comes on this day… he sits out on the Northern pasture of our ranch, tending to his little fire… he stands when he see me… and motions for me to come…

… we stand across from one another now… sprinkling our sacred herbs into the fire that is between us… and we are bathed in the sacred smoke we make… until we become one with it… and we rise above ourselves then… into another (a higher) knowing…

… the feeling of being formless and free… of being light as air and yet aware of all that is my life… brings new perspective to that which I struggle with daily… and it is from this place that we… the Old Man and I… sing the prayer songs for all people…

… and as we return to the physical plain… we struggle to fit back into the shapes of our physical bodies… and the answers and knowing we bring with us… are from a place far above and beyond the structures and confines we have created for ourselves here on Earth…

"… whatever it is you believe limits you and keeps you from moving forward… is just that… your belief that you are limited and cannot move forward… it is a structure that you built way back then… and though it was once your protection… it is now your cage…,

… much has changed, child… and you must build a new structure now… one that is higher and more sound… flexible and able to expand…,

… your new structure must be open to and for others… and may even require the assistance of others to build… for there is strength and wisdom to be found… whenever many gather to build something together…,

… in this time when many are stuck, and feel only hopelessness… there is a need to join together… to draw together rather than to separate…,

… expand your belief now, child… change your thoughts, which will change your words… put only positive out into the space around you… and let the negative go… believe in your ability to grow and expand… believe in the goodness of others… and in their ability to grow and expand…,

… then look at the door of that cage which resides within you… and see that it is open… and as you walk toward that door to go out… see that there is no door there at all… and not even a cage to move out from…"

… a s qua di s di… and so it is good

One of the most ancient and fundamental teachings of my ancestors, is that of silence. We honor and respect silence in every way. From affording it to others through our own silence, to allowing others their own space of silence (and all ways in-between). The greatest form of respect we can offer to an Elder of any kind… is our silence.

What many may have forgotten over the generations in regard to this teaching, is the gift we receive through honoring silence. For when we offer our silence to an Elder, we allow them to speak out their wisdom to us… through which we receive the gift of experience, knowing, and wisdom of many years (and generations) gone by.

Another forgotten aspect of this teaching has to do with our own personal integrity. For the Elder can sense whether we are one who can honor and respect the information given to us, or if we are one who goes about telling all we know (or think we know) just for the sake of doing so. There is a right time and place to express what we have learned, discovered, or been told about, and in the case of Elder teachings, there is the fact that these teachings need to be taken in and worked with before being passed on.

The message I received in ceremony this morning had to do with the keeping of secrets…which is a word that has a different meaning today than it did in ancient times. For today, we know that secrets and gossip are two things we want to keep away from.

But the Elder who spoke to me this morning was talking about secrets in the old way of knowing them… secrets, as in… ***the original knowing of… the inner workings of… in the beginning… and… that which has taken years to understand, uncover, or discover… the secrets of our own inner-sacred…***

"… you are past the halfway place in this year of transition, children… and as it prepares to fade away… you will be seeking more intensely, passionately, and eagerly to discover the secrets you hold within…,

… but know, children… that which you seek is already available to you… it is right there before your eyes… but your eyes will not see it until you are ready to honor and respect what you are shown…,

… reassess your own personal integrity now, children… redefine what personal integrity is to you… reexamine the reasons you seek what you seek… and what you plan to do with theses secrets once you have awakened them…,

… for the Highest of all Elders… is the one you must give your silence to now… and this one knows for sure… how (and if) you will honor and respect the knowing you wish to receive… so think on this for a time, children… make the necessary adjustments within… and then go seeking again…"

… a s qua di s di… and so it is good

Driving home last night, the Cowboy and I were greeted by two Owls and a Hawk. They sat atop the telephone poles (at the entrance to our little valley) like sentinels. All on the East side of the road, and leaving three poles between them, they stood in the shadows of dusk and kept their eyes on us as we drove by.

It had been a bit of a strange day (too much energy in the air, so much that even the afternoon storm could not clear it), and so we went to bed early… and I fell asleep with the image of our three **Winged** friends in my mind's eye.

… *"Ah yes, there you are"*… are the words I heard as I found my way into the Dreamtime. Hawk and the two Owls were waiting for me… and we began our journey immediately…

"… two-legged… it is time to release again… but remember… that in order to truly release… you must first recognize the value of each disappointment, challenge, lesson, set-back, hurt, loss, (and so on)… remember that you must celebrate the *gift* of these as you release them… and remember to keep the wisdom they offer, too… or the release cannot be complete…,

… come with us… we will guide you to all the places within… where you store and hide all that really must be released now…,

… look for the little things, two-legged… the smallest and seemingly insignificant things that have been pushed into the corners… for these have the power to create great chaos within you… they will collect together and become very heavy… and they can build-up and attach together, too… then they will create an even bigger hurdle than any one event or issue ever has or could…,

… we have (all) come to assist you with this, two-legged… as those things that you hide within… tend to be difficult… and when many combine into one… all that is negative within them… becomes bigger and stronger… like a gang of negativity… and the challenge they present can be overwhelming…,

… use us now, two-legged… use our medicine… use our strength and wisdom and power… use all that you know of us… for we have come to assist you… and we will stay until it is done…"

… a s qua di s di… and so it is good

The Star People called me out last night. They stood in the deep-black of Father Sky, in rows and circles and villages. The ones whom I know well, standing right in front and close (as always), and there were more behind them, and even more behind them… and then I saw a Shooting Star (my very dear old friend) who guided my vision in the direction of the Southwest… where my Raven Sister was waiting for me…

… and so it is Raven who calls me out this morning (just a few short hours later)… and as we walk the prairie on this cool and breeze morning… I see us through the eyes of the Star People… one black and one white… the Raven and the Swan… each a bridge into the higher realms… each with our own specific Medicine… each strong in our own Medicine… but blended together now to bring forth our message for today…

"… it is the equality of shadow and light that you must consider at this time, two-legged… the message and power and purpose of each individually… as well as the balance and wholeness… the completeness… when the two blend as one…,

… in order to shift from separation to oneness within your world… you must begin with that which is within you… embrace your shadow as well as your light… for they are equal and sacred… and one is as necessary to your wholeness as the other…,

… look through the eyes of the Star People then, two-legged… and see the animal (totem) who is symbolized within you… get to know yourself in this most telling and intimate way, two-legged… and do not be surprised if the animal who represents (symbolizes) you… has changed or is not what you expected to see… for you are ever changing… and most two-legged carry many animal (totems) within…,

… then look, two-legged… to see both the shadow and the light of this (animal totem) aspect of you… and blend your abilities to create and shift… with true, sincere, and deep trust in yourself… for today your message is about bringing together… in every way, in every realm… (within and without)… and the knowing of what can be accomplished… when that which has been separated… is brought back together again as One…"

… a s qua di s di… and so it is good

There is an unusual stillness on the prairie this morning, and I feel as if I am standing within a large building, someplace holy and built for the sacred. I can feel the gathering of Cloud People who have moved in close, but the air around me is cold and damp. I can sense the presence of Grandfather Wind, though he seems to be holding back for now, but it is the absence of the Winged and their joyous morning song that occupies my mind in this moment.

I set ceremony at my altar on this day… and I feel the kinship of all my relatives rise up within me through the Stone People who create the prayer circles here.... and so I walk the Labyrinth... in and out... and I walk around and through the seven other stone prayer circles... and I sing the prayer songs for all people as I walk...

... and the prairie begins to breathe... as I feel the first breath of Grandfather Wind upon my skin... and the Winged join me now... for I hear them singing along with me ...

"... wherever you find yourself today... breathe in the joy of friendship, companionship, fellowship, and humanity... the love and comfort of family, friends, and neighbors... and recognize, too, your co-workers and the people in your communities... all and any whom you may know only causally... by mere acquaintance... and especially those you don't even know at all...,

... it is the joy of life and living that is your message on this day... the appreciation of all and every one... for the simple gift of their being... for the simple gift of your being... of being connected to and with one another... together as **one tribe**...,

... allow your hearts to expand now... to open and embrace... to reach out for one another... and to feel the joy of coming together as one great family...,

... be with your relatives on this day... even if it is impossible to be with your closest loved ones... know that all whom you encounter on this day are your relations... your family... your relatives... and so stand in gratitude for each of them... and feel the joy they bring... as you offer joy to them in return..."

... a s qua di s di... and so it is good

I heard the Drums begin from deep within the Dreamtime. First it was just one beat at a time, slow and perfectly spaced... *Creator's heart calling.* Then I heard the double heartbeat of our Mother the Earth awaken and answer back to Creator... her song full and deep and rich... *for she represents all of **their** children.*

Then in perfect rhythm, they joined their hearts together, and played a ancient song that I know and love…

… and I saw the people coming (then), as I gathered my ceremony bundle… and I saw the circles begin to form, as I walked out onto the prairie… and I saw that the gathering of all people (all Nations, all children of the Earth) had found its way to this little piece of ground I have been called to care take…

… and the circles became full (then)… as the Drums beat loud and strong… singing the songs of each tribe and village… of each nation and people… and bringing forth big medicine… as the people began to dance… and the Buffalo moved in close… as the energy began to build…

… and the ceremony began (then)… through the power and strength of all hearts beating as one… and all people came together… as the words to their song were sung…

"… this is the coming together… the blending as one… it is the singing of each other's songs… and the dancing upon the same ground… the sharing of the same air… and the hearing of the same sound…,

… this is the honoring of your Mother the Earth… and of your Father, your **Creator**… by coming together here… and knowing that you are one…,

… this is the knowing of life in its purest form… and gratitude from the truest place within… and this is the affording to one another… the same respect and love…,

… this is the coming home to one another… and the promise to never be separate… this is the dance that *is* your ceremony… and it is the ceremony of your life…"

… a s qua di s di… and so it is good

There is a heavy mist sitting on the prairie as I walk out on this day. The cool wet air is visible from my upstairs porch (it looks like a soft white veil covering the land), and it becomes a part of me as soon as my feet touch the ground. The smell of wet Cedar overwhelms me as I take my first few steps onto the prairie, and I look around to find the Old One who seems to want my attention.

I am drawn to the West, to the high meadow where the Buffalo are grazing (and the Antelope are here on this morning as well). I walk carefully out to the place I am drawn to, for the Cowboy opened this pasture for the Buffalo this summer, and it is ground I have not walked in awhile.

The smell of wet Cedar is even more powerful here, and the heavy mist that hangs in the air has become visible to me again… it looks like smoke rising… and there is a vision within it…

"… children… it is time to seek more than direction… for it is the **course** of your life-path that must be considered… whether you have found your true path… or are still searching… it is the **course** you take that is important now…,

… it is one thing to find your direction… another to trust enough to actually set out upon the path you are directed… and still another to discern and follow a course… for even when you tread upon ground you have walked before… it is possible the land has changed … and so you must always be mindful of your footing…,

… see that you find yourself in the West on this day… know it is the voice that speaks from deep within you that has called you here… and know that it is **this** voice you must listen to and truly hear…,

… once you hear the voice from within… pay attention to what you feel… engage all of your senses before you open your inner-eye to see… for in order to truly see your vision… you must first look with only your senses… for your eyes can deceive you… they will show you just what you want to see… rather than that which is true and real…"

… a s qua di s di… and so it is good

It is the soft whisper of Grandmother Aspen who wakes me on this morning. I feel her healing touch before I even open my eyes, and her wisdom flows into my knowing without the need of words.

We stand together for a time now, Grandmother Aspen and I... and I feel my entire being take root in the soft soil here as Grandmother Aspen whispers... *"come with me child"*... and I feel myself expand... deep into my Mother the Earth... into the place of her heart... while at the same time I feel myself rising up... into the infinite love of my Father the Sky...

"... an opening for transformation is just up ahead on your path, two-legged... and the space you will find there is vast... there is no time limit in this space... nor will there be a limit (or condition) as to how much (or what) you can shift and transform...,

... keep in mind then, two-legged... that your spirit is pure and perfect... and that whatever you feel needs to be transformed... are simply those things you have picked up along your Earth Journey... and so transformation will merely be the shedding of these illusions... so to uncover the truth within...,

... think of Snake now, two-legged... and think of transformation as a Snake shedding its skin... and remember... that even after its skin has been shed... the Snake is still the Snake..."

... a s qua di s di... and so it is good

The Cloud People lay like ribbons above me. I can see the Star People just behind them in the blackness of Father Sky (but they remain distant and come only for support). I can feel the presence of someone on the prairie, but it feels as though they are hiding. I walk to my ceremony place for today, and it feels like eyes are watching me.

I sing my gratitude to Creator, as I prepare to set ceremony for today... and from somewhere behind the Wind... out steps the Warrior...

He is younger than I... and he wears a traditional Warrior outfit... his entire face is painted white with black stripes down one side... and he walks from out of no-where leading his horse beside him... (a black and white paint who is perfectly marked with exactly the same amount of black as white)... he is magnificent, and I know him... he is my Warrior... and he only comes during especially trying times... during times when I am experiencing intense internal struggle and conflict... or when a great change is upon (me) us...

"... the ability to blend in with your surroundings is important... it is a good skill for the Warrior in you to master... but you must not allow yourself to blend in too firmly with the opinions and visions of others... for it will be through your own perception... and your own way of seeing, thinking, and reasoning... that you become most valuable to the Tribe...,

... it is good for many to see with the same eyes... for much can be accomplished when all are walking the same path... but remember... if the path continues to return you to the same place again and again... it is time for new eyes to look (then)... eyes that can see above the illusion... and lead the people to a higher path..."

... a s qua di s di... and so it is good

T is a cool Fall-like morning that greets me on this day. I pull my shawl around me as I walk, but it is no match for the comfort and safety of the blanket that the Cloud People have provided for me on this day.

I set ceremony in my altar space, and feel the closeness of all people and all things move in around me. I sing the prayer songs for all people, loud and strong, and I smile at the incredible acoustics of the prairie (which is provided by the closeness of the Cloud People on this day).

I look up and out and around, before I move into stillness, for I can see the black of Father Sky turning a lighter (but still deep) blue. I can feel the sacredness and wisdom of Grandmother Moon and the Star People, who are hidden just behind the Cloud People...

... and a voice from above begins to speak, as I begin to slip into stillness...

"… hidden deep within you… are the memories of let-downs and disap-pointments… missed opportunities and endeavors… that fell short of success or fruition…,

… you may wish to keep these hidden… or even rid yourself of these completely… but know, children… these memories are sacred and carry great wisdom…,

… honor each experience of your life… and use the wisdom gained from each fall… to rise up again and again… and to acquire more strength and determination…,

… there is a force within you that is ready to be reborn… it is your own life-force and energy… that which rekindles your excitement for creating… and for living life to the fullest…,

… look now, children… just behind that smoky mist within you… and see the sacredness of all the experiences you wish to forget… go through the emotion of each… and then let that emotion flow away…,

… for it is the wisdom of every dream, idea, and wish… that you are to consider now… and it is the wisdom of each of these… that will show you the sacredness of you… and ignite within you again… the desire to begin to create…"

… a s qua di s di… and so it is good

It is the Woman Spirit I see as I walk out on this day. The beautiful pear-shaped Goddess spirit, that instantly brings comfort to my soul and joy to my entire being. The knowing of walking in good relation with all beings rises up in my thoughts now, but it is remembering that which has been given and shared so generously by others that brings forth the feeling of unconditional love within me.

I hear her song as I walk the paths and trails of this ranch. I hear and feel the joy that comes from deep within this beautiful Old One, and I sing the prayer songs for all people soft and low… as I blend my songs, my voice… with the song of the Woman Spirit…

… and her energy expands around me now… as I am held within it…

"… I am the Spirit of all that is waiting to be born… and I speak of that which is lasting and enduring… I come with assurance that your world will continue on… and with a reminder of how important it is for you (each) to walk in good relation with one another…,

… it is through the sharing of yourselves that your hearts will expand… and the movement from *give a little and take a lot… to give generously and receive in balance*… will be made…,

… open your hearts and minds to embrace all… open your hearts and minds to share unconditionally as well… for there are partnerships waiting to be born… and from these partnerships… solid and enduring relationships will come to be… and it will be these relationships… that will keep your world turning and thriving…"

… a s qua di s di… and so it is good

I walk with Wolf on this day, or did she come to me deep in the night? I know it is she who woke me on this day, but it also feels as though we have spent several days together.

We walk out onto the prairie together and greet the morning with excitement and joy. My sister, the Wolf, wastes no time in finding the path we are to follow on this day… and together we walk this path with the prayers for all people singing out from deep within our hearts…

"… come, two-legged… follow me into the place of purity and grace… come with me to the place of perfection and truth… for there… deep within you… is the knowing of all that is possible… to and for you, and in your life…,

… look now, two-legged… and see in this place… all of the versions of you… the ordinary and the magnificent… and see, too… that you have the ability to choose… whichever one of these you wish to be… see that it is never too late to let go of the old… to take hold of the new… and to choose whichever path or destiny… is best for you…,

… and know as you walk within this place of inner knowing… that even though you had another path to follow first… one with lessons and experiences that you needed to learn and receive… you have come upon a time to switch directions… to let go… to shift up… to leap onto another path… and I can take you to the jumping off place… the place that will lift you out of the mundane and into the exceptional…,

… breathe with me now for a time, two-legged… breathe with me and allow your heart to beat with mine… for I will attune you with my highly developed senses… so that you too, can see as I see… know as I know… and sense as I sense…,

… then relax, two-legged… and listen to the wisdom from deep within… and use all of your gifts and abilities… to know what it is you seek to know… and trust, two-legged… with the heart of **Wolf**… for you must finally trust in this most honest and complete way… in order to accomplish all that you came to accomplish…"

… a s qua di s di… and so it is good

Grandmother Moon sits behind the Cloud People on this day… I feel the softness of her spirit as I sing the prayer songs for all people. I open my eyes for a moment as I move into stillness, and I see her there… sinking into the horizon… almost completely full. She is round and yellow and warm…

… and she whispers to me just before she moves completely out of sight…

"… honor yourselves, two-legged… look up at me… and use me as your mirror… see yourselves in my reflection… as Creator sees you… **whole and pure… perfect and beautiful**… see the light within you, radiate out… and see if you are balanced… if you walk in harmony with **all that is**…,

… know that the most important qualities to focus on and set for yourselves… are balance and harmony… for once you find balance… you will know harmony in all things… your vision will click into focus… and you will see with great clarity… you will see the sacred path you seek to know and walk…,

… and know, too… that once you have discovered your sacred path… you must remain in balance… (of spirit and emotion, of mind and thought, of action and all things physical, of male and female, of light and dark)… in order to truly walk your sacred path…,

… balance and harmony are the keys for you now, two-legged… so look into me… and see your reflection… see yourself as you are seen from above… and know, two-legged… that you are far more perfect and beautiful in our eyes… than in your own… and that we see you in absolute, complete, and perfect truth…"

… a s qua di s di… and so it is good

The sense of a new Season greets me as I walk out on this day. Although our calendar does not show the Season changing for a few more weeks, Mother Nature has another plan. The cool evenings and crisp mornings are already telling some of our Standing Relatives to change into their Autumn attire, and I find myself craving a good hearty stew.

My own thoughts seem to have a pressing matter to discuss with the High Ones on this day, as I find myself thinking about this last quarter of our transition year… and how best to use it…

"… seek the innocence of a young child… seek to know true innocence and trust… for you walk with wide and open eyes then… and you walk without expectation as well…,

… as you work through the remainder of your transitional year… know that you release the last of what you cannot take forward with you (that which will certainly hold you down and back)… and you prepare for the actual transformation and changes… that you have been working so hard to make… the solid transformation that will be the **work** of your next year…,

… returning to a place of innocence… opens you to every possibility… for when you walk with expectation… you confine yourself to a space the size of your expectation… and no matter how grand this expectation may be… it is not (nor could it ever be) as grand as the possibilities Creator has in store for you…,

… refresh your spirit… in the time that lies before you… and return to a place of innocence and trust (within and without)… open yourselves to receive all that is new and fresh… and walk with childlike wonder into your own transformation…,

… then smile, children… the sweet and joyous smile of a child… for you will truly be a child again… ready to run forward and explore… and to learn and know… all that is waiting for you to learn and know…"

… a s qua di s di… and so it is good

Grandmother Moon is waiting for me as I step out into the morning. She sits high above me on this day, round and bright, shining her light upon the whole of the prairie. I stand for a time and let her soft healing light wash over and through me. I stand for a time longer, listening for what it is she wishes us to know on this day.

I hear a voice call out to me now, but it is the voice of our Mother the Earth who speaks. I quickly make my way down the seventeen steps and out onto the prairie… following the voice of our dear Mother Earth… and sitting quiet and still until she begins to speak…

"… dear children… it is time to shift the attention you have been giving me… from how to heal and protect me… to allowing me to teach you how to heal and protect yourselves… for it is time that you begin to recognize the magnificence of *you*… and for you to begin to trust in your own healing ability… and know that you have the power to restore that which has been damaged to its perfect state of being… and to make use of all that you have experienced… so to become stronger and wiser…,

… stand upon me and connect with the **Universal Conscious Intention**… allow yourself to be grounded… and allow your heart to beat with mine… know that I am your solid foundation… and that I provide more than a place for you to walk upon… for I am your teacher… and even within the cold of Winter… the connection we make on this day… will allow you to journey deep within me… whenever you need the knowledge and wisdom (the answers and teaching) I carry within…,

… listen now, children… for it is time for you to go seeking within me… it is time for you to be quiet and still… and to allow me to awaken a knowing within you… for as you move into the last of this (your calendar) year… you will be as an unborn baby… gestating and developing… and waiting to birth…,

… and you will see then, children… with the purest of eyes… which will show you the beauty and perfection of each and every **one**… and as you witness your own formation… you will understand one another in a deeper way… and you will let go of that which makes you feel separate… and you will remember everything that makes you **same**…,

… I am eternal, children… and so are you… and in the time that is before you now… it is important for you to remember this…"

… a s qua di s di… and so it is good

I am awakened by the nun ne hi (little people - fairies) on this day. I walk out of the Dreamtime upon flower petals of all kinds (which have been scattered about on the path that I walk). I hear the wisdom of each flower as I walk along, and the intoxicating fragrance of each one stands out for a moment as I pass by… waiting for me to recognize it.

I hear the nun ne hi giggle and whisper now, and so I rise and move quickly out onto the prairie. I walk to the *Purple Smoke Bush,* for I know that the *nun ne hi* live here

"… there is an opening coming soon… a space where it will be easy for you to awaken and adapt to that which resides in the higher realms… the information will come in different ways for each… through sound - through dreams - through sensing - through inner-vision - (and such)… and so you (each) must pay attention now… for you (each) must be alert and prepared…

… a difficult time is passing… for all, as well as for each… and in the space just beyond this… the opening will occur

… soften now… and let go of anger and rigidity… of stubbornness and entitlement… for you must be ready and able to adapt to the higher vibration that follows…

… but keep your feet on the ground… you must stay solid and grounded… for it is not for you to rise up and fly away… but to expand all that you are… in spirit, heart, body, and mind… so to enhance the experience of your Earth Journey…,

… and a deeper sense of trust in yourself will come then… for as you connect to and with the higher vibration… you will connect to and with a higher knowing of yourself as well…"

… a s qua di s di… and so it is good

Grandmother Moon illuminates the entire prairie as I walk out on this day. I stand for a moment before I make my way out to my ceremony place, and I breathe in all that is Grandmother Moon. I breathe her in through my crown, all the way down to my toes, and I allow her to fill me completely…

"… reach high children… set your goals and aspirations high… for you have everything you need to reach and accomplish whatever you set your mind to…,

… reach beyond now… for the boundaries have all been removed… reach out and up… and grasp with both hands… for the prize is yours for the taking…,

… be inspired… and inspire others… breathe in the fresh and clean air of this fresh and clean day… and with that breath… breathe in the brilliant white light of the *High Place*… for it is the **new** that you must be aware of now…,

… it is time for you to become your new **lighter** self… to become more spirit, less physical… to become more light, less shadow… to create a new "cleaner" way of living (of being)… to know and understand that *"all things really **are** possible"*… and to accept within you… a new and stronger (deeper) trust and belief in yourself…,

… for today you begin anew… and all you have to do now… is to dream and trust and believe… to aim high… and to reach up…"

… a s qua di s di… and so it is good

It is hard to wake on this cool morning. I feel like a child who has to get up for school, I just want to pull the covers up over my head and sleep some more…

… but I rise and gather my ceremony bundle… and make my way out to the ceremony place for today… for my spirit is awake and joyous… it is only my body that is tired…

… school has already begun here in Colorado… which inspires much talk about growth… for as the children return to school… they have grown and changed… and they move along their ever-changing circle of beginning over and over again… in perfect rhythm with the greater plan…

… it is easy as a child to notice, mark, measure, record, and even strive for growth… for growth is what it is all about as a child… and even though physical, mental, and emotional growth are all that is required to be tracked in the school arena… there is spiritual growth as well

… we as adults sometimes fail to notice our own personal growth… and whether the growth we do recognize is spiritual, emotional, physical, or mental… often depends on our job or circumstance… our hobbies and our recreation…,

… once we become adults and set out into the world… we really need to pay attention to our own personal growth (in all aspects of our being)… for we do not change from grade to grade every nine months… and noticing our own growth is extremely important to our overall experience of life…

… an Elder once told me that everything we do in our lives is spiritual… and everything we do… is connected to everything we do… nothing is separate… so if we are growing emotionally… that is expanding our spirit… if we grow physically and/or mentally… that expands our spirit… and of course, when we grow spiritually… well, you know…,

… as I sit in ceremony on this day… I hear the voice of this wise old Elder… and as I sing the prayer songs for all people… she whispers…

"… look in on your own personal growth, children… look at your physical and mental and emotional growth… as well as your spiritual growth… notice how far you have come… or if you have stopped to rest for a time… and set your goals then… so you will begin to move again…,

… know that you are always growing and moving forward… even when you do not pay attention… but as you look in and notice how far you have come… and how much you have grown… you will be inspired to go further… to continue your growth… and this will expand your spirit... and this is good…"

… a s qua di s di… and so it is good

And so it is the beating of the Sacred Drum… that calls me out of the Dreamtime on this day… I hear the sweet ***double-heart-beat*** of child in womb… the mother's heart beating and the child's heart softly answering…

… I make my way out onto the prairie… and follow the sound of the Sacred Drum… and soon I am standing upon the rich, soft soil where the Buffalo walk… and I feel the strong and healing heartbeat of our Mother the Earth… beating beneath my feet…

… I quiet now… and I breathe in the oneness of all that surrounds me… I allow my own heartbeat to slow and wait for a time… as it listens for the call of my Mother the Earth… and something within me stirs… as my heart softly answers back to the heart beat of our dear and eternal Mother…

… I sing the prayer songs for all people now… in rhythm with the sacred ***double-heart-beat*** of mother and child… of sacred mother and forming child singing together through feeling rather than voice…

… and as I move into stillness… I feel my spirit release… as I begin a deep and sacred journey within…

"… find your own rhythm, children… feel for that which is your own beat… your own pace… and listen for your own sound…,

... for there is a song that is yours... and it must sing within you... it will not match that of any other... but when all songs are sung together... they become the music for the dance of life...,

... and once you have found your own beat and rhythm... you begin to know where you fit... and once you know where you fit... you can journey out as far as you like... and know for certain... there will be a place waiting for your return..."

... a s qua di s di... and so it is good

And so the song of the Drum calls to me again on this day... this time it is the single heartbeat of our Mother the Earth I hear... slow and deep and ancient is her sound... and so powerful is she... that she draws me back into the Dreamtime... to show me the message for today before I even step out onto the prairie...

... I set ceremony... as the Drum continues to sing out the heartbeat of Mother Earth... and together the Drum, Mother Earth, and I sing the prayer songs for all people...

... I can feel the prayer songs moving within me... taking me back and back... out of the present day... and into a time long ago...

... and the Drum and Mother Earth are beating strong and steady now... as their song fills the space of this land... and I walk with them... in that place of long ago...

"... it is time to go deeper within, children... it is time to build your *new*... from that which has been your *past*... for there are many jewels that you will find hidden... in that which you have let go and walked away from...,

... consider the experiences of your lives (of past lives as well as of this present one)... consider those which you have learned from... and consider those experiences that have changed you completely... the positive ones as well as the negative ones...,

… and stay with the experiences that have stopped you completely… created a block… and shut a door… turned your face to look away…,

… for it is time for you to remove these blocks… to bring the issues out into the open… to heal them and to understand them… it is time now, children… for you to allow the old dry leaves to fall away… so to reveal the jewels that lie hiding beneath…,

… and it is time for you to know, children… this is one of the secrets of the **Circle of Life**… and you must know now, too… that as you remove these blocks… old doors are revealed… old doors with new thresholds… and new opportunities for you to cross over and experience…,

… and the circle will go on and on, children… as you build your **new**… from that which has been your **past**…"

… a s qua di s di… and so it is good

There is an unusual energy on the prairie this morning. I have felt it before, but not for some time. It is the knowing that something is hidden or hiding… and wants very much for me to find it… but it is not hiding by its own plan or action… it has been hidden by me… and it is concerned that I have forgotten all about it.

I walk the prairie now, in walking ceremony… I sing the prayer songs for all people silently within… so to allow this one (or thing) that is hiding… a safe space to come out into… I feel feline energy… and I hear the sound of her paws softly padding upon the land…

… and I follow her now… into the place of stillness…

"… yes, two-legged… come with me… for you have hidden something deep within you… and I can help you find it… mind you, we will not go seeking… for that is not the way to find this hidden treasure… you see it is your own personal integrity that must be checked and placed in high order… before your sacred gift can be found again…,

… it is time to examine your respect for that which is sacred and personal… it is time to look in on how trustworthy you are… and how you keep safe (care for and protect) the sacred secrets of that which is your Medicine...,

... for you are in search of an even higher knowing... a knowing that you have always had access to... a knowing that is ready to emerge into the world... a knowing that you owned and made use of throughout many lifetimes... a knowing that requires the highest of integrity and trustworthiness to possess...,

... and each and every being possesses this gift, this treasure, this Medicine... somewhere within them... but it is personal and different for each....

... sit, two-legged... sit and look in on how you respect the sacred secrets, knowing, and Medicine... yes, there are those which are to be shared and explained, and even taught... but then there are those which are so sacred and personal... that they are to be kept within... for each must discover these on their own...,

... and to offer your own personal Medicine to another... cannot be done... for it will bring about confusion and frustration within them... and set them out on a journey that cannot be made... in search of a place that does not exist for them...,

... so go now, two-legged... go in search of your hidden treasure... but know that you will not find it... until you have found your own highest place of integrity and impeccability... and when you have the utmost respect for yourself and others..."

... a s qua di s di... and so it is good

SEPTEMBER
2010

Last night was the seventh night in a row that I was greeted by an old and wise Elder who lives in the body of an Owl. Each night as I drive through the gate I see him sitting on a large fence post in the North area of our ranch. He remains silent and still as I drive through the gate, but as I drive around the curving road to park, he flies right in front of me and then circles back to sit upon my altar.

I know he has something to tell me, and so I listen for him in the Dreamtime. I look for him each morning as I walk out to set ceremony, but I know he will speak only when it is time. And so I go on about my daily routine as usual, day after day... only to be surprised by his presence, again and again, each night.

As I walked out for ceremony on this day, I heard the deep and distinct song of the Elder Owl. It stopped me for a moment, and I stood silent and still as I looked toward my altar... just in time to see him change...

... I saw the Owl sitting there... quiet and still... and as he spread his wings to take flight... the Owl flew up... and the Elder appeared... it is an old and wise *Elder of Wisdom* who stands before me now... tall and lean, in a dark colored robe... he stands cloaked in light and motions for me to join him...

"... it is time for you to begin a conscious and deliberate course of learning... one that you set for yourself... and does not necessarily involve formal education... it is time for you to look within... to find what you need most at this time... to determine if this phase of your education will come through teachers, books, or experience... and if you will learn with your mind, your heart, or your spirit...,

... seek out seven things that you wish to study... seven things that you wish to look in on and finish (or strengthen)... that you need to balance and/or understand...

... it is possible that for some... you will revisit seven things that you have just learned (or uncovered within yourself) throughout this year... and for some it may be a combination of that which you have just learned and that which you seek to learn...,

… get yourself a journal and spend some time with this… list your seven subjects and provide a chapter for each… for this will be your teaching guide as well as your learning book… and once you agree to this assignment… you will be surprised at how much information awakens within you for it…,

… the knowledge you gain… will be for your personal growth and development… but remember… with knowledge comes responsibility… and this is **most important** for you to remember… for you must remain responsible and respectful of this newfound knowledge at all times… for it belongs to the **Elder of Wisdom** who lives within you…"

… a s qua di s di… and so it is good

I find myself in the Sky Place on this day… high above the Earth but with a very deep knowing of all that is upon and of her… I do not fly upon the Wind… for I feel as though I am the Wind on this day…

… and I know who is with me… here in this place above… it is the Old Grandmother… the one who lives deep within the Earth… but reaches out to the ends of the Universe and beyond…

… there is great healing and vision in the space where this Grandmother lives… deep wisdom and ancient knowing… secrets of how to shift and change… to create and manifest…

… I sing the prayer songs for all people now… and I see and feel them (each) within me… I sing joy and laughter and gratitude into their hearts… for I feel they are weighted with worry, fear, and despair…

… and the Old Grandmother begins to speak… from deep within the Earth and from high up in the Sky Place, at once… as I find myself sitting back upon the prairie… bathed in the sacred smoke of ceremony… and held in the presence of all that is…

"… awaken, children… to a new vision that is just coming into focus for you… adjust your sight to see as far up and out as you can… and then look even farther… close your eyes and breathe in deeply from this high and far place… for you will breathe in all that is pure and perfect and possible… all that is new and fresh… all that is real and true…,

… and feel as you breathe… feel your physical being standing solid upon your Mother the Earth… and know that the two must work together… know that the vision and power of the High Place… needs the ability and strength of the physical (earth place)…,

… and understand in this instant… the power of true cooperation between spirit and body… know the importance of the spiritual and the physical working together as one…,

… for you must align yourself with these two magnificent forces… and bring them together within you… bring them together around you… for all to feel and sense and share… and know in this instant, too… that this balance is essential… in order for healing and peace to be present in your world…"

… a s qua di s di… and so it is good

I wrap my shawl around me as I walk out on this day. It is a cool morning and I walk briskly across the prairie to the place where I will set ceremony for today. I see the bunnies run and scamper as I near their territory, but I see it is Deer who has come to speak to us on this day…

"… release the static from within, two-legged… release the fear and the doubt… connect with the softness that lives within you… the trust and the kindness… that which is gentle and unconditional…,

… honor yourselves with these, two-legged… for though it is important to offer trust and kindness, gentle words and actions, and unconditional love to others (all beings)… it is essential for you to offer these to yourself…,

… you are the healer of your own self, two-legged… and as you heal… you become stronger and more able to assist others… this you must trust and as you trust… you expand the energy of trust within the world… and as you trust even more… you let go of that thing you know as fear… and the overwhelming sense of fear that presides over your world… will begin to lessen… as one by one (each) begins to trust and release…

… there is much to be done yet… in the way of healing the wounds that keep all people living as separate (rather than in **oneness**)… and this work must be done from within the hearts and minds of each and every two-legged… and in order for this work to begin… **someone must begin…**,

… so begin now, two-legged… begin to honor and respect yourselves… begin to love and cherish yourselves… begin to trust and love yourselves… **unconditionally**… and allow all negative feelings to fall away…,

… and the world will heal and change then… and become a place of peace and light… through the gentle, kind, and compassionate **Medicine of Deer**… as it awakens within each and every one of you…"

… a s qua di s di… and so it is good

The season is already turning into Fall. Everything feels as though it has been shaken up. I keep a close eye on all of the critters and wildlife as I walk out today, for I have already seen evidence of the Prairie Mice setting up their winter home in our barn…

"… it is time to get some things in order… to organize… and to reduce the clutter… use this Season to make a transition… and to minimize all that you keep as **necessities** within and around you… pick up your rugs and shake them out… dust out every corner… and purge that which is no longer of any use…,

… for as your rest throughout the Winter… you will receive much wisdom… new information will awaken within you… knowing will rise up… and you must provide a place for these to live and grow and expand…,

… look to your physical environment first… and then to that which has cluttered up your emotions and your mind… next look in on that which has attached itself to your physical body… for as you begin to sort and clean and tidy up these areas of your life… your spirit will naturally expand… and you will become open and ready to receive… all the wisdom that awaits you…"

… a s qua di s di… and so it is good

I find myself deep within Mother Earth on this day… I feel the beating of her heart even before I hear the sound of it… and I feel the vibration of all that lives deep within our dear Mother… every stone… every jewel… every crystal…

… and I see light now…and color too… I see all of the stones and jewels and crystals as they each step up to speak… to tell me something of their Medicine that I am to know and use and keep… and I listen… wishing that I had a journal to write it all down…

… but I am assured that the knowing and medicine I am being told of today… is not new… it is old and ancient… truths from the very beginning… and wisdom I am to remember… rather than learn…

… and I am told on this day as well… that all people are awakening to the knowing of their ancestors… and that all of what I am being shown today… is for my own personal expansion and use… that is except for one…

… and so it is the **deep purple** of Amethyst that comes forward to speak on this day… offering her wisdom and Medicine to me… as well as to all of you…

"… it is important for you each to distinguish… whether the energy that you attract… is the positive energy of others (that you bring out)… or if it is the negative… and look to see now, too… if you are in charge of your own thoughts and visions… or if you are allowing others to take this lead for you…,

… bathe yourselves in the deep purple of my being… draw it through you to cleanse and heal (to purify) yourselves completely… for as you do… you will be lifted higher and higher in consciousness… and you will have access to all that is awakening to and for you… and you will gain the ability to make your own choices as well…"

… a s qua di s di… and so it is good

I wake from many Medicine Dreams on this day. The Snake and the Bear… Horses of Many Colors… the Dog and the Water… and two-legged of every Tribe, Culture, and Nation…

… I stand for a moment before I make my way out onto the prairie… and I breathe in the purity of a morning not yet begun… I feel the peace of this place within my entire being… and I listen without expectation for what I am to know of my dreams…

… it is the Old Shaman who calls out to me… "Come, this way… follow me…" … and so I follow the sound of the Old Shaman's Drum… up into the place of the Standing Ones… and together we set ceremony for today

"… Bear is from the West… and Snake came in from the North… Horse has come to carry you wherever you need to go… and Dog is here as your companion…Water speaks of the place where you stand on your own personal Medicine Wheel… and tells you that it is your heart and emotions that need healing and attention now…

… Bear tells you to go within… so to truly see that which has been disrupting your flow… and Snake shows you how to shed the old… so to begin again, fresh and new… with its belly completely connected to and with Mother Earth… Snake moves along smoothly… flowing like water upon its path… and encourages you to strive for the same…

… Dog is your companion… loyal and devoted… and Dog walks alongside of you as your protector… for Dog is your eyes and ears, and represents all of your senses… and so Dog will see and hear and sense that which you might miss… but Dog represents your Spirit as well… and is your connection to Creator… and so Dog is also a representation of you…

… the two-legged of all Tribes and Cultures and Nations… represent two things… first… that you are all people… that all people are the same… valuable and necessary and deserving… and second… that you are to share this message with all people… for it is time now for all people to take this Journey…,

… and although this Medicine Dream came to you… it is for many to follow… all others will need to call for their own Medicine Dream… but all should look within anyway… to find what it is they (each) are called to do at this time… for it is time (for each) to walk straight ahead… and to assist in the creation of the future…,

… or maybe you will just ride in on your trusty Horse… with your loyal companion Dog by your side…"

… a s qua di s di… and so it is good

A cool evening has turned into a cold morning. Or at least it seems cold compared to the warm mornings of Summer. I step out on this day wrapped in my blanket, and welcome the new season with a smile and gratitude. The time of Fall seems to be upon us now, and in the season of Fall we find it easier to allow that which we have been trying to release… to simply fall away.

Fall is a time of transition, a time when the grasses die and the leaves dry up and fall away… it is a time when we can physically see what transformation is… we can see that it is a process… and we can see that this time of transformation coincides with our own personal transformation… and it becomes easy for us to recognize, too… that it is only after we have allowed the old to die and fall away… that the new can be born again in Spring.

This helps us to trust and respect and honor the process of transformation… for during the time of Fall we begin to understand… that we must make time for transformation… in order for transformation to take place.

I am told that whether the changes we make are positive or negative… is always left up to us… and I believe this is true… but oftentimes it is difficult to see and know… here and now… what would be a positive change… and what would be a negative one…

… and my heart begins to beat faster now… and I feel myself begin to worry… the more I think on this…

… but the Old One I am sitting with assures me… that the process will be simple… and that all will go smoothly forward in a good way… as long as we do not move forward presuming we know what would be best… (which would be a positive and which would be a negative)… for this would only incite great conflict among us… the key is to focus on our own personal growth and development… and the rest will fall into place (move and shift) naturally…

"… it is for each to strive to be the highest and best version of themselves… to work toward their own healing… and through this process… begin to see one another as their own… to respect and honor one another as they would like to be respected and honored… to let go of any and all judgments that one would not like imposed upon themselves… and to live each day in gratitude for life itself…

… find your way to this place, two-legged… and you will have assisted in the greatest transformation you could ever imagine…"

… a s qua di s di… and so it is good

There is a Porcupine who lives on our ranch. I see her every night as I drive across the cattle guard. She is always in the same general area, just shuffling along the edge of the road just above the ditch. But last night as I drove in, she was all snuggled up in a ball trying to stay warm.

I sent warmth for the night to my Porcupine friend as I drifted off to sleep, and so she came into my Dreamtime to thank me…

"… feel the Wind as it blows… stand up… and allow it to blow around and through you… see if you can feel the dance it wishes to teach you… for there is a new way to move now… as the vibration of the Earth is shifting…,

… see with new eyes… and feel the excitement of looking upon that which is new and different… be as a child in this way… for you have become a child again in many ways…,

… look with wonder at all you believe you know… for everything is shifting… and even though the changes may be subtle… they will be important…

then wander along in your own way… but notice everything as if you have just encountered it for the first time…,

… learn that which you may have overlooked before (or forgotten)… for there is new information to be found… and it is time to rediscover everything… including yourself…,

… there is wisdom and knowing within you… from the past as well as from the future… and as you wander along your path… know that you walk along that narrow place between the ditch and the road…,

… so remain steady and true to yourself… for if you become too heavy in the words and opinions of others… you will find yourself out of balance… and you will begin to lean to one side or the other… which will cause you to wobble… and your movement forward will begin to slow… ,

… and if you stay this way for too long… you might find yourself falling into the ditch… or too far out in the middle of the road…"

… a s qua di s di… and so it is good

The Old Ones who wait for me on this morning stand in circle, they are the *sacred stones*. I see the Grandfathers in their physical spirits on this day… and it is their hearts that I see expanding… it is their hearts that I feel… it is their hearts that hear… as the Grandfathers begin to speak…

"… there is much emotion rising up within you, (all) two-legged… you will feel it on your skin… you will feel it stirring within… you will feel that which you have been avoiding… and you will wonder how to find the balance again…,

… allow the *sacred waters* to flow through you, two-legged… allow the tears to flow… allow the pain to rise up… and allow yourself to feel it… for once you get to this place, two-legged… the sting will fade away… and the balance will return…,

… and your clarity will return too… your mind will clear and so will your sight… you will breathe with ease again… drawing in and breathing out in a smooth and even flow… you will sigh for the relief…. and you will move forward again… with strong and steady steps…,

… it is important to honor the emotions that speak to you now… and it is necessary to acknowledge the pain as a gift… just as you would a moment of happiness and joy… for all things that come up within you… are guiding you to a higher place… especially those which cause you pain… and beg to be released…"

… a s qua di s di… and so it is good

I wake on the west coast of our Turtle Island, in the home of my childhood. The movement of Grandmother Ocean is strong within and around me. I feel the emotion already beginning to stir within me, as I gather my ceremony bundle and walk out into the warm California morning.

My family sleeps as I sit in ceremony here, and the sound of the cars on the freeway blend with the sound of Grandmother Ocean, to create a balanced place between the physical and the spiritual for me to set ceremony within.

I sing the prayer songs for all people as Grandmother Ocean moves in close to me… she is strong yet she is gentle… wise yet unassuming… and I listen with deep respect as she begins to speak…

"… consider your relationship with the physical world, children… consider your relationship with one another… quiet your minds as well as your voices… and listen with your spirits and your hearts…,

… bless with love your relationships (with others) that are ending now… and stand in gratitude of those that remain strong and constant… be grateful, too, for all of the relationships in your lives that have come and gone… for each has had purpose and value…,

… then look to how your relationship to and with yourself has grown and developed… and at how your relationship to and with your Creator has deepened and expanded…,… find the greater meaning of life… as you experience the world around you through sense and feeling… rather than thought and judgment… and hear what is being said on all levels and in every way…,

... for as you work through the details of your relationship to and with one another... as well as to and with the world around you... you will become stronger and more balanced in your relationship with yourself, your spirit, and your Creator..."

... a s qua di s di... and so it is good

A sense of safety and protection flows through me as I set ceremony on this day. I sit for a moment in this energy, as it wraps around me (holding me as if I were a small child). I look up to acknowledge my Star Relatives, and they draw me up into the place where they are.

The Star Place is my home... the place of my origination... I know this deep within my heart and soul... it is the source of the purest and most powerful Medicine that I carry... and the purity of the energy here cannot be explained... for it is completely pure... completely perfect... and the knowing of Oneness in this place... is absolute... for here in the Star Place... we are simply Spirit... and each and every one of us is equal and same.

The notion of safety and protection is of great concern for the two-legged of our physical world on this day...(9/11)... and so our Star Relatives have brought me home with them for a time... for they have a message they want to share with us...

"... here in the place where we reside (the Star Place)... there is no thought... only feeling... all are same here... pure and perfect and same... there is only peace in this place... peace, and the knowing of being safe and protected... and all beings should travel here from time to time... to experience this place of peace and trust...,

... you know about feeling... there in the place where you reside... but *thought* is used (there) much more often than feeling is... for it is the stronger of the two in your world... thought is the thing that assisted you in creating the magnificent world in which you live... and *thought* is also the thing that brought you to the place where you are now... open and exposed and in need of protection...,

… think on this for a time, two-legged… then release your thoughts and *feel* for a time… begin to balance your thoughts with your sense of feeling… and feel for the sameness of one another… go beyond what you have been told of any individual… go beyond what any other may look like… and then go directly to the **Spirit** of each and every **one**…,

… for this is where you will find peace… this is where you will find safety… this is where you acquire the knowing that you are protected… for when you find your way to this place… you will not think with your mind… but feel with your heart, soul, and **spirit**… and this is when you will know (truly know)… without question or judgment… that purity and perfection reside within all beings…,

… and there will be no need to be protected from any **one** or any **thing** (then)… for you will have found safety and protection in the knowing… that you are all **one and the same**…"

… a s qua di s di… and so it is good

It is still and quiet as I wake on this day… cold and damp and overcast (here in Southern California). I walk out the front door, and take a short walk down the street before I set ceremony on this day… and I walk right out of the dense cloud that is sitting on our house.

I sit in the backyard (now), immersed in the white cloud that seems to be covering about five other houses here on this street. I sing the prayer songs for all people, and feel warmth rise up within me… … and it is in the peace and grace of this moment… that I move into stillness… or does the stillness move into me…

"… seek peace, and you will create it… seek balance, and you will become balanced… seek to live in harmony, and you will bring harmony to all who surround you… love and accept yourself just as you are, and you will know the world in a much higher way…,

… know that whatever it is you wish to create in your life… it begins within your heart and is guided by your spirit… but your thoughts and beliefs will determine how and if you manifest that which you desire…,

… negative thoughts toward yourself and/or others will hold you in one place… keeping that which you wish to create or achieve… just beyond your reach… open your minds and thoughts to see and know the goodness of all people… open your hearts and prayers to all people too… and seek for all… that which you would seek for yourself…,

… your thoughts will change as you begin to live in this way… and the thoughts of others will change then too… and all will begin to bring forth that which is good and positive into their lives… and each will share their peace and joy with one another… and this is harmony, dear children… and this is good…"

… a s qua di s di… and so it is good

I journey on the back of my spirit friend, the She Cougar. It is an old place that she has taken me (deep within the night), and we return from this faraway place with a message from the Old Ones who live there…

"… you are getting closer to knowing who you truly are, (all) two-legged… and you are beginning to see the unlimited possibilities that lay before you… as you discover even more of your abilities and strengths…,

… take no direction from the physical world… but make a solid connection with your highest spirit… and allow your highest *self* to be your guide… for it is time for you to achieve your full potential… and to become as comfortable in the higher realms (and with the higher vibrations)… as you are and have been in the physical…,

… you are your own teacher (now) as you move forward… and it is your higher self who leads and guides you… it is time for you to discover what is already there within your knowing… and so you must set aside some time (now)… to be the student of these lessons and wisdoms… and to learn that which only you can bring up from within yourself…,

…set yourself a place that is free of distraction… a place where there is no influence from the physical world… as you will need to pay close attention to that which is awakening within you… so that it can remain pure and clean and true…,

… this is an important transition that is upon you, two-legged… and a difficult one as well… for once you become both teacher and student of your own Medicine… you will live your life in a much higher way… and your presence within the world will make a greater impact… than it ever has before…"

… a s qua di s di… and so it is good

The weather has been cool and pleasant here in California (mild for this time of year). I sit in the darkness on this morning, listening to the quiet. I listen beyond the white noise from the freeway (just a quarter mile away), and connect with Grandmother Ocean (less than seven miles away).

There is a freshening that stirs within me, as I breathe in the sweet fragrance of this morning… jasmine, gardenia, and roses blending with the damp salty air of Grandmother Ocean… it is a freshening for sure.

I sing the prayer songs for all people… and I am bathed in the cleansing of this morning's ceremony… fragrance rather than smoke… which proves to be even more powerful than I had expected.

I sit in silence for a moment now, before I move into stillness, and allow myself to become completely immersed in the sacredness that surrounds me here…

"… take time now to refresh and renew… drench yourself in the spirit of Father Sun… allow Grandfather Wind to blow in and through you… breathe in the healing power of the plants and trees and flowers that surround you… for each of these will fill and freshen your spirit… as they push out all that is old and stale…,

… this is an important part of preparing for the Winter that is coming… to push out the last of that which is old and heavy and stale… to freshen and renew… so to create a space which is clean and clear… for moving into the next year… will require you (each) to be as light and unburdened as possible…,

… so become empty now… and ready to receive… for deep within the stillness of Winter… you will have access to a much higher vibration… and you will need to be lighter (then)… in order to reach that vibration…"

… a s qua di s di… and so it is good

I awaken from a place of old wisdom on this day… and a vague memory of an old building… a large room… a place where books are kept… a library or a monastery of some kind…

… I can still smell the sacredness of this place… the books… and the wood of the ancient furniture, walls, floors, and doors… I can still feel the holiness of this place… the years of history… and the sacrifice of lives and experiences held within the pages…

… there is a peace and a comfort I feel… as I remember standing in such a place… a knowing of something magnificent… a knowing of something simple… the promise of wishes granted… and a teaching of the true fruits of life… *explanation and meaning…*

… and I feel the presence of an Old One now… one who has followed me back from the sacred place I have just been… and this Old One quietly waits for a moment of silence… before speaking to us on this day…

"… whatever your doubts or concerns about the future… understand only knowledge can free you from the confines that restrict your movement forward …,

… the flame that lives within you… is also a light… a light that guides as well as reveals… allow this light (your light) to guide you to your place of knowing (within)… for there is a sacred place within you… where *your* books of wisdom are kept…,

… spend time in this place as often as you can… and discover the gifts that await you there… the fruits of your own *tree of life*… that teach and assist… awaken and assure…,

… be in this place daily (if you can)… for your awakening will come with grace and ease… when you go in search of what you have forgotten that you already know… rather than leave it to chance that you will remember…,

… then that flame (that light) within you will expand to its fullest… and become a light for others to follow… a light that guides as well as reveals…"

… a s qua di s di… and so it is good

As I sit in ceremony on this day, I feel a shift in my space. For the space in which I exist has opened, and I stand before a narrow hallway. There is light in this hallway, and warmth too. I feel no sense of dread or fear (not even apprehension) as I begin to move into and through this hallway…

"… there are times on your journey of life… when you must move away from the crowd and spend some time alone… and this is a good time for many of you (two-legged)… to look for a place to simply *Be*…,

… find the solitude within yourself… find a space that is empty and clear… go with no questions to be answered… with no agenda or purpose… set no plan and take no action… just go so to simply *Be*…,

… find your way through all of the contents (and clutter)… that you have stored so carefully in your mind and thoughts… but do not attempt to understand or even explain to yourself their presence within you… simply allow all that is stored there within you… to be revealed in its own time and way…,

… for this is not a journey to release… and this is not a journey to become… this is a journey to explore and discover… that which lives in the deepest places of your being… to recognize, realize, and remember… all that has been there within you… for lifetime upon lifetime…,

… and these things are not right or wrong, good or bad… but they are simply just so… just part of who you are… and the purpose of taking this journey of exploration and discovery… is so that you will know and understand… that you get to decide what you want to use now… in this, your present life… and what you will simply leave for use in another lifetime to come…"

… a s qua di s di… and so it is good

It is interesting how quickly we can go from certainty to indecision. How one minute we can be sure we know exactly which path to take (what we are going to do, that we have the answer to a deep and nagging question)… and then in the next moment something happens (something unexpected, something big) that brings us right back to that place of question and indecision… and we find ourselves seeking direction all over again.

The Old One who sits with me in ceremony on this day… is one who looks after those who find their lives suddenly taking an unexpected turn… facing a path that has never been there before… given options that were not in their master plan… or have had their whole world turned upside down… the rug pulled right out from under them…

"… seek peace as you go forward… look ahead… find that place of peace… and then move toward it… know that you have the right to choose… and that you can create your future… so brush away the rubble now… and begin to build the life you want to live…,

… you must honor the questions that rise up within you… but do not linger too long for the knowing of *why*… for that is not the answer that will move you forward… ask instead, *how*… how do I find peace?… how do I go on?… how do I begin again?… how do live and breathe and make a difference that will matter?…,

… but sit with these questions for only a short time as well…,

… for then you must ask the question *who*… who am I?… who am I and what is my purpose?… who did I start out to be?… and who have I become?… who am I now and who can I become?… who do I want to be?…,

… and approach theses questions with the intention of finding peace…,

… for now it is time to look beyond that which is the easiest… that which goes along with the flow that others have set… and to find what is right and perfect for you… for when you find your place of peace… you bring peace to others as well… and inspire others to find their own place of peace…,

… and soon the flow of others will become the same as yours… as all will begin to search for their own place of peace… and each will think with their higher minds (then)… and you will finally have the answer to that question **why**…'

… a s qua di s di… and so it is good

The air is heavy with moisture as I wake on this day. I walk within this healing mist, and become one with both Earth and Sky as I make my way to the place where I will set ceremony for today.

I notice a balance within myself. A balance of all that I have learned and experienced to this point in time, and all that I have yet to learn and experience as I go on. It seems that I am standing in the middle of my life, and can see all the way back as well as all the way forward.

I sit with this for a time before I begin ceremony on this day, for that which I am feeling does not match the questions in my mind. I *feel* content and calm and perfect, yet my mind is *reeling* with thoughts and questions…

"… calm yourself, child… for all is well… settle your thoughts… and let your emotions speak… for they are your truest guide at this time… and if balance is the question… there are many ways to find balance within your life and being…,

… as you stand upon the misty path… that shows both where you have been and where you are going… consider all the places you have struggled… all the times when you have fallen or become lost… for as you move forward now… you will need to afford others **unconditional** compassion and understanding… as they set out to find their way… as they stumble and fall… as they get lost and become in need of assistance…,

… the path before you… is one of bringing together… of seeing one another as you see yourself… and of giving in whatever way is needed… from monetary assistance… food, goods, work, and money… to advice, teaching, opportunities, and such… but what is most important at this time… is that **(each)** must be afforded compassion and understanding… for this is the way of bringing together…,

… remember the many paths you have walked… honor the healing and wisdom you have found along your way… share what you have learned from your experiences with others when appropriate… and hold compassion within your heart for *(each)* at all times…,

… for your journey forward… is one that requires you to stand tall and strong… and to be the one who walks the higher path (in and as your highest spirit and being)… the one who sees the good in all beings… and who sees the unlimited potential in (each) as well…"

… a s qua di s di… and so it is good

The Star People are very near on this day. I stand with them for a long while (before making my way to the ceremony place) just enjoying this reunion with my Star Family. I feel extremely high energy stirring within me, as I stand in honor and respect of all who have come from the High Place to join in our ceremony…

… and their sweet and airy voices sing with me, as I sing the prayer songs for all people

"… what you think you may be missing… is just hidden deeper within… consider this as you go searching for answers, wisdom, knowing, and truths… (those things you know are there within you)… for if you are still searching… it is just that you have not gone deep enough… not that they are not there…,

… be patient, children… but be alert as well… for there will be a stirring within you soon… one that you will not be able to ignore… and you will find a way to go deeper within… and you will find what has been calling out for you to find it…,

… and you will meet your **highest spirit** then… and you will **know** the divinity that lives within you… and this will bring about powerful changes for you… even if you only get a glimpse… a whisper… a breath… of this, your highest spirit… even if you reach this place within for only a moment…,

… for this is the power of Creator…,

… and this will be only the beginning… of your newfound relationship with your Creator… and with that which is known as your **highest self**… and great changes will come to you then… and you will know peace…"

… a s qua di s di… and so it is good

Grandmother has come on this day. I smelled her Sweet Almond Oil even before I woke. I walked out my front door to see Grandmother Moon just beginning to set in the West… and that is when I heard my Grandmother's call…

"… quick, Grandchild… stand with me here in the West… stand in the light of our Grandmother the Moon before she sets… and see as new light is offered upon an old issue…,

… for soon our Grandmother will be full… and you must know… that the time between her fullest point of this month… and her next time of fullness, in the tenth month… will be a powerful for you… and it will be a powerful time for **all**

… the skins between the High Place and the Earth Place become very thin during this time… and you will be able to draw advice and wisdom from the Elders and Ancestors very easily then (instantly)…,

… and, our Mother the Earth speaks louder during this time as well… so you will be able to hear her wisdom and teachings without even settling down to ask… for her voice will become strong enough for **all** to hear…,

… listen then, Grandchild… for what she tells you… listen to all that she speaks… and know that only some of what our Mother the Earth brings forward will be for you (personally, at this time)… but know this too… that you will learn and benefit from all that she reveals… for you begin to understand others better… when you understand the lessons that they are learning (the paths that they are walking)… for each has their own path to walk… just as you do…,

… and, Grandchild… know that as new light shines down upon you… all and anything can be repaired (renewed, regenerated, restored, reshaped, and reborn)… and that you have been given access to the most powerful assistance of all… to all that is of the High Place… as well as to all that is of the Earth Place…,

… and this means, Grandchild… that a time of great and magical change is upon you now…"

… a s qua di s di… and so it is good

The Keeper of the Dreams and Visions came to me in the night, and together we traveled into an ancient time. We traveled through many lifetimes and realities, weaving a web-like path that brought us right here to my own little space upon this world, and to the exact moment that I was to wake.

As I walk out into the morning (now) my Grandmother the Moon is here waiting for me, and as I turned my face up to greet her… she calls me into her light… "… come child… come and sit within my light… for there is much you have experienced on your journey with the Keeper of the Dreams and Visions… and it will take years (possibly lifetimes) for you to unravel and understand all of the knowing you have been given on this journey…,

… look back to the place where you began… and follow your movement as you traveled along… see the web that you created as you moved along your life(times)… this is your own pattern… your own design of your own life… it is every choice you made… and every road you took… it is a picture of you… as well as an expression of your life… and it is an acknowledgement of your existence…,

… now step back farther… and see all of the webs that interconnect with yours… these are the webs of everyone you have touched along the way… from your very beginning to now… (and do see how all beings are connected?)… for even after one has left your physical reality… their web still remains…,

… it is a common practice among two-legged… to search within for answers… for it is known that your true spirit lives within… but you (all two-legged) are coming to a time now… where you will be asking questions that cannot be answered from within… for the answers that you seek now involve creating a new reality… building a new future… completely changing your way of life… so to bring peace, balance, and harmony to the world you live in…,

… and so it is that you must seek the knowing of the web… for everything is recorded here… everything that has lead you (and your world) to this exact place in time…,

… you don't go looking for the mistakes and wrong choices here… (because everything is just as it is supposed to be)… you go looking for the **understanding**… you look to see the reasoning behind every choice and action… and you learn from these… for it will be the shifting of mind and thought… that will move you (all) forward into change…,

… listen to the wisdom of the Keeper of the Dreams and Visions… for it is time to shift from the place of Dreams… to the place of Visions… for dreams are of the mind… and visions are of the spirit… and it is time to let your spirit guide you now…"

a s qua di s di… and so it is good

I walk the sacred paths that lead to my ceremony place as I sing the gratitude song. I stand in the center of this valley, and feel gratitude within my entire being (for myself as well as for all people). I stand for a time longer now, as feelings of gratitude radiate out into the world from deep within me…

… and through this prayer… I offer abundance and prosperity to each and every being…

… an Old One from the Star Place calls out to me now… I see him as I turn… he waits for me in my ceremony place… and so I walk to him…

"… as you share the gift of abundance with all people… you must also tell them how to receive it into their lives… for abundance of every kind is available to all beings at all times… but the knowing of how to receive abundance remains a mystery…,

… express gratitude and appreciation for all that you have… no matter how much or how little it may seem… no matter how difficult the path… or how many times you stumble upon it… for it is by feeling **(being)**… appreciation and gratitude… for every detail of your life (for your very existence)… that causes positive energy to awaken within you and expand out into the world…,

… but positive energy does not simply attract abundance and prosperity randomly… it brings for each exactly what they call for (through that which occupies their minds while they intentionally feel gratitude and appreciation)… the positive energy will bring you exactly what you need then… the job… the work… the demand for your product or the service you provide (for what it is you do)… the opportunity… the opening… the knowing of the right place to be…,

… just as complaining about all that you do not have… brings about more lack… keeping prosperity and abundance just out of your reach… for the negative energy you create by complaining… blocks abundance and prosperity… and allows negative energy to expand out into the world… which will begin to affect all people… if it is allowed to expand too much…,

… begin now, (all) two-legged…to feel gratitude and appreciation for all that you are and have… no matter what… be grateful for and appreciate every-thing… for this will cause the negative energy that has taken over your world, to diminish… and allow the positive energy to rise up and expand…,

… and you will (all) see and feel this shift… and abundance and prosperity will return… and you will be even more grateful and appreciative of all that is available to you then… and you will treat with respect and honor… all that you receive…"

… a s qua di s di… and so it is good

Soft, healing rain began to fall yesterday afternoon, bringing much needed moisture to the land. The Rain Keeper a ga s ga ~ u (ga) se di came to me during the night, and took me into an ancient place. I woke on this day to the wonderful fragrant smells of the prairie after a Rain, and to Grandmother Moon standing big and round and full above me.

The morning is cold… and soft rain continues to fall… so I wrap up in my blanket as I make my way to the ceremony place… and I stand, quiet and still, as I breathe in several deep breaths before setting ceremony… for the fragrance of the air is so rich and pungent and full of Medicine… that I cannot resist filling myself with all that is here… with as much healing as I can take in… so to share it with all people through the song of my prayers…

… and as I sing the prayer songs for all people… I begin to smell the Old Village… the Old Village that I knew long ago…

… I smell the fire that burns in the center of the village… I smell all the fires that burn within each dwelling… I smell the Elk Stew that cooks on the Old Woman's fire… I smell the new fresh hides that are ready to be scraped and tanned… I smell the old hides and bones that have become shelter, tools, clothing, and such… I smell the grasses and the gardens… I smell the Standing Ones who watch over and protect this village… and I smell the sacred smoke of ceremony… calling for all people to come…

"… sit within this smoke… close your eyes and become quiet and still… and see what you can see… for there is much that waits for you to see it…,

… call upon the wisdom of your inner knowing… call to it and allow it to speak… for there is a knowing within you that must be acknowledged… and consciously seeking this knowing… is one of the ways that you will prepare for the coming Winter…,

… for in the coming Winter… you will have access to that which you are to **know**… and once you have discovered this knowing… you will need to be patient… and wait for the right moment to put this knowing to use… and this is important… for this discipline is part of your growth and wisdom… your maturity… for understanding the importance of waiting for the right time… is equally important as the work you are called do…,

… and there is much for you to gather now… before the Winter comes… whether it be physical materials and strength… or spiritual knowing, materials, and strength… understandings of the mind and of the heart… or some of all of these… for you are preparing to assist in the shaping of your future… and this will begin soon… so begin, now, the task of gathering… so that you will be ready when the time becomes right…"

... a s qua di s di... and so it is good

Grandmother Moon sits high above me as I walk the prairie on this morning. Her light is bright-white, and exposes every detail of this land. I set ceremony in complete clarity, and I share this clarity with all people as I sing the prayers songs...

... and I move into stillness now... and I hear the voice clearly... the voice that speaks our truth...

"... if it is clarity you seek... begin with truth... for deception creates a smoky veil... a veil that will eventually become solid... and if left too long... it will become a tether... a tether that holds and restricts and binds you... which will then become an anchor... an anchor that will stop you completely...,

... deception is what blocks all of your wants and dreams and desires... for it tells the Universe that you do not trust (or believe that you deserve)...

... seek truth and you will know clarity... live in truth and you will find abundance... dissolve all deceptions (even self-deceptions) that live within you... and you will become strong, protected, and healed...

... deception creates static... truth removes the static... truth brings about a smooth flow of thought and emotion... when there is a smooth flow of thought and emotion... there is no tension or stress put upon your physical body (mind or heart)... leaving it free to work with ease (as it was designed to)... and your connection to your own spirit (as well as to all things spiritual) opens wide then... and you have a clear channel... a clear connection... to and with all that is of the High Place...

... and remember... this channel... this connection... carries your thoughts, feelings, actions, and words to Creator... in just the same way that it allows you to feel, hear, sense, know, and receive... all that is there for you in the High Place... all that Creator has waiting for you... all that is just waiting for you to recognize and claim it..."

... a s qua di s di... and so it is good

I see images of the past as I walk out on this day. I see the Old Ones who walked this land long ago preparing their ceremony. I stand quiet and still as I attend this ceremony, and I struggle to keep my balance…

… for I feel as if I stand here in this time and place (my world)… while the Old Ones stand there in theirs…

"… not all of what is in the past is bad… look to all of the good that you have created along your (many) Earth Journey(s)… seek those extraordinary moments of *your many lifetimes*… and bring them through… for you can make good use of these as you continue forward…,

… use the strength and energy of your youth… to assist you in what you wish to create now… build something new… from that which you knew and experienced before… remember the feeling of excitement that comes from standing on the edge of something new… and engage every part of yourself (spirit, emotion, mind, and body)… as you design a new path to walk upon…,

… that which is before you now… is higher than where you stand at this time… so remember to look up and to step high… to stretch beyond that which you believe are your limitations… and to trust in the assistance from the High Place…,

… bring the best of your past through… as you set out to create a better future… and make it your intention to release all that holds and blocks you as you do… for your time is now and your direction is forward… and this requires you (all two-legged) to move without restriction… to let go of all that holds and binds…,

… look upon the lessons of your past as the *gifts* that they are… for it is their wisdom that you will carry forward with you… and it is their wisdom that will assist you as you set out to bring a strong and loving future into being…"

… a s qua di s di… and so it is good

I wake on this day to the feeling of being held... nurtured and cared for like a child... comforted by a Mother who holds me... and a sense of being safe... a sense of being home...

... I stand in the darkness... singing gratitude for this moment... for that which I feel so strong within... and I relax into the very earth that I stand upon...

... I hold onto this feeling as long as I can... for I know it is this feeling that will shift my awareness and perspective... and I become still now... as I feel the prayers of all people move from within my heart... out into the world...

... and I quiet... as I hear the soft, sweet voice of the *Mother* begin to speak...

"... what are you willing to sacrifice for the life of a child... would you give time, so to teach and guide... would you give attention, so to instill worth and value... would you give comfort, so to provide a sense of being safe and cared for...,

... and would this time be a sacrifice at all... for the knowing of all that is given to a child in this way... also brings comfort and joy to you...,

... sit with this for a moment, two-legged... find your perspective... come to the knowing that whatever you put into a child... ***be it the nourishment of food, education, being loved, or the grace to love and respect others***... is also what you put into the world...

... and pay close attention to your thoughts and feelings on this subject, two-legged... for the child I am asking you to look after, is you... it is a new time you enter now, two-legged... a time for you to begin anew... as an infant... as a child...,

... and so what are you willing to sacrifice for the life of this child... would you spend time on learning... and would you accept guidance... would you give to yourself the attention you require... would you offer yourself comfort and understanding when times get tough and difficult challenges arise...

… and will you come to know (then)… that sacrifice is not about pain and suffering… for when sacrifice is made on behalf of one you love… it is a gift of the heart…

… look to that which you need at this time… and give to yourself whatever it is you need… give to yourself the comfort and nourishment and understanding that you would give to a child… and see yourself safely into the future…,

… for you are valuable and important… and you are a child of the Universe, **always**… and you deserve all the time and attention you need… to bring your unique gift into the world…"

… a s qua di s di… and so it is good

I wrap my blanket around me as I stand at my ceremony place on this day. I smile, for I love this time of year. It is the season just before we settle in for our Winter rest. *The Harvesting Time*, a time when we can clearly see, harvest, and use all of what we have dreamed of, planted, and tended to throughout the course of the year.

All seasons come with challenges as well as rewards, and this may be especially true for *The Harvesting Time*. For as we look to that which we have accomplished (grown, developed, manifested, even released, let go of, and transformed) throughout the Winter, Spring, and Summer, we can also see (all too clearly), that which is still to be done. That which we were not able to accomplish, that which we are still holding onto, and how much more growth and development is still before us.

And so the question becomes, do we look positively to that which we have accomplished, and set plans for the next season… or do we sink into disappointment and despair over that which still remains?

It is a familiar question, to be sure… is our glass half full… or is it half empty… are we sad to see each ending… or excited for each new beginning?

The Old Ones who stand with me in ceremony on this day seem to believe that although the difference in perspectives comes from within each individual, and is specific to one's own nature (time of birth, parents, childhood, environment, and such)… that a new perspective and way of seeing and feeling about life and self can be learned, changed, and shifted… and… they tell me that knowing how to use disappointment, is the first step in making this shift in perspective…

"… understand two-legged… feeling disappointed is natural… but to allow disappointment to get a hold of you… is debilitating… and will set you out upon a crooked path…,

… look to each disappointment as an opportunity… allow it to shake you up… allow it to shake out all that weighs and holds you… but then, welcome disappointment as an opportunity… use it to inspire you to dig deeper within… to use your mind and your senses… your will and your determination… to get to and find whatever it is you need… so you can move on and accomplish that which you set out to accomplish…, … then acknowledge and honor all of what you have done… all of what and who you have been given… all of the experiences of your life… for these are the happenings of your life…,

… and know, too… that there are times when that which you have set about to do… is simply not meant to be… but may have come about only to get you from one place to another… or to assist you in awakening a gift that lies sleeping within…"

… a s qua di s di… and so it is good

I have only the slightest memory of the place I have just awakened from. I stand at my ceremony place, and feel this place from within my dreams moving toward me (awakening here in the physical). I hear the song of an Old Medicine Woman echoing through the silence of the prairie… and I stand now… at both my altar and the opening to a hidden cave from a long-ago time…

… I see her there… the Old Medicine Woman… out among the shrubs and trees… she is gathering herbs and roots into a large handwoven basket… and she moves toward me as if she does not even see me… she moves past me without even a nod… but she turns when she reaches the opening of her cave… and motions for me to follow…

"… sit here by the fire, child… and listen as I tell you of these roots and herbs… you called me here, you know… and I heard you… so listen as I tell you of what I can see of your time… from where I stand in mine…,

… the channels of vision into the future (the future of your time and people)… are bringing through messages for all to receive… but very few are giving attention to what is being told… too many are content to allow another to begin the process… while even more are happy knowing others are doing the work…,

… but it does not work that way, child… this is work that **each** must take part in… even if it is only to become aware of the movement of energy… and of the knowing that it is time to make great changes in the world as they know it…,

… breathe in the aroma of theses herbs and roots that I have boiling here… allow them to open your airways and to clear away the stuffiness… breathe in and out now, child… deep, strong breaths… feel the ease in which the air moves through you now… and notice the clarity that follows…,

… you see now, don't you child… you see as if you have just stepped out of this cave and into the light… and this is what I have come to show you… for the path before you is wide and bright and open for **all**… but **most** can see only a small tunnel… as if they were standing inside a tiny cave… facing inward, rather than out…,

… it is time to turn around now… it is time to step out of the tiny cave and into the whole of the wide, bright, open world… it is time to listen for the messages that come to and for you **all**… and for **each** of you to walk forward with your heads high and your eyes open…,

… it is time to get excited about the possibilities that lay before you… for all things are possible as you walk forward and work together… and there is power within you all (within each and every one of you)… to bring forth great changes and healing… and the power of all working together… is more than even I can see…"

… a s qua di s di… and so it is good

Ilooked for Grandmother Moon as I walked out on this day, for Father Sky was very black and the Star People were very close. I found our Grandmother the Moon straight up above my head and very high, she seemed to be keeping her light far away so that the Star People could stand near.

I found my way out onto the prairie, and set ceremony in the center of this land we have been called to care for. The sound of the prairie took on a hollow sound then… and I saw a Star drop right out of Father Sky…

… I saw a figure move in the darkness… as a Star Man emerged and moved right toward me… and the space around me became sacred… and my breath began to slow… and I heard a soft voice speaking… as the light from this being became clear and bright…

… and I saw this light begin to expand then… as the Star Man stood before me… he seemed to be suspended in mid-air… and he seemed to be connected to the High Place as well as to Mother Earth… by this powerful pulsing light…

"… remember, two-legged… it is important to create a sacred space and use it daily… to set aside time… no matter how little… and go to a space that is set just for you… a space where you can be separate from the movement of your physical life for a time… and simply be connected to and with the Earth and the Sky…,

… whether you go out to a special place upon the land… or into a quiet space within your dwelling… go to the same place each time… for your spirit will expand in this space… and it will call you to return there as well…,

… and all the knowing of your highest *self*… will begin to awaken there… and you will find trust in this space… as you spend more and more time within it… and you will discover more of who you are there, too… and you will know more of the world you live in as well…,

… and your life path will become clear to you then… and you will begin to walk upon that path…"

… a s qua di s di… and so it is good

Grandfather Wind speaks on this day, as he blows around and through the Standing Ones who live up on the hill. He whispers stories of long-ago times, and sings soothing lullabies for us, the babies of this Star we know as Earth.

I sit in the North now, wrapped in my blanket and breathing in the sacred smoke of my ceremony fire. I rock forward and back, singing the prayer songs for all people in time with Grandfather Wind…

… and it is Grandfather Wind who guides me softly into stillness… out into the place where the Buffalo stand… and deep into the heart of the herd… where I find myself standing face to face with the Story Keeper of this majestic Tribe…

"… stand for a moment, two-legged… stand quiet and still… allow yourself to feel the vibration of your Mother the Earth… and allow this vibration to become a rhythm (a flow) within you…,

… now, begin to feel the vibration of your Father the Sky… allow this vibration to flow in and through you… and allow this vibration to blend with that of your Mother the Earth… quiet your mind… and simply **allow** this movement… ask no questions… and expect no teaching…,

… for what I show you on this day… is not about receiving answers… it is about finding balance… and connecting with the natural flow of your life… there is always a tendency to want to push ahead… especially once you begin to see the path before you through clear eyes…,

… but you must remember… there is a flow and a rhythm to your life… and much for you to experience, encounter, and discover… as you walk the paths you came here to walk… so do not run ahead like a rabbit… (who must continue to begin again and again)…,

… but walk steady and sure… in right rhythm and time… like the turtle… who experiences everything he has come to experience… and makes it to his destination in perfect time… ready to receive his next task… and completely prepared for it… without having to go back and begin again…"

… a s qua di s di… and so it is good

OCTOBER
2010

I carry my ceremony bundle close to me as I walk the Stone Prayer Circles on this crisp morning. I feel the changing season all the way down to my bones as I sing the prayer songs for all people. I stand at my altar for a time, connecting with the oneness before beginning ceremony... and it is the warmth of the Woman Bear who greets me as I settle into the silence...

... I see her as she steps into my ceremony circle... I feel her as she guides my breathing... and I follow her as she leads me into the place she has come to show me (us) on this day...

"... we are in the West, young one... for it is time to prepare your place within... to let go of the last of what your ego has been holding onto... (through this time of growth anyway)... so that you can move about more easily... so that you have a good space within to receive, acknowledge, and accept that which is ready to be revealed...,

... do you smell the sweetness now... can you smell the Sweet Cherries... listen as I tell you of their Medicine... for they bring to you many gifts...,

... be relieved of any stress... and be revived, too... as you take in deep, full breaths... as you breathe in completely... for as you walk among the Cherry Standing Ones... you will be calmed and soothed... as well as cleansed and cleared and prepared for a new awakening...,

... focus on only true nourishment now... on only that which will sustain you throughout the time of Winter... and focus only on that which is of absolute use (necessity, need)... for your strength and endurance, and the ease of your journey forward... will be directly affected by that which you choose to carry...,

... it is possible that you may encounter a bit of turbulence... as you move through the next two seasons... and you are bound to experience turbulence at any time along your Earth Walk...,

... keep the Medicine of the Cherry Standing Ones with you at all times... or call upon them when you see the Great Winds begin to stir... when you feel the ground beneath you begin to shake...,

… for Cherry Medicine will guide you through with grace and ease… and help you to keep the time you spend in upset, short… while allowing you to get the full understanding of each experience…,

… the doors are all opening now, young one… for you, and for all… you have but to find your way to them… and, of course… be prepared to step across the threshold…"

… a s qua di s di… and so it is good

The prairie is still and quiet as I walk out on this day. I carry my ceremony bundle with me as I walk the paths and trails here on the ranch, stopping now and then to close my eyes and feel the earth beneath my feet, the spirit in the air around me.

I set ceremony up on the flat space where the West blends into the North… and I feel the energy within this space shift… it is as if I have blended in with all that surrounds me… and I feel myself expand into all four directions… into all that is above and beneath me, too…

"… yes, two-legged… stop frequently and notice how far you expand… get a sense of where you sit or stand… and then ask your mind to ease back… as you use all of your senses to tell you how far (outward) you can reach …,

… walk in nature… through a wooded area or in an open field… along a sandy shore or a mountain trail… and feel how far your energy reaches… and notice the distance between you and that which you encounter along the way… (winged, animals, other two-legged, standing ones, stone people, and such)…,

… for it is time to recognize and develop your relationship to and with the world around you… so that you can recognize and develop the relationship between your own spirit and the High Place… and this will lead you to understand, know, heal, and tend to your relationship with one another (with all people)…,

… this exercise requires trust… but it will also build trust within you… for once you begin to sense and feel as you move about within your life…

(rather than using only your mind to tell you about all that you encounter)… a relationship will begin and develop… between you and everything…,

… and you will feel that which cannot be spoken… and you will sense the heart of others within your own… and you will realize more in a momentary encounter… than could ever be told (or learned) within a lifetime thinking… and this is good, two-legged… this is good…"

… a s qua di s di… and so it is good

I feel cleansed and renewed as Grandfather Wind blows through me. I open the blanket I have wrapped around me, and turn in each direction, asking Grandfather Wind to cleanse and purify my entire being (spirit, heart, body, and mind).

I set ceremony as my Star Relatives draw near. I feel the spirits of dear friends and beloved family members gather around me, and I see the Elders gathered together in circle. I see the gatherings in small towns, in big cities, and in all places in between… from generations gone by… to this very moment in time…

… I see the people truly expressing their love for one another… as they celebrate one another… as friends and as relations… and I whisper a prayer for all of my family and friends… no matter where they are… in heaven or on Earth… and I feel them each move in around me…

… and I have no use for my blanket now… for I am warmed and held by the love that surrounds me

"… find comfort in the love of family and friends… reach out to one another and celebrate each and every one… give love, attention, comfort, and support… and draw together often… for celebration as well as for companionship… for it is time to know what a gift you have in one another…

… there is a loss of trust in your world… but it can be regained in simple ways…,

… gather together people… spend time together… know one another through the touch of your hands… thorough the love in your hearts…

gather in groups for celebration… but sit with a friend or loved one, too… just you and them… so you can know the comfort of time spent together… without having to speak a word…,

… communication can restore trust… but remember… your words represent only one form of communication… and know this, too… it is your actions that will speak the greater truth… of who you are… as well as of what you are trying to say…"

… a s qua di s di… and so it is good

I see a light shining up from the altar at my ceremony space, or does it shine down from above? I stand for a moment to see what I can see in the darkness of this morning. I search my mind to know if I have left something there, something that would be lighted. I hold my ceremony bundle close to me as I make my way to the ceremony space, and I walk straight toward the light… which becomes brighter with each step I take…

"… the light is for you, child… (all two-legged)… it is time for you to stand within the light… and see yourself completely… it is time to let the light shine upon you… and burn away the illusion… it is time to adjust your sight, while you stand within the light… and to see with the eyes of your highest spirit… the beauty and grace and magnificence of who you truly are…,

… step into the light now… and see the magnificence of you… step into the light now… as if you are stepping onto a stage… feel yourself expand… and see that even your clothing has changed… for as you stand in this light… you are free to express yourself completely…,

… reach deep within yourself… and draw up all of your gifts and talents and abilities… for the stage is yours… and it is your time… so show the world all that you have to offer… and let go of the fear, child… for fear will only keep you small…,

… the changes that you have been working to make… have seemed difficult and out of reach… but it is time for you to see… with the eyes of your highest spirit... that the changes you wish to make... can be as simple as changing your clothes... as simple as donning a new costume... or stepping into a character as part of a play...,

... or maybe it is not about what you will put on (take on)... but what you will remove... and so it is upon you (now)... to remove that costume you have been wearing... to step out of the character you have been playing... for the role you have been playing for so long... has served its time and purpose... and you are ready to take on a new role... ***the role of a lifetime***... the role of your lifetime...,

... so look again, child... look into that bright and shining light... do you see the truth... do you see the stage you stand upon... and do you see yourself as the ***character*** you have been playing... and are you ready to step out of that costume, that character... and do you see how simple it can be...,

... for the truth of who you really are... is more magnificent than any part you could ever play... and that which you offer to the world... as your true and original ***Self***... will be real and true and lasting (then)...,

... and it is the light of your Creator... that lights you when you're real... and it is he who supports you most... as you stand upon the greatest stage of all... as who you truly are..."

... a s qua di s di... and so it is good

Grandmother Moon is in her last stage of waning as I walk out on this day. I look for her as I step out my front door, but I do not see her. I ask the Star People, who are close and bright right now... "Look up high"... they tell me... "Follow us into the East... for she waits there for Father Sun on this day" ...

... and so I walk into the East... and I find my dear Grandmother the Moon... waiting there for my Father the Sun...

"... it is a time of many questions for the two-legged... Father Sun and I have come together to assist you in finding the answers and solutions that you seek...,

… during the time when I am dark… what many of you call "the New Moon"… your minds become sharp and your thoughts become clear… that which has been difficult for you to understand… begins to make sense… and that which you have struggled to reason and plan… falls smoothly into place…,

… but emotions become intense at this time as well… so feel that which rises up within you… but let it go quickly… for this is a good time to use your mind… but you must have no emotional distractions…,

… and this is a good time to look to the past, too… for many of the answers you seek… will be found through examining past experiences… and by looking in on that which has already been…,

… it is a time to believe in that which seems fantastic and impossible… to open your mind and let the bright light shine in… for there in the corners of your mind… you will find great wisdom and knowing… but this wisdom and knowing will provide just a glimpse of what you can create… (when you put your mind to it)…,

… then put your mind to it… and find the answers you seek… and then set about to create… that which you have come to create…"

… a s qua di s di… and so it is good

The Cloud People greet me as I step out on this day. I can feel their warmth, for they sit low and close. I stand for a moment before singing the prayer songs for all people, for I can hear the Cloud People speaking quietly among themselves… it seems as though they are trying to tell me something…

… and I quiet myself as I look up now… for suddenly I can see very clearly… I can see exactly what I am to see on this day…

… in the darkness of the Morning Sky… as Grandmother Moon prepares to go completely dark… I see the Cloud People are all gathered there… dark and heavy… they provide just the slightest contrast between themselves and Father Sky… and I see there is an opening there… and through that opening I can see just the outline of Grandmother Moon…,

... ah... I see it now... the Black Shield as it stands before me... completely empty... and ready to bring forth whatever our hearts desire...

"... it is a time of all potential... a time to release the hold you have on anything that weighs you... a time to allow your deepest (truest) desires to be known...,

... look upon this empty shield... see that it is black and clear... see that it carries no image... no rules... no right or wrong... just pure and true potential... and see that it waits for you...,

... when Grandmother Moon goes dark... your heart expands... it opens wide and reaches out for her... your emotions rise up then... and you feel with great intensity... that which has been kept deep within...,

... sit with this for a time... allow your heart to speak... listen to that voice within... and allow it to guide you as you design your **Shield**... for the designs you paint upon your **Shield**... are the desires of your heart... they are your deepest desires for your own future... for all that you seek to do and be... and all that you know you are...,

... and so do not paint your **Shield** with your mind... but paint it with your heart... allow your spirit to guide your hands... for together they will they show you that everything is possible...,

... this is a time of great change as well as true potential... and the Empty Black Shield is a powerful tool for you to have... honor it by using it... and use it to set yourself in motion..."

... a s qua di s di... and so it is good

I wake from a Medicine Dream on this day, and I remain still for a moment, remembering all of what I was shown in this dream. My heart expands as I see the Old Woman waiting for me, and together we set ceremony... together we sing the prayer songs for all people... together we listen for the words that come from the High Place... and together we bow our heads in silence...

"… look now… back into your dream… see the people of the village as they prepare for the Winter… see the harvest they tend to… see their store houses filled and overflowing…,

… look now… watch as the people honor the earth from which their harvest has come… see the care they take with each step… see the care they take in deciding the placement of their dwellings, fires, work places, and gathering circles… see how they protect the earth they live upon…,

… look now… see how the people care for themselves and for one another… see the respect they give to every living thing and being… see that they honor life itself and that this is how they show gratitude for all that they have…,

… look now… see that you do not stand watching a ceremony… but a simple way of living that speaks with honesty and truth… for it is in the way one lives… that one truly tells their story… it is in the way one lives… that tells Creator what they feel within their heart… it is through the way one lives… that the healing will come… it is through the way one lives… that inspires another to begin…

… and then it will be through the way *all* live… that peace will come about…"

… a s qua di s di… and so it is good

I remember the image of a face as I wake on this day. A *mask* that reminds me of an old traditional ceremony of my people. These masks, meant to ward-off intruders and scare away "bad spirits," were ugly and carved purposely to frighten.

These ceremonies came about during the time when our people were being moved from the land they knew and loved… to reservations in places far away… and the masks were carved in the likenesses of the "white eyes" who came in and disrupted their lives… destroying and taking… as they went about their business.

I carry a strange emotion with me today… as I make my way to the place I will set ceremony… I see the image of a Mother Deer scooting a young one along to follow its Father… they walk swiftly… but with caution… for it is

Hunters they are dodging as they set out to cross a large open meadow... searching for the safety a thicket or a forest... a place where they can blend in among the Standing Ones... a place where they can rest...

"... young one... it is the awareness of protection that we bring to you on this day... but it is not the fear of being chased or hunted by another... that we bring to your attention... for we ask you to look to your own self... to see if you walk out into the open meadow... or if you have found your way to the safety of the Standing Ones...,

... you are in charge of your own protection... and it is through your own choices... that you will find the inner-peace you seek...,

... you protect your physical body and health... through the way you choose to nourish it... you keep it strong and swift... through the activity you choose to engage in... you keep your mind sharp and alert... by using it daily and testing it often...and you keep your spirit strong and pure... by spending time in the High Place...,

... if you spend time... every day... connecting to and with the highest energy you can reach... (and then reach even further)... if you sit for (even) a moment... with the intention of "being" in the presence of your Creator... if you spend time in meditation and/or prayer... or gathered in ceremony with others... you will never have to worry if you are crossing an open meadow... or if you are safely disguised by the forest... for there will be nothing for you to be protected from...,

... yes... it is the awareness of protection we bring to you on this day... but it is not another you are trying to out-run... it is you, dear child... it is your own insecurities and sense of lack that chases you... and it is time for you to stop running for a place to hide... and to stand strong and steady... in the strength and ability you already carry within...,

... spend time in spirit... spend time with spirit... allow this part of you to grow and develop and strengthen every day... and you will feel your balance return and click into place... and you will know peace..."

... a s qua di s di... and so it is good

I see the Old Man as I wake on this day. He stands at the center of a cross-road, tapping his drum and turning to each direction. I feel the vibration of his drum, but I cannot hear the song he sings.

I call to him as I sing the prayer songs for all people. I look for him as I move into stillness…

"… it is not the words to my song that you need to know… but how to connect with the vibration of my drum… for the vibration of the Earth is shifting… and you must allow your own vibration to shift as well…,

… close your eyes… and *feel* as I play my drum… see the Hummingbird with your inner-vision… and call to the Medicine she brings… yes, she vibrates faster than you do now… but you will soon find a way to sync with her rhythm… and then she will teach you… how to move (spiritually and physically) in all directions…,

… spend time with your sister Hummingbird… begin to know her Medicine… feel her move within you… and begin to move as she does… for the vibration of the Earth is shifting… to a higher and more loving (place) energy… and you must find a way to sync with it… so that you can move higher too… smoothly and with ease… into the joy that is there for you…"

… a s qua di s di… and so it is good

I stand within the Medicine Dream… awake and aware… even though I am sleeping.

… I live in the small village… even though I look upon it from above… I see the happenings there… and I feel them as they occur…

… I see hundreds of Horses have found their way to the small village… and the people run out of their hut-like dwellings… cheering and singing gratitude songs for this gift…

… for it is the gift of abundance and prosperity… and a sign that all will be good and right… that whatever lack and scarcity the people have endured…

(has ended) is ending… and the abundance has returned… the means to live and thrive is upon them again…

… and the Old Ones who walk with me within this small village have something they want me to know… they tell me that my Medicine Dream is a sign for all who live in my time (in present time)… that today marks a shift… and that scarcity and lack live only in our minds now… for prosperity and abundance have returned…

"… look within now, children… look at what you hold so tightly to… and let go of it… release your hold of all limiting thoughts and beliefs… and open your hands to receive… stretch out your arms as you look up… sing and feel and speak out your gratitude… and smile as you look up and forward… and welcome in all that is ready to pour upon you… to come into you…,

… it is time to shake off all that limits… for holding onto beliefs of limit and lack… will surely stop the flow of goodness that has now begun… you are creative and intelligent beings… and it is time for you to put your creativity and intelligence to good use… to make a plan and to focus… to know and trust and believe… that now is the time to take action and begin…,

… shift your sadness to joy… your despair to gratitude… be thankful for all that you have… for all that you do not have… and even for that which you have lost… for the slate is clean now… and it is time to begin again… but go forward this time… wiser and stronger and more compassionate… and working for the good of all…"

… a s qua di s di… and so it is good

And so the Medicine Dream continues… as I stand in a place so far away from my home… and yet I know this land and these people… and they know me, too…

… and I feel their ever-growing excitement… for the possibilities of change that is upon them… and I feel their ever-growing fear and apprehension as well…

... for there is comfort in that which we know... and a space (or time) of discomfort and uncertainty that usually accompanies change...

... and we, two-legged human beings, love the idea of change... we think about it until it consumes us... we talk about it incessantly... but when it comes to taking action... we seem to lose our steam... we slow and idle and wait... until it is too late... (or so we think)...

... for just as I know I will return to my home (so far away from this place where I stand)... I know this too... I know that just as we rise up to that place we have worked so hard to reach... we sink back into that which we know so well... back into our old habits and ways... and return to the places that comfort us... even if that comfort is uncomfortable...

... I am told by the Old One who stands with me again today... that it is simply our human nature to resist change... even the changes that we have fought to bring about... for the **dream** is much easier to manage... and there is fear in that which we do not know...

"... embrace your own now, children... that which is truly you... your strength and wisdom and creativity... and especially your curiosity...,

... use your mind to explore new possibilities... rather than to focus on fear... and see that which is before you now... is what you have always dreamed of...,

... for the earth has evolved... and so have you, children... and you have been given the ability to create as you move forward... and to move forward into what you create..."

... a s qua di s di... and so it is good

I sit before an Old Standing One on this day. This is a very old and ancient one, to be sure, for I do not recognize the shape or size or smell or energy of this one. It is no matter though, for the Medicine of this Elder is as strong as it is kind, is as much male as it is female, and is as giving as it is receiving...

"… I am your message as well as your messenger today, two-legged… for mine are the qualities that will serve you best at this time… awaken them within you… as you stand beneath my protection and cover… and then come closer to sit with me for a time… but be still and listen close as you do… for after a time I will ask you to tell me what you heard…,

… you can see that I stand deeply rooted in the soil of our Mother the Earth… and that I reach up high into the Sky Place (so to remain in constant connection with our Creator)… but do you hear the water that flows through me… and do you hear my heart beating…,

… now look at me again, two-legged… do you see fingers at the end of my branches… where others see only leaves and twigs… can you see my hands… now step back a little further, two-legged… and see that thousands of hands reach out from within me…,

… I am spirit and heart and physical body… I bring nourishment and protection… and I stand solid and true throughout time… I reach deep into the earth and stretch up high into the sky… and I have recorded all of the happenings of this world in which I stand…,

… I carry great wisdom within me… and I offer it to you whenever you seek to know it… but you must go deep within yourself… and call to me from there… for the knowing that I carry deep within me… is held within you, too…,

… and as you begin to ask from within… you will be inspired to call out for more… and you will begin to explore (then), two-legged… to research and experience, to ask and to listen… and to learn all that you can learn…,

… and your own ingenuity will ignite in this time… and you will begin to create… and you will go forward as if there were thousands of hands reaching out from within you… and *this* is why I came…"

… a s qua di s di… and so it is good

Fog has moved in around us on this day. I walk into it as I walk out in search of a place to set ceremony. I make my way to a high spot (moving into and out of the fog as I go), and I see that the Fog lies like ribbons across the land. It looks like smoke from a ceremony pipe as it streams across the land, and I follow it with my eyes to the place where it originates.

I hear the drums begin to beat from there, playing the slow and constant heartbeat of our Mother. Ah, this is where I am to set ceremony on this day, and so I make my way there, moving (again) in and out of the ribbons of Fog… that have begun to smell of sage…

"… keep aware of the foundation you have set for yourself in your physical world, two-legged… and if you have given this no thought… begin now… for in order to move about freely (into and throughout) the higher realms… you must have a solid foundation upon which to land (return to)…,

… sit within the sacred smoke, two-legged… breathe it in and be filled with it… allow it to cover you like a cocoon… and remain still as your breathing slows… relax your muscles as your mind lets go and begins to sleep… then release your spirit into the smoke…,

… all negativity from within and around your physical body will be cleansed then… and your spirit knows where it is called to go… as it moves into the higher realms… for there is knowing for you to receive from the High Place… which your spirit does naturally and often… and so it is the cleansing of your physical body, mind, and heart… that is most important now…,

… for though your spirit can retrieve this knowing with ease and grace… your physical body must be prepared to receive it… and in order for you to make use (in the physical) of all that you receive in spirit… you must have a good (physical) foundation… you must be balanced and grounded… and know how to keep negative energy at bay…,

… and so it is that communication with the High Place is essential… so to keep the openings wide and clear and easy to move through… but if you have not prepared (cleansed and cleared) yourself physically (body, mind, and emotions)… that which you bring through from the High Place… will be locked within… unable to be used…,

… so mind your health, two-legged… and keep your spirit healthy as well… take in proper nutrition and spend time in prayer and/or meditation daily… for the wisdom of the High Place is beginning to flow now… and you must be able to use (and share) all that you receive… in order for the flow continue…"

… a s qua di s di… and so it is good

I see the Old Shaman through my inner-vision. He stands dressed in a sand-colored robe and carries a tall staff. A dark leather pouch hangs from one shoulder and across his chest, and he is reaching out his empty hand toward me.

I hear no words, but am filled with knowing. I cannot move, yet I feel I am in motion. The sound of my own heart beating fills my ears, and it is my own breath that seems to be creating the wind that blows around me.

I do not recognize this place where I stand… though the people seem familiar… and I hear them singing a song I know well… it is a healing song that brings about thorough change… and I feel intense energy building within me… as I begin to sing the healing song, too… and I feel each one sigh with relief… as something from within them is released … as the healing occurs… and *each* is changed completely…

… and I look for the Old Shaman… but see only a tall, full branched Scottish Larch… and then Grandfather Wind arrives… blowing around and through this magnificent Standing One… and with him comes the song and the words… that we are meant to hear on this day…

"… it is the balance of heart and mind that has been created here… the syncing of will and desire… for as the song is sung… it awakens the heart… which convinces the mind to sleep… so the desires of the heart can direct the will of the mind…,

… close your eyes, children… and see the seven who stand around you… breathe in the clean fresh air they provide… and feel your feet sink into the rich earth beneath you… open your eyes, children… and see the sacred grove of Standing Ones before you… for these are the seven who represent the **seven sacred direction**s…,

… acknowledge your spirit, your heart, your body, and your mind… give thanks to the earth and to the sky… and honor the sacred fire within… stand in complete balance, children… and know that you are not **one part, but all parts**… and all parts are equal… just as the earth is equally important to your existence… as is the sky…,

… be balance in every way, children… and remember how it feels to be balanced… for then you can hear when one part begins to speak too loud… and you must listen to what that part has to say… but listen with your heart, children… for your heart always knows what to do… yes, the wisdom of your heart will keep you aligned and in balance…,

… and when you are aligned and in balance… you will have no need for a healing… and you will be free to follow your heart's desire then, too… to be who you are… and love without fear… and to live as you came here to live…"

… a s qua di s di… and so it is good

It is the sound of hooves running on hard ground that awakens me from the Dreamtime, or am I awakened within the Dreamtime? I stand upon an open prairie, somewhere in the middle, for there is nothing but bare land as far as I can see. I look to find a trace of the herd that drew me here… was it Horses… Cows… Buffalo?…

… and I see them now, far off in the distance, waiting for me to follow…

… and so I begin to walk… obediently following those who have come so far to tell me something… I move like the Wind… here within the Dreamtime… without effort or obstruction… and I can see the herd clearly now… they are Buffalo…and I stand among them somehow…

… but am I one of them… or am I the air that got me here so swiftly… do they see me… or am I only here in spirit… or is it that I am merely watching from in the Dreamtime…

… and the ground turned coral-red… and the sky turned turquoise-blue… and tiny crystals rained down from the sky… and all the Buffalo turned white… and a place appears before me… where you can walk right into the sky… it is a bridge made of light… though it is solid enough to walk upon… and the Buffalo call out to me…

"… walk in truth, two-legged… for you walk upon the sacred **red earth**… see with clarity, two-legged… for you walk beneath the turquoise-blue **medicine sky**… know that you are sacred, two-legged… for you stand among the **White Buffalo Nation**… live for all people, two-legged… for they are the **crystal rain** that fell from the sky…,

… step upon the bridge, two-legged… and climb as high as you can… now look to see what is above and below you… for you stand somewhere in the middle… look with truth and clarity, two-legged… as the sacred being that you are… and see that the crystal rain which covers your land… are your brothers and your sisters…,

… they are just like you, two-legged… made of the same light from above… with each, its own shape and distinction… and its own message to share… they are perfect and magnificent just as they are… one just as important as the next…,

… so give respect to them **each**, two-legged… hear what their hearts have to say… know that **each** has made their way here from your same home… and have come with their own task to complete… (just as you have)… know that there is no **one** who is more… and no one who is less… for they are all the same in the eyes of Creator… and they all look just like you…,

… now go to stand among them again… and tell me from your heart… is there any that you would toss away… or would you keep them all…"

… a s qua di s di… and so it is good

The Star Nation has come to greet me on this day. I feel their unconditional love as I stand out on the prairie. It is pure and soft, powerful and strong, wisdom and knowing, nurturing and compassion. It is love that fills (and overflows within) me.

I feel myself illuminate in the darkness of this morning. I feel warmth move within and through me. I feel as though I am rising up, and that I am suspended somewhere between Earth and Sky.

I hear the tones now. The tones which are the voices of those who reside in the High Place. And they speak to me in their tones, that vibrate to the place where I stand… and I hear and know and understand… exactly what they are saying…

"… call on us, two-legged… open your hearts to feel us… open your minds to know us… and through your spirits believe that we are here…,

… whatever it is you need in your physical life… for yourself or for another… ask us… for we are here to assist…,

… do not be concerned with why and how… and do not worry about your past… or consider whether you are deserving or not… for your past does not matter… and you are always deserving… *always*…,

… call on us, two-legged… trust in us, two-legged… believe we can help you… and you will know we can… and you will see how your life can change…,

… with the faith and trust of a young child… look up into the Sky… and feel or think or speak out your need… your greatest wish or your deepest desire… and then… with the faith and trust of a young child… know that we have heard you… and that we are taking care of it…"

… a s qua di s di… and so it is good

It is a bright shining Star Being who wakes me deep in the night. His light fills my room, yet I am unable to move… I am half asleep and half awake (or so it seems).

We move into the in-between space, to a lighted opening surrounded by Star People. This is a magical place that I do not recognize, but the two of us just slip right through… into another dimension…

"… love what you do, two-legged… do what you love… find joy and fulfillment in something of each day you live… for life is to be a good thing… and far too many of you settle for sadness (unhappiness)… when joy is the gift your Creator intended for you…,

… here in this place… see all the colors of the rainbow… here in this place feel the warm and healing fire… here in this place… allow yourself to dream your heart's desires… here in this place… you are given permission… to receive all the goodness and joy that is waiting for you (that you have been waiting for)…,

… now look out from here, two-legged… look from within this place of all possibility… and see with clear eyes… the truth of your existence… from beginning until now… can you see the good that has always been there… hidden within the happenings of each day…,

… within you there is conflict… between the life you believe you are living… and the life you want (wish) to live… and then there is the life that you are truly living (seen by us in the High Place)…,

… settle the inner conflict within you, two-legged… and you will find contentment… know it is your own mind that tells you "you are unhappy" … or that keeps you from taking the action that will help you find joy…,

… love what you do, two-legged… do what you love… and see the goodness that has been given to you throughout your life… from beginning until now… then move forward to embrace and acknowledge that joy and goodness… so that you can begin to accept and receive all that is still there… waiting for you to claim it…"

… a s qua di s di… and so it is good

I
t is the Buffalo who call to me on this day. I hear the voice of an Old Elder Buffalo and quiet my thoughts as I listen…

"… come to the give-away ceremony, two-legged… come, I will show you the way… step into the circle and follow the dancers… as they make their way around the inside of the hoop…,

… give away as you dance, two-legged… give away all that restricts your purpose… whether it is fear or doubt that keeps you from moving forward… old thought patterns and beliefs that hold you back… the negative words someone spoke to or about you that you cannot let go of… or even your own excuses… know that it is time to giveaway…,

… for it is time for you to walk strong now, two-legged… with confident, determined, forward moving steps… and holding onto to fear and doubt can only weaken you… it will cause you to walk slow and your steps to be timid and apprehensive…,

… old thought patterns and beliefs… are just that… old ways of thinking that do not serve you now… for they do not vibrate in rhythm with heightened energy that you have created/become… just as the negative words of anyone who tells you, you can't… carries no weight… unless you allow them to… and then all they are is weight… extra, unnecessary weight that holds you down and back… and feeds your pocket of excuses…,

… look at these places within yourself, two-legged… draw them up to the surface of your being as you dance… and once they are all there… change your direction and release them… as you dance counter-Sun-wise toward the center of the circle…,

… and once you reach the center… sing your gratitude song for the healing you have just received… and then move back into your life… walking with strong and certain forward moving steps… walking forward with determination and confidence…"

… a s qua di s di… and so it is good

I was told we would have rain yesterday, and I was glad for it. Mother Earth needs the water and we need the healing. But no rain came to the place where I live. So the guardians of our hearts came and found me in the Dreamtime, so to provide us with the healing waters that fall from the High Place, and a way to connect with the flow of unconditional love… for ourselves as well as for others…

"… truth lives within the heart… and it is because of your heart, that you feel… your heart will not lie to you (it cannot)… if you feel happy, it will tell you… if you feel sad, you will know it… if you are hurt or angry or excited or afraid… it is your heart that knows this first…,

… you will always feel the emotion… although it can be difficult to distinguish exactly which emotion you are feeling… if you use your mind too much… or if you are one who holds emotions within your heart… rather than allowing them to flow in their own natural way…,

… is it love you feel for the boy, or is it the excitement of getting to know someone new… is it truly sadness you feel, or is it the fear of not knowing how your life will be without him…,

… emotion is good… even when it is negative… but all emotion… even the positive… is meant to flow in, and then flow out… just like the tide that moves in and washes up onto the shore… only to move back out again… in a smooth and natural rhythm… the water remains clear and fresh then, alive and healthy…

… it isn't until you capture the water… and confine it to a small area… that it becomes stagnant and unhealthy… if you create a dam or a block… with no way for the water to flow out and no way to clean it… the water will become sick… and it will make you sick as well…,

… much of the action and choices you take and make in your life… are driven by what is going on in your heart… and so begin to know the condition of your heart… and care for it daily… for there is a natural flow of unconditional love… that flows into and through you at all times… and it comes from the High Place… it is always there and always available for you to use… in fact you are meant to be connected with it at all times…,

… so check in now… and see if this connection is open and flowing… or if it is blocked and cut off… then make it your intention to release the block… or reconnect the flow… and allow the old emotions to flow out… so the healing of unconditional love can flow in… and look in on this daily… to be sure that all is flowing well… and that what you are feeling is real and true… and not old distorted emotions of the past…"

… a s qua di s di… and so it is good

I t is the Bear within me that speaks on this day. She stands at the opening of her cave and reminds me that it is time to begin our dreams for the future. Whether our dreams are for the next year coming or for our entire future, we must set aside time in the Dreamtime (each day or night), to plant and tend to the seeds of our dreams.

The She Bear tells me that if we begin now, dreaming and nourishing our dreams for the future, they will have developed enough by January One for us to step into. And that which we have set for ourselves to do or be, or take on or take off… will begin to become so…

"… go into the shadows of your sleep-time… and discover what is there… for that which lives in the space of your most deep and intimate (inner) thoughts… become the dreams that guide your waking movement…,

… go and see what is there… ruling your dream space… and if it is not the dream you have put there… then you can replace it with one that is your own… remember… that you must intentionally set your dreams in place… into your soul and spirit… and intentionally connect them to your mind and thoughts… or random thoughts (and even fears)… will become your dreams… and they will lead you into places you may not wish to go…,

… tend to your dreams… and spend time with them daily… nourish them well… and trust them too… for when you do, you will begin to see… how your future becomes your dreams… and your dreams become your future…"

… a s qua di s di… and so it is good

Grandmother Moon guides my walk on this dark morning. It is by her light that I see just the faintest image of myself. A slight shadow of me appears on the road before me as I walk. And though I have seen myself in this type of shadow before, I look very different on this day. I thought it was the shadow of someone else at first, but after taking a moment to look around, both physically and spiritually, I see that it is me…

"… you are changing, Swan… you are doing your work and following your path… and as you let go of the old… you make room for the new… you shift and change as the old falls away and the new flows in… and this is why your shadow looks different… because you are different…,

… this is a critical time, Swan… for it is when a person first notices they are changing… even after all the work they have done to bring about these changes… fear rises up… they become uncomfortable with the new, and long for the old… and once others see, feel, and sense the changes you are making… they begin to draw you back to the old (much of the time without even realizing they are doing so)… simply because they fear losing you… they begin to feel uncomfortable and sense a difference in your relationship…,

… but life is about change, Swan… it's about growth and movement, and rising and falling, and getting back up, and finding your way to the highest most expanded version of yourself… and to do this… one must accept the changes that take place along the way…,

… remember when you were a child… from your first memory until now… all you did was change… and changing was natural and easy and acceptable during your childhood and youth… it was what you were supposed to be doing… and so everyone around you (including yourself) supported you through all the changes you made…,

… but as one becomes adult and set in their life… even though they are still growing and changing… the growth slows to an almost undetectable pace… and one becomes comfortable with who they are and what they do… and so changing becomes more difficult (if one even has the notion to change at all)…,

… the key to making it through and making it last… is to acknowledge the work you are doing every day… to embrace the changes taking place within and around you… to replace the fear of losing the old… with the excitement of bringing in the new… to consciously support and assist yourself at all times… and to trust and allow the guidance of all that is of the High Place to support and assist you as well…,

… allow the flow from the High Place to fill you at times of confusion and doubt… and remember at all times… why you set out upon this journey of change… for it is also why you came…"

… a s qua di s di… and so it is good

The Cloud People have gathered on this day…I felt them moving in late last night. Grandmother Moon is almost completely full now, and though her light is dim, I can see her there, just behind the Cloud People. I look up as I walk the prairie on this day, for there is something drawing my attention to the Sky Place…

… and I see it as I stop at the place where I will set ceremony on this day… for the Cloud People have woven themselves together like a blanket… and with the assistance of Grandmother Moon's light… I can see the pattern of the blanket they have woven… it is one of peace and hope and trust and future… it is a Medicine Blanket… and it is here to cover all of us…

"… feel the warmth of this blanket, children… and feel the life that lives within it… for it is a time of healing… and the Medicine of this blanket we have woven… is alive with the ***healing waters of life***… and the ***healing waters of life*** fall upon you (each)… as rain and snow…,

… take in the wisdom carried within each drop and flake… as the rain and snow falls upon you (each)… and learn the patterns of this Medicine Blanket… for held within these patterns are the weavings for peace and hope and trust… ***and future***…,

… then begin to weave these into the pattern of your own Medicine Blanket… (the story of your own life, told by the weavings created through how you have lived your life)… and you can fill in any holes and tears that you find…

with the patterns of peace and hope and trust *and future*… that you have learned from weavings of our Medicine Blanket…,

… then step back for a time, children… and see the strength and beauty that is you… see the Medicine that has awakened within you… for just as you have drawn a strand from each experience of your life… you will draw a strand from the High Place to balance it… and your Medicine Blanket will become strong and beautiful… and reflect the strength and beauty that is (and always has been) you…"

… a s qua di s di… and so it is good

It is the Old Man who greets me on this day. I stand in the cold and dark of this morning, shivering to the bone, and the Old Man reminds me how to warm myself from within. I draw in the light and love from the High Place through my crown, and then the nourishment and compassion of Mother Earth up through my feet. And I begin to feel warm and comfortable, as if the Old Man has wrapped me in a blanket, and the warmth of his fire heats only the place where I stand…

"… you have been experiencing the world in a two-dimensional way, children… but as the vibration of your Star (Earth) rises… you will find there is more to see and know and experience in every happening… so you must understand your world, yourself, and your life in a three-dimensional way now… for there is so much more to see and know and experience…

… to begin… you must release control of your mind… for your mind knows and understands the value of expanding itself… for although your mind has been content to work separately from your spirit, heart, and body… connecting with these only in council… it is preparing to become completely blended (and work together as one) with your spirit, heart, and body… as well as with all that is of the High Place and all that is held deep within Mother Earth… so that you can see and know and experience your world, yourself, and your life in a more complete way…,

… you will notice a significant difference in how you live your life… once you have allowed your spirit, heart, body, *and mind* to truly integrate and Be as one… and joining with Creator and Mother Earth will bring about an even greater shift and expansion in your experience of life… for your perception of each happening will be influenced by every aspect of you at once… rather than by each of them individually (one at a time)…,

… you become wise then, children… and your reaction to each happening of your life shifts from hazy to clarity… from confusion to understanding… tranquility takes the place of static… and you begin to see the divinity in all things… you understand thoroughly… in mind, heart, body, and spirit… and this is what it is to know peace within…"

… a s qua di s di… and so it is good

I walked the prairie last night, under the light of Grandmother Moon. The air was cool, but not too uncomfortable. I sat and then lay upon Mother Earth, for it was the wisdom of these two feminine beings that my soul has been calling for.

As I closed my eyes I saw a Star Being shoot across Father Sky. I watched the trail of light that followed this Star Being, as it lingered there for a moment. Then, without even the slightest effort (notion or warning), my vision was magnified, and I could see this trail of light was actually many Star Beings all lined up, and creating a pathway for me to follow…

"… as this year nears its end… you must begin preparing for the next… in fact… much of this year has been a preparation for that which will be significant and available to and for you in the next…, … there has been much seeking inward… much letting go… much discovery of the gifts and abilities that had been hiding within… much drawing out of your inner strengths and wisdoms… and much ridding of that which no longer serves you…,

… you have engaged your spirit in this work… and found a way for all aspects of yourself (spirit, heart, body, mind) to work together… and this has been good… but now it is time for you to awaken an aspect of yourself that has been left sleeping for too long…,

… we speak of your intuition, dear children… which lives within all two-legged… it is usually linked to the feminine… but remember, all two-legged carry both male and female energy within them… and one does not have to be male… to have allowed their intuition to slip into to the background for this long…,

… and so, dear children… close your eyes and feel the presence of Mother Earth below and Grandmother Moon above… align your heart with Mother Earth and your breath with Grandmother Moon… ask your **Feminine** energy to rise up… and your intuition to awaken… and then follow the trail of the Star Beings as they guide you deep within…,

… feel yourself expand… as your entire being engages… as every aspect of you (spirit, heart, body, and mind) opens to acknowledge your intuition… and know that your intuition has now become an active part of you…,

… for that which awaits you on the path ahead… will speak to you in subtle ways… through what you know as feeling… but will begin to come as energy first… and your intuition is the aspect of you that senses energy…,

… so awaken your intuition, dear children… respect it and use it for all that it has to offer… and find confidence in the knowing that you are aligned and balanced and ready to receive… as you move into the coming year…"

… a s qua di s di… and so it is good

I wake from dreams of my childhood. The sound of my childhood friends and I laughing and playing, lingers in my ears. I remember a simple joy as the feeling of this time of innocence expands throughout my entire being. It is a feeling I almost fear, for it is so pure and perfect… it is the feeling of childlike trust… of no worries… of complete and total contentment…

"… it is time to find within you… the simplicity of a child's trust… the knowing that you are cared for and that all your needs are met… so as you prepare for the time of Winter Sleep (that is just ahead)… remember to awaken your trust and innocence as well…,

… for once the Winter has passed… and you step out into the Spring… you will find a new playground awaits you… and you must know that it is safe to play there… you must be certain that your (Father) Creator is always there and watching over you… and that (your Mother) the Earth will always provide for you (care for, nourish, and nurture)…

… and that this will be a time to explore and discover… and you must go forward with childlike wonder and curiosity… you must go forth with the open trusting heart of a child… and begin to live in a playful and joyous way…,

… for if you go forth guarded and serious… with an expanded ego and cynical attitude… you will be set out on a lower level of experience and possibility… one that is restricted and confined… where there is no sense of trust or security… (and all of this will come to be through your own sophistication and suspicions)…,

… so call to the child that lives within you… heal all and any wounds that linger within her or him… be the trusted parent (guardian, guide) that she or he needs… to soothe away the pain and restore the trust… do all and anything you can or need to… so to heal this blessed child…,

… for it will be this part of you… this your playful, trusting inner-child… who knows the way and leads you forth… and together you will do and become great things…"

… a s qua di s di… and so it is good

I sat on the prairie with the Old Man for hours this morning. He was there, waiting for me as I walked out early this morning. I laid out my ceremony blanket and lit the sacred fire. I sprinkled sacred herbs into the fire and breathed in the sacred smoke. I waited for the Old Man to speak, but he kept silent.

I sang the prayer songs for all people and began ceremony for today. I moved into stillness expecting the Old Man to speak, but still he offered only silence. I sat still and silent waiting to hear the voice from above, but it was only silence that I heard.

I waited patiently, for what I now know were hours, until I finally let go of my mind and allowed my spirit to guide me… and that is when I heard our message for today…

"… it was not my words you needed on this day, young one… but my presence… it was not my teaching… but my compassion… it was not what you needed to see or hear that brought me to your side on this day… but what you needed to feel…,

… this is the message that you are to share on this day, young one… for as the energy of the world you live in… moves and shifts and expands… it will be by your presence that you make a difference… by the love and the light that you carry within…,

…it will be by your willingness to sit with a person… providing a safe and protected space for them to be in… allowing them to find their way… by the love and light that lives within them…,

… and as you learn how to assist another in this way… you will understand… that life is more about what is within you… than it is about the words you speak… it is more about how another feels in your presence… than what you tell them of yourself…,

… for when you sit with another in this way… you will feel what is within their heart… and they will know what is within yours…,

… go into the silence, young one… and find your way into the stillness… sit in that sacred space… and examine what is in your heart… feel the joy and the sacredness there… the pain and struggle too… find your triumphs and accomplishments… and the places that make you smile… as well as the ones that make you cry…,

… and know that for each one of these within your own heart… there are millions of the same within the hearts of others… and then find within yourself… the compassion to love them all… and then give them each your silence… as you sit with them in stillness and prayer… for this is how you bring *Medicine* into the lives of others…"

… a s qua di s di… and so it is good

By the light of Grandmother Moon, I can see the Antelope who have gathered in the back pasture (there must be at least a dozen of them). They stand with the Buffalo (who share the space generously with their Antelope relatives), and together they provide an amazing and irresistible energy.

I set ceremony here on this day (as close to the fence line as I can), in the front pasture that connects directly to the back pasture where the Antelope and Buffalo stand grazing…

"… it is time to pay attention to your physical being, two-legged… to respect and care for your physical body… for it houses your spirit… and in order for you to accomplish all that you came to accomplish… you will need your physical body in proper working order…,

… as you align and balance every aspect of your being… you will find they communicate with one another continuously… and you will notice that many of the messages you receive from your spirit and heart… are first spoken to you through your physical body… (a feeling, an ache, a spasm, or a pain)…,

… it is important to keep every aspect of your being strong and healthy and clear… to tend to the whole of yourself each and every day… but remember, two-legged… your physical body is the pasture that nourishes your heart, mind, and spirit… and without it… you would not be here to share all of that which you came to share…

… a s qua di s di… and so it is good

It is natural at this time of year, to begin preparing for the Winter (at least it is in Colorado, where the weather can feel like Winter as early as September). So it does not surprise me that Squirrel Medicine has been poking at me for the last few days.

Usually Squirrel speaks to us of gathering and storing, making sure we have enough supplies to last through whatever the Winter may have in store for us. But on this day, Squirrel offers us another way of preparing for the Winter…

… for it is during the time of Winter… that we receive the important gifts, abilities, and attributes that will serve us best in the future…

"… be sure to create the space within and around you, two-legged… make room for all that you will receive during your Winter Sleep… for as you slow your pace… and the nights become long… you will find time to receive knowing and energy from the High Place…,

… release all of the un-serving worries and doubts… that still linger in the corners of your mind and being… for these only take up space… and even if they once had value and necessity… they no longer have purpose…,

… prepare your space, two-legged… even if you must choose only one thing at a time… so to clear away the negativity that it produces… continue with this work… for as you clear away each un-serving emotion, worry, and fear… you create a space for knowledge, talent, ability, and wisdom to move in… and not just for fleeting moments, mind you… but to stay and to become a part of who you are… of who you are growing into to *Being*…"

… a s qua di s di… and so it is good

I walked the Labyrinth this morning. I stood at the opening and tried to settle my mind. I breathed out and in, trying to untangle my thoughts and searching for clarity. Then I realized… this is why I am here.

So I walked the twists and turns of the Labyrinth, watching my feet as I took each step. Making sure I did not stumble or fall in the darkness of this early hour. I stood in silence at the Altar in the center of the Labyrinth. I stood there without words or prayers or song or expectation. I just stood there in the presence of God, and allowed the Labyrinth to do its work.

It was on my third journey through the twisting pathways of the Labyrinth, that I heard the words… "Look up child"… and so I began walking with my eyes looking upward, trusting that I would not stumble or fall.

And although I walked a bit slower my mind began to clear, and I could physically feel the webs within it untangle… and it was then I heard the words that came from above…

"… look to me for direction, children… look to me for your power as well as for your grace… for it is your trust and belief in all that is beyond you… that awakens your personal power… and it is here in this space beyond yourself… that you find the grace to accept yourself, all things, and others… just as they are…,

… to accept all things and all beings (including yourself) just as they are… does not mean that you do not work to make changes for the better… it simply means that you do not impose judgment upon anyone or anything (including yourself)…,

… and once your mind stops worrying about the state of all things and other people… it will realize that its first purpose… is to assist you in realizing that whatever changes you set out to create in the world around… always begins with yourself…,

… look up now, children… look up and find your own personal power… look up and find your own purity and grace… combine these with the determination of your own will… and you will be able to move mountains… with the gentleness and grace of a feather…"

… a s qua di s di… and so it is good

I spent most of the day yesterday, tending to my altar and the sacred ground around the stone prayer circles. The beautiful Fall afternoon enhanced the sacredness of my work, and I could hear voices from the High Place murmuring low all day.

It was a day I had planned to work alone and in solitude, offering this day of sacred work as a prayer for all people (a day of giving). I could feel my prayers rise up as I breathed them out from deep within me, and some prayers, I could actually see moving upward on the soft Wind that kept me company all day.

I worked diligently throughout the day, sitting from time to time, upon the large Grandfather Stone in the West. And it was this Grandfather who followed me into the Dreamtime last night, as he had something to tell me, something I apparently failed to hear while I was working there yesterday.

And so I sit, on this morning, upon the Grandfather Stone in the West, listening as he tells me what I need most to hear…

"… as you set out to offer a day of giving… you must remain open to receive as well… for this kind of energy flows in a circle… and will become less (and even distorted) if the flow is interrupted…,

… this does not mean that you set about with a request for some kind of compensation for that which you give… or with an unspoken motive… it simply means that as you offer your day of giving… or any kindness or assistance to anyone in any way… you must be open to receive as well…,

… there is a flow, child… and if you close your eyes and quiet your mind… I will show it to you… look and see the people… see the energy that surrounds them each… see the people giving to one another… see that as one gives, another receives… and see too, how when one gives… that **one** also receives… see the balance… see the flow…,

… and concentrate on the flow for a moment, child… see how the energy of receiving moves through one… and becomes the giving to another… there is no entitlement here… no demand… it is simply the way it is… but if one breaks the flow… by refusing (or denying themselves) to receive… the balance is disrupted… and the flow becomes broken…,

… so set about on your day of giving… and set out to give to others… whatever and however you can (and do)… just remember to be open to receive, as well… for each and every one of you… all people and all beings… play a part in maintaining the balance here upon this Star… and each and every one of you… are valuable and special and worthy to receive…"

… a s qua di s di… and so it is good

The fresh scent of oranges fills my senses as I wake on this day. I have just the slightest memory of where I had been in the Dreamtime, but a very clear understanding of the message I was given.

I sit in ceremony singing the prayer songs for all people, and the fragrance of oranges intensifies. I feel a cleansing in my heart, and clarity in my mind.

I become still as I quiet my thoughts so to hear the message for today…

"… focus on your heart and emotions, two-legged… for it is time to cleanse away the negativity from within your heart… fear lives within these emotions… fears that began long ago… and it is a good day to release these fears… it is a good day to cleanse and clear… so to begin anew…,

… if left unattended for too long… negative emotions will create physical ailments… your inner-vision will become cloudy… and your mind will become foggy…,

… these emotions are very difficult to clear (if not the most difficult)… and so you may need the Medicine of a kind and compassionate **Standing One** to help you… go to the place of the Orange Standing Ones… align yourself with the energy there… for although theses Standing Ones are kind and compassionate… their Medicine is powerful…,

… fill your senses with the sweet smell of oranges… and use their oil to remind you that you are safe and cared for… that you are protected as you journey deep within to release theses old and un-serving fears and emotions… and keep the scent of Oranges around you at all times… for as long as you need to… in order to cleans and heal your heart…,

… for there is much that your heart will feel and experience in the year that is ahead… good things that will expand within you and fill your heart… and you will need to be prepared for these, two-legged… and make ready a clean clear space within your heart… which is ready to receive…"

… a s qua di s di… and so it is good

NOVEMBER 2010

Rain. At last the Rain is falling (at least in my little portion of the Earth). I have felt the need for emotional release so strongly over the past several weeks (for myself as well as for all people). I understand the healing that accompanies such a release so deeply, that I have been singing and dancing the prayer songs and dances that call to the Rain Keeper for weeks now.

It is not as if we can only release and heal when it is raining, but the kind of emotional release (and healing) we are in need of at this time, is so much more effective and thorough when accompanied by the Rain

… for the Rain washes us clean… it brings up those deeply seated emotions (which brings up our tears)… and it nourishes and fills us with the new (at the very same time we are releasing; cleansing out and filling us, at once)… the Rain makes sure our healing is complete… it makes sure that we are filled with love and goodness from the High Place while we cleanse… so that no void is left within us… no space of any kind for us to call back (and place within)… that which we have just released (or any other negative emotion that may be lingering around us either

"… today let your soul be nourished… let your inner-spirit-self be strengthened and renewed… for then you will know peace within… and it is easy to remember the stability with which you walk… when you walk with peace within you heart…

… the gift of self-renewal… is not given only to the plants and trees and things in nature… you (two-legged, human-beings) possess such a gift as well… be reminded daily of this gift… and use it as you need to…,

… look to the seasons if you cannot find something in nature to inspire you… for the seasons will show you how life is renewed each Spring… how new life always springs forth after the ravaging of Winter… and how beautiful life grows to be… each and every time it renews itself…"

… a s qua di s di… and so it is good

I am joined on this day by the Old Woman of the Tee Pee. She is moving around in the circle of stones that mark the place where the Tee Pee once stood, and she calls to me as I move into stillness…,

"… come child… sit within the space of this sacred dwelling… for there is much I have to tell you on this day… ask your mind to fade back so your spirit can come forward… and relax into the warmth of my fire… feel your heart open and stand with your spirit… for your spirit knows the message I bring to you… and you must hear this message with your heart…,

… look into my fire and see the sacred Tree of Life… see that it is strong and sturdy yet gentle and kind… and feel the peace and tranquility of its heart… and see how its branches reach up… naturally, gracefully, honestly, prayerfully… reaching for the Father… and see that its roots have grown deep within the Mother… clinging, grasping and holding her (as she holds them)…,

… and hear the song that comes as your Grandfather the Wind blows gently around this sacred Standing One… and see the shadow it casts as your Father the Sun rises above it… feel the emotion that is released as your Sister the Rain washes gently through its leaves… and tell me, child… what do you feel as you look upon this sacred being… what do you know as you stand in its presence… are you satisfied by that which you can see with your eyes… or do you look further, with your heart and spirit…,

… and look closer now, dear child… at this sacred Tree of Life… and see that this Tree is you… that it is (and represents) each and every living being… and because of this… you can experience anything/everything of life from any place within this Tree… from as deep within the Earth as it goes… to as far up into the High Place as it reaches… and you can influence those around you… with the shadow that you cast…,

… and when you look upon this Tree… you will see each and every living being there within it… and you will know your sameness as well as your sacredness (then)… and when you see yourself within this Tree… stand against its trunk until you feel its heart beating… and listen as that heart to speaks to you…,

… and see that people have gathered in your shadow now, child… and what does your shadow offer them… is your shadow cool and pleasant… comfortable to stand in… gentle and kind… welcoming and nourishing… or is it cold and harsh… damp and uncomfortable… and does fear rise up within them there…,

… and learn from this, child… as you look at others in this way, too… as you stand in the shadow they cast upon you… and know then, child… that each of you casts a shadow upon whomever gathers around you… and that you influence one another within these shadows… and that you can choose what you want your shadow to offer…,"

… a s qua di s di… and so it is good

The Cowboy and I walked the ranch last night (what a perfect evening). We watched Father Sun sink slowly into the horizon as Pikes Peak Mountain seemed to move in closer, its lines and shape becoming more clear and distinct in the blue-orange of Father Sky.

As Father Sky grew dark and then black, the whole of the Star Nation came quietly down to sit with us upon the prairie. We gazed upon our Star Relatives for a long time then, noticing how they gather together in small villages, but still live together as a whole…

… and it was this images of my Star Relatives that I saw in the darkness as I closed my eyes to sleep… and they moved in even closer, there in my dreams… and formed patterns that became faces… and then there were faces within the faces… and like watching clouds… I began to see stories in the movement of the Stars…

… and they spoke their messages to me again this morning… as I walked out among them and settled into ceremony…

"… gather together, two-legged… become joined in community again… see that you are part of a whole… but that you can draw together in small groups as well…,

... for each of you have your own purpose and value... and if you look you will find others who are of the same heart and mind... and if you look again... you will see the value in knowing and respecting... those who see from a different point of view...,

... for as you share your different perspectives... you will each become more... your lives will be enriched by the expansion of vision... and then you will find... that even if you never change from your own values and beliefs... you can still love (and be loved by) one another... unconditionally... and this will be the beginning of the healing that you seek..."

... a s qua di s di... and so it is good

I stand wrapped in my blanket on this very cold morning, singing the gratitude songs and prayers for all people. I walk the sacred paths that lead to the sacred places here on this ranch. I find myself in the center of the large front pasture, and I stop for a moment to feel for the direction I should go next...

"... listen to your heart, two-legged... feel with your heart... for all directions are open to you... and there are many paths to walk in each... and you could set out upon any of them...,

... it is all about choices... and your own ability to connect with your inner guidance... for each path will offer you a different experience... and it is up to you to discern which of these is best...,

... the question is really not which path to choose... but who will benefit most... for each path will provide you with a gift of some kind... but which path will bring about the most good to all...,

... it is time to look beyond your own self now... and to seek direction for all people... it is time to look for the path that brings about peace and goodness for all... for this is your divine purpose... this is the divine purpose of all people...,

… so release your fears and worries… let go of your mind and thoughts, and even your physical being for a time… allow the grace of all that is of your spirit to guide you now… and you will find your way…"

… a s qua di s di… and so it is good

It is hard for me to wake on this day, as it is Grandmother who sits with me in the Dreamtime. We sit in one of my favorite places, along a hidden creek next to her Medicine Lodge. There is a sacredness here that seems to awaken deep memories within me, and they are so powerful that is easy to get lost within them. Sometimes I return from this time with Grandmother with clarity and answers… and other times I return filled with questions…

… Am I within myself here, or am I beyond myself? Do the words I hear now come from my own knowing, or are they the words of my Grandmother, or maybe of my Creator. And aren't all words that come in this way, the sacred knowing given to us by our Creator?…

I have no concept of time as I wake… for I am so deeply held within the Dreamtime… and I choose to remain in this deep sleep… for I am captivated by these questions…

"… within each two-legged… is **knowing** from the beginning… wisdom and answers that bring about the understanding they need to live a full and happy life… and this knowing can become hidden and buried throughout their life… by fears and insecurities (inner-conflicts) which come about though everyday life experiences…,

… as you begin to release your fears… you become more secure in who you are… which makes it possible for you to conquer the inner-conflicts that shadow your wisdom, bury your knowing, and hide the answers you seek… and all of this begins with a deep and solid connection to and with your Creator…,

… breath is one of the truest and strongest ways by which Creator (God, Spirit) connects with you… and so breathing deeply, with conscious and focused intention… is essential for one who wishes to expand their spiritual knowing and connect with their Creator…,

… going within and tending to all that has been left there over the years is also essential… for that which is stored and carried within… inhibits the movement of breath… which is Creator moving through you constantly… (without condition or prejudice)… and once that which has been stored within has been released… your breath becomes deeper and stronger and moves more easily…,

… and the voice of your wisdom will call to you from deep within then… and you will find yourself asking the question…

… Am I within myself here, or am I beyond myself? Do the words I hear now come from my own knowing, or are they the words of my Creator. And aren't all words that come in this way, the sacred knowing given to us by our Creator?…

… and you will know the answer…"

… a s qua di s di… and so it is good

In my ceremony place, there stands a lovely Paper Birch. She is a young Standing One with an old spirit. She stands between the Labyrinth and the Circle of Grandfather Stones, and she has become the Keeper of the Stones (though the Stones speak of her as the Lady who watches over and cares for them).

I hear her singing as I walk out on this day, and I feel the stillness offered to her by the entire prairie. The Lady Birch sings the *Song of November*… a song which is meant to assist us in renewing and rededicating ourselves for the coming year…

"… stand here on the edge of time… with one foot in the old and the other in the new… see from both places as you balance here… and decide what to take forward and what to leave behind…,

… look back and see who you are now… look forward and see who you can become… and draw down the light from the one above… to illuminate your spirit which lives there within…,

… for there is a birthing before you… and a death behind you… and as you move forward you must honor them both… the death is of that which can no longer serve you… and the birth is of that which can bring forth your best… the elusive one who waits there within…,

… with the support of the soil you know as your Mother… find strength that could carry many more of you size… and with the grace of the **One** who requires no name… receive the messages that cannot be seen with your eyes…,

… for a change is in the Wind now… and you ride upon the Wind… and there is an opening before you… and I see you looking in… so speak out your dedication… and cast your dreams into the light… and the one who sleeps within you… will find you in the night…"

… a s qua di s di… and so it is good

Emotion is what I notice as I wake on this morning, and a stirring within that creates a bit of confusion.

As I step out into the morning, my cognitive mind begins to reason… *it is the combination of the uncommonly warm weather, and the fact that it is a New Moon which creates this unrest within me…*

… but as I begin ceremony, I find my Spirit has another explanation…

"… emotion that is rising up now… is the ever growing anticipation of what your next year will bring… and the stirring within… is excitement mixed with fear… that familiar feeling of wanting to move forward… combined with fear over what the new will hold… and the question of whether you will be able to step up, stand up, live up… do it, be it, accomplish it…,

… but it is the New Moon… a perfect time to set your goals… a perfect time to get clear… but you must begin with a very clear intention… and you must keep that intention clear and focused throughout… and it is important to set your intention with positive words and visions… and to spend time daily… reaffirming your goals and intentions…,

… and if you cannot find the clarity within… to define your goals and intentions for the coming year… begin by aligning yourself with your highest spirit… and then align your highest spirit with your Creator… and from that place… trust what comes… (trust what you are shown)…,

… allow your mind to fade back then… and listen to your spirit… for your spirit knows the answer to the questions that will not let you sleep… "what is my purpose?… and where do I put my energy?… what is it I am to do now?… and where am I going?… does my life have meaning?… and am I where I am supposed to be?… am I following or am I leading?… and is all of this for the highest good?" …

… so it is a time of blending now… as you use your mind to speak the words that your spirit has brought through… and it is a time of trusting, too…as you release your physical hold… your need to control and structure a plan for the coming year… for it is better to allow your spirit to guide you now… and to watch as it all unfolds…"

… a s qua di s di… and so it is good

The laughter of a child seems to be echoing through my head as I wake on this day. A feeling of happiness and joy that is so pure and simple it fills my entire being. I hear the voices of young children singing silly songs and giggling… *where am I?* … or should I ask… *who is here?*…

"… it is time to get serious about not being so serious… for the energy of this season and the next is very dense… and it can be difficult to maneuver through… unless you can remember the simple joy of playing (being silly) in the way that children do…,

… it is your Higher Self speaking to your *Self* on this day… and the conversation is about your *Self* and your inner-child… and the topic is about having fun… for it has been too long worrying… too long under too much stress… too much work and not enough play… and too much stored-up hurt… with no outlet for release…,

... laughter is a wonderful healer... for laughter opens every aspect of your being... (your mind and heart... your spirit and body)... laughter allows the static to dissipate and the energy to smooth... laughter brings about a lightness to your entire being... and it brings the light in as well... it cleanses away the built up toxins that have gotten caught up within you... and laughter can even inspire you to go out and play, and dance, and have fun... to forget about the serious part of life for a while... and to just be like a child for a while...,

... this is not to say that your troubles will magically disappear if you give yourself a recess... but it is important to understand that when you are worried, under stress, filled with hurt or pain or sadness or anger... your energy becomes very dense... and if you are trying to maneuver through extremely dense energy while your own energy is so dense... the will struggle exhaust you... and you could develop serious health issues, too...,

... you may not be able to control the density of the energy around you... but you *are* in charge of your own energy... and you can lighten your energy just by laughing and playing and having fun...,

... you have all of the power, wisdom, knowing, and tools... to solve all of the issues that keep you stressed... but you cannot access them if your energy is too dense... and you know this somewhere deep within... and the child within you has the answer of how to heal those things that have been stressing and distressing you for far too long... and that is to find a way to shake them up, shake them loose, and get them out for good... and it all begins with laughing and playing and giving yourself a break..."

... a s qua di s di... and so it is good

Ihave noticed that many people (myself included) struggle to understand what blocks them from sincerely addressing the big issues in their lives. I presented this question last night in ceremony, and this morning the answer came. It was brought to us by a fully decorated Warrior... complete with feathers, a bow and arrow, medicine pouch, and the most magnificent Warrior Horse I have ever seen...

"… it is fear, Swan… fear which is very deeply rooted and hard to detect… for this fear did not come bursting in by way of some trauma or tragic experience… this fear began as a small thing… and like a seed… it began to grow and develop over the years…,

… it has been given just enough attention (over the years) to keep it alive… and sometimes a situation occurs that feeds it so well… that it begins to grown quite rapidly… it stays there in the background, though… just beyond your reach… on the inner edge of that shadow-place within you… where all of the uncertainty that is woven into your life continues to feed it…,

… this is a debilitating fear, Swan… for it has been there within you for so long… that it has become a part of you… and this makes it very difficult to locate… and very difficult to remove… for in a way it has become attached to you now… and for some, even the knowing of this will create more fear…

… but for most, the knowing of this fear… is just what they have been search-ing for… and that is good… for once you know what you are looking for… half your battle is won…,

… and it is time to face this fear head on now, Swan… and to reclaim your own strength and courage and will to go forward… and it is important to know that this fear is all emotion… and that the barrier it has created for you… must be dissolved… you cannot simply break through it… you must find a way to dissolve it…,

… ride with me now, Swan… and I will take you to the highest place my Horse can reach… we will stand in the place where Father Sun drops into the Ocean… and he will call this fear out from within you… for there is a strong pulling here in this place… as Father Sun moves from our sight… and his fire is very strong here, too…,

… but you must release then… as your fear is draw out… and trust the power of Father Sun… for his fire is Big Medicine… so big and so powerful that it will dissolve your fears away… quickly and completely…,

… then stand with me as the last of Father Sun fades away… for the healing power of your Sister the Ocean… will fill you with the healing and nourishment you need… and the barrier will be dissolved completely… and you will be strong again… and you will go forward in a good way then… and so it is good…"

… a s qua di s di… and so it is good

I stand in snow on this day… the first snow of the season… and I breathe in the cold, clean air (which feels so good… like renewal)… I light the ceremony herbs and breathe in the sacred smoke… (freshly dried cedar mixed with cold clean air… it is renewal)… and my spirit emerges… and I follow her

… I sing the prayer songs for all people… as I walk with my bowl of smoking herbs… and I follow as my spirit leads me to the Labyrinth… I trust her as she leads me in and around the pathways there within… and we stop when we reach the altar… and sing out our prayer songs (strong and clear)… before making our way back out again… and we offer blessings to all who have ever walked this path… as we carefully trace our footsteps… around and around

… I find myself in the Grandfathers Prayer Circle now… and I walk the inner circle until the last of the prayer songs have been sung… and I sit upon the Grandfather Stone in the North… and the silence becomes loud… as I move quietly into stillness…

… and the wisdom of this Grandfather rises up within me… as my own spirit circles around and around us… and a feeling washes over me… it is compassion… contentment… peacefulness… tranquility… perfection… purity… joy…

… and I feel an understanding now… an understanding that comes from very deep within me… like I understand it a*ll* now… (here in this moment)… and yet I am sure there is more for me to know…

"... you see your spirit as a being on this day, Swan... and this is good...for it is time to understand the relationships in your life... and how they reflect who you are **being** at this time (or at any time)...,

... your first and most important relationship is (and should always be)... the one between you and your Creator... but you know (and should always remember)... that this relationship includes the relationship you have with your own **self**... (that is, between your self and your spirit)... and that it is from this relationship... that all other relationships in your life come to be...,

... honor your **self**... care for and nurture your **self**... be kind and loving and compassionate and attentive to your **self**... for what you give to your self... you give to Creator... and when this relationship (between self, spirit, and Creator) is strong and solid and loving and respectful... your relationships with others develop in this way as well..."

... a s qua di s di... and so it is good

There is a sweetness in the air as I walk out on this day. I breathe in deeply as I pull my blanket up snug and walk out to the place where I will set ceremony. There is a woodstove burning, warming someone's home, and I can smell the sweetness of the wood... it smells like peach.

I light my ceremony herbs and breathe in the smoke, singing the prayer songs for all people silently within. I reach into my ceremony bundle, and feel around for my Rattle... for Rattle is the Medicine that is called for at this time.

I listen as the tiny stones within my Rattle begin to speak, and I open my eyes as I hear another Rattle begin to sing close by. It is the Old Man who has come to sit with me on this day. I offer him a welcoming nod, and together we blend our voices through the Medicine of our Rattles... listening for the message we seek on this day...

"... it is easy to stiffen and become hard... as the air grows cold and the snow begins to fall... you want to protect that which is precious and lives deep within... but your heart is strong and resilient... and must be used if you are to keep it open and alive... and so you must remember to keep a softness about you... so that your heart can be felt by others... and so that you can feel their hearts, too... for it is far too long before the Springtime comes... for you to wait to know one another (again) in this way...,

... and deep within you... there within your very heart... a wisdom hides... it is safe and protected there... like the tiny stones within your rattle... like the precious seed within the peach... but in order for this wisdom to be awakened and known... you must find a way to release it... (to make use of that which it has to offer)...,

... and so you shake your rattle... and you eat the peach ... and that which had been hidden within... will awakened into the world... and the Medicine that comes to all who hear the song of your rattle... (inspiration, healing, knowing, wisdom, vision, and such)... will grow tall and wide and infinite... just as the seed of the peach, when planted... will grow to produce more peaches... and from these more seeds will be planted to grow... and they will produce more... (and so on and on)...,

... and so it is with your heart... and the wisdom held within it... for that which is hidden deep within your heart... is pure and true and soft and warm... and anyone who feels the softness and warmth of your heart... will be inspired to know the wisdom of their own... and the wisdom their hearts will tell them... to be open, soft, and true...,

... and the voice of each heart will begin to speak then... and blend with one another... just as the song of our rattles did on this day... and each will know their sameness... and each will know their truth... and each will begin to soften... and Oneness will begin to grow..."

... a s qua di s di.. and so it is good

D o I dream of the Bear on this cold morning, because I would like to be tucked away (warm and cozy) in her cave?... or does the Bear offer me her warm and cozy cave, because it is so cold ?... no matter... I am here within the cave of the She Bear... and her message is just what I needed on this day...

"… ah yes… it *is* time to be within the cave… and for two-legged, this is a symbol of going within… but you do not just go within to find protection from the cold… (although my cave will bring you warmth and comfort)… there is purpose to going within… and though there are many reasons to go within… today I will teach you only one of them…,

… you see, two-legged… everything you take in is nourishment of some kind… the food you eat… that which you read… that which you hear, see, feel, and sense… even that which you imagine and dream… everything you experience throughout your day (your life)… is taken within and feeds you somehow…,

… and so it is that you nourish your mind and your heart, your body and your spirit… with everything that surrounds you (all the time)… now your body will naturally process the food and drink that you take in… it will use that which is appropriate and necessary to keep you alive and strong and healthy… and it will eliminate the rest…,

… but it is up to you, two-legged… to process all that you see and hear and read and feel and sense, and even imagine and dream… it is up to you to sort through all of these things… and determine what is valuable and what is not… what nourishes you in every way… and what simply must be eliminated from your being…,

… and this is one of the reasons you go into the cave… for once within the cave… there is silence (stillness)… and the feeding stops… and the processing begins… without the continued (distracting) influence of anything or anyone…,

… and as you process all that you have taken in… you begin to eliminate that which does not serve your highest good… you let go of fears and confusion… and you find clarity and truth… and even though you respect that which does not serve your highest good… for you know it has purpose for some… you eliminate it from your being with love and gratitude…,

… this is a cycle of life, two-legged… it is meant to keep you from getting bogged down with too may question… it is meant to be a way for you to find the answers to those questions that effect your future (as well as the future of all people)… and it is meant to be used regularly… so that you remain healthy in every way and at all times…"

… a s qua di s di… and so it is good

The Star People are very present as I walk out on this day. Their energy is intense and it pulses… I can actually see it pulsing… like a heartbeat or blood pulsing through veins. My own heartbeat begins to sound in my ears… and I can feel it in my chest, too… it seems to beat in rhythm with that of the Star People…

… and the ancient beat of ceremony drums begin to sound now… from somewhere off in the distance…

"… the skins between the worlds are thinning, two-legged… and the knowing that was brought forth in times long-ago… is now just a heartbeat away… and within your reach are answers and tools and forgotten pieces of the great puzzle that you seek to complete…,

… but do you know, two-legged… that these have always been so close to you… that this knowing (the secrets of the ancestors)… has always been within your reach… just as we, The Star Nation, have always pulsed with the flow of life…,

… it is you who are changing, two-legged… you, who are expanding your energy… you, who has found your way past all that blocks your view… and you, who has connected with your inner place of trust… and this has opened the door for you… to all that is beyond… (that is all that came before, as well as all that is yet to be)…,

… and so it is a time of remembering now, two-legged… rather than a time of learning… it is a time to trust your own intuition… for your intuition is simply that which you already know, but sleeps somewhere within… and it is awakening within you now… and calling out to be used…,

… so take some time, two-legged… to notice all the ways you have grown and expanded… to acknowledge that which has awakened within you… and to draw forth that which is still yet to be remembered… for as you move forward to create your future… you will be required to remember… some of the knowings of the past…"

… a s qua di s di… and so it is good

I sit wrapped in my blanket on this cold and frosty morning… singing the prayer songs for all people (silently within) as I breathe in the sacred smoke of ceremony… there is a blanket of frozen air between me and the Star People on this day… but I know they are there… for I can feel them…

… the space around me begins to warm… as I bring to mind each one for whom I pray… as the inner-sacred of each one calls out… reaching for one another… and somehow the pure and perfect light within each… bridges the gap between all people…

… and I can feel my Star Relatives reach out for me now… and I can feel my inner-light reach out (and up)… (as theirs reaches down to me)… and I know we are connected… today and always… no matter what stands between us…

… and I know in this instant, too… that it is we, the two-legged human-beings… who let go and look away from one another… for the light and the grace of all that is perfect and pure… (of all that is of The High Place)… is constant and present and connected to us at all times… and the sacredness that is our soul and spirit… (the truest part of our beings)… is always present, too… reaching out (and up)…

… and I know now… that it is our minds that let go and look away… not our hearts… and so we must engage our minds… and ask them to remember… and ask them to make time each day… to create a sacred space within our lives… to consciously acknowledge and connect with the light from all things and all people… as it reaches out for us…

… and as our own inner-light reaches out to connect with the light of all things and all people… we ourselves begin to expand… our consciousness expands and our knowing awakens… and we understand from a much higher level then… and we let go of lower attitudes and opinions… and we love one another without judgment or condition…

… a s qua di s di… and so it is good

Eagle came to our ranch yesterday, I saw her late in the afternoon as I was coming in for the night. She sat on a fence post exactly midway between the West and the North, and told me she would be back to show me something important…

… she returned to me in the night and took me to fly with her… high above our Earth Mother we flew… and we saw the *Great Mother* (Turtle Island) swimming beneath us… and I saw that we were exactly halfway between the West and the North… and I understood the message I am to share on this day… as the *Old Mother* and the *Oldest Grandmother* called out to me from deep within the land…

"… you are not at the beginning… nor are you at the end… you are somewhere in between, dear children… there is much you have come to know by now… and much more for you to learn… and so you must look to see… exactly where you stand…,

… West is the place of Earth… and of all things material and physical… it is the place where you come in to adulthood… and where you harvest much of what you have planted in your youth… but there is a place of balance in the West… for just as you are given a new harvest here… you are also given a way for the old to die away… it is death and rebirth here in the West…,

… North is the place of Air… of thoughts, and of all of the workings of the mind… it is the place where you can organize all of that which you take in physically, emotionally, and spiritually… so to comprehend and make use of… but the Old Ones live here, too… the Eldest of the Elders… and you are given access to their wisdom here in the North… as you stand upon the highest of their mountains… and see all there is to see… you are offered complete understanding here in the North…,

… and so you find yourself somewhere in the middle, children… and you wonder "what does this mean?"… and you ask me for the answers… but it is I who must ask you…,

... have you completed your harvest?... or is there more you must bring forth?... have you let go of that which no longer serves you?... or do you hold it within you still?... have you sat upon the mountain?... and seen all that you can see?... have you head the Elders whispers?... and felt their wisdom stir within?...,

... there is a knowing that you have yet to find... and more for you to be... that which you can shape and form... and that which cannot be seen... so ground yourselves to the Earth, dear ones... stand steady, strong, and tall... then call for the Wind to blow upon you... so you can know it all...,

... and look out as the dust settles down... and the Wind becomes quiet and still... to see where you stand now, and what surrounds you... for your mountain has become a hill..."

... a s qua di s di... and so it is good

The shifting vibration of our Star (our planet Earth) is becoming more and more perceivable these days. I believe that all beings can sense this on some level or another, whether they know what they are sensing or not. I set ceremony in the Grandfathers Prayer Circle now, for the Old Grandfathers are awake and holding council there... and they are speaking about the vibration of our planet...

"... ah, Children... come and listen now... for just as the vibration of your Star is rising... so is your own vibration... and for some of you... this can be a difficult transition to make... especially for those who do not know what is happening...,

... first you must know that everything has a vibration... and that not all things vibrate to the exact same frequency... but most things do vibrate within a certain range... and so it is that you feel comfortable around certain people and in certain places...,

... now you must take this knowing... and combine it with the understanding that the vibrations you have become accustomed to are shifting... they are becoming higher as well as stronger... and for those who are not aware of (or prepared for) this kind of shift... it can bring about chaos and confusion...,

… you many notice a difference in the foods you like… the music you listen to… and even in the people you choose spend time with… you may notice that some folks are getting on your nerves… and others seem to be making perfect sense… or that certain foods you used to eat with no problem… do not agree with you now…

… it is all about the vibration…,

… and so, dear children… it is time to pay attention… for as your *own* vibration shifts… you will become more and more sensitive to the vibration of all things and people… be mindful of the foods you eat and the music you listen to… feel the vibration of each food before you eat it… and notice how much better you feel… notice the clarity of your mind…,

… *feel* the vibration of the places you move around in (the place where you work and live)… for it could be time for you to change the location of your job or dwelling… to move to a place that matches your vibration…,

… and remember to make no judgment of anything or any person/being… for as your vibrations shift out of a certain range and into another… those who vibrate within different frequencies will be somewhat repelled by yours (and you by theirs)… and this is just so… it does not make any *one* more or less… for everyone is shifting in there own time and way… and each will make it to the same place (the same higher vibration)… when they are ready and as they are meant to…"

… a s qua di s di… and so it is good

The morning is cold and clear, and though I want to walk briskly because of the cold, I walk cautiously because of the ice. Grandfather Wind has gone back into the North to sleep now, but he spent most of the day yesterday (and all of the night) blowing hard and strong, offering us his wisdom as well as his cleansing.

I sit wrapped in my blanket as I breathe in the ceremony smoke, and I sing the gratitude song for all people before I sing the prayer songs. I ask for abundance for all people as I sing, by feeling within my body the positive flow from the High Place as it connects to and with each

"… open your hearts to receive… as you let go of worry and doubt… feel gratitude from deep within you… as you call to mind all that you have… be joyful and giving as you walk briskly through your life… be loving and caring when you see the ground is uncertain…,

… breathe in with intention… to bring in the new and let go the old… and as you do… feel that breath move throughout your entire being… then recognize the gift you have in breath… for it is always there, infinite and abundant… and breathe it out completely… without thought or concern… for you know without even thinking… that another breath will be there… and that you will breathe it in…,

… feel your prayers of gratitude… for the simple gift of air… and trust all of life… just as you do your breath… and begin to live… in this divine and perfect flow… giving out without out worry, question, or doubt for what you will receive… but in appreciation for each and every moment you are alive and breathing… for this is how you transform the negative to the positive… and draw to you all that is good…"

… a s qua di s di… and so it is good

The Star People called me out deep in the night. It was 3:33 am when I walked past the clock and grabbed for my blanket. I walked the prairie gazing up at Father Sky and watching my Star Relatives dancing there before me… *"It appears to be a celebration of some kind… an honoring ceremony perhaps"* …

… and then I woke… at 4:00 am… just as I always do… with no memory of returning to my bed… only the memory of going out at 3:33 am… and my blanket is still wrapped around me…

… I sit with my ceremony smoke now… and I sing the prayer songs for all people… I feel movement above me… and I see that the Star People have gathered near…

"… we come to celebrate the growth and development of all two-legged… for the lines of connection between the physical *self* and the Higher Self are appearing now for each…,

226

… and so an alignment has begun… not only for one, but for all… and those who have already found their way to their Higher Self… are lit-up now, and shining… so to guide the way for others…,

… and the alignment is between the *self* (the physical body, the mind, the consciousness the spirit, and the heart)… and all that is divine… and there between the self and the Divine… is the Higher Self…,

… and there is a knowing of importance… as one connects with their Higher Self… and a difference in how one lives their life and thinks about who they are… it is the difference between feeling you are important… and knowing you are important… it is the difference between believing another who tells you that you are less… and knowing they are wrong…,

… and there is no arrogance here… only the knowing of the truth… and there is compassion here… for each can clearly see the pain of another… and so it is that the words do not affect you anymore… for you do not take them in… and you cannot be diminished by the words of another… when you are so aligned…

… and there is an expansion of love… as each becomes aligned… love for self and love for others… and the very deep and certain knowing of how much you are love by God…"

… a s qua di s di… and so it is good

Grandmother Moon sits perfectly in the West on this day… and just below her I can see the Buffalo grazing… I walk straight into the West… as far as I can go without disturbing the Buffalo… and set ceremony as close to Grandmother Moon as I can…

… my ceremony smoke rises easily on this day… for the air is still, and warmer than it has been… the smoke rises up and lingers… hanging in the air before me like a shield… and I can see the visions that speak within the smoke with great clarity now… as they are illuminated by the light of Grandmother Moon…

… and there is a voice that comes… as I watch a story unfold within the smoke… and the story seems familiar… and the voice belongs to one I know well…

"… look into the smoke and see your own story… watch as you have grown and developed along your Earth Journey… see that there were times when the smoke brought you confusion and uncertainty… and see (too) the times when it brought you clarity and truth…,

… the reflection you see in the smoke is your own, two-legged… and in that reflection you will see the truth of who you are… as well as the illusion you try to present… the illusion that you sometimes believe… and you can also see the illusion others have placed upon you (here within the smoke)… the illusion that you have accepted as truth…,

… you see the shadow and the light here within the smoke… and as you can see… one small breath will change the image completely… so if you ask for truth as you breathe upon the smoke… it is truth that you will see… and if you hide within the illusion as you breathe out your breath… it is illusion that will show…,

… and so you come to a place upon your Earth Journey… where it is you who must decide who you are (and who you want to be)…,

… so sit *within* the smoke, two-legged… and dream your dream… breathe in the smoke… and set your intention… remove the illusion… as the sacred fire moves within you… for as you breathe it out… you will release the veil that stands in your way…,

… and your path will be clear then… and you will stand up tall and strong… as you see with perfect clarity… that have become the person you have decided to be…"

… a s qua di s di… and so it is good

The beauty of this morning takes my breath away, and I find myself standing for a time just taking it all in. Grandmother Moon is so bright as she prepares to set there in the West, that I cannot see even one of my Star Relatives. The Cloud People lay in ribbons behind her and Father Sky is the most incredible color of blue.

If you have never watched a Moon Set, I highly recommend you take a chance some day and do it. It is one of the most beautiful sights you'll ever see and the feeling you experience could very well change your life… for it brings you back to a place of child-like wonder in witnessing such majesty.

I walk to my ceremony place while keeping my eyes on the ever-changing Sky. I feel giddy, like a child in an amusement park, for the privilege of being here to experience such splendor, and I set ceremony is such a way that I am looking directly into the face of our magnificent Grandmother…

"… find the child within you now… and call her/him to come out… for the qualities and innocence of a child… will assist you more than you could ever imagine…,

… your mind is overwhelmed… your body is stressed… and your heart just aches to beat freely… but your spirit calls to you … "Come on… let go… come out and play"… and as you continue to strive for the higher perspective… it will serve you well to remember the perspective of a child… where there is laughter and wonder and purity and innocence…,

… can you remember a time when you believed in everything magical and wondrous… when you could spend a whole day just watching the Ants crawl around the Ant hill… and before the woes of the world came to sit upon your shoulders…

… as you grow older in age… and higher in vibration… it will serve you well to realign with the energy of a child… to remember to stop from time to time and experience life from a child's perspective… and to experience that child-like wonder…

… and as you begin to feel within your heart… the purity of the faith and hope and trust of a child… (these which have not yet become tarnished or distorted in a child)... you will be filled with innocence and grace as well... it will all be renewed within you... and it will expand within you and become permanent... as you allow it to flow freely throughout your entire being...,

... then share this magnificent gift with everyone you can... for much of what the years ahead have to show you... will require you to see from a place of trust and belief... through the eyes of a child... and from a place of truly knowing... that anything and everything is possible..."

... a s qua di s di... and so it is good

Grandmother Moon is spectacular on this day. She is full and bright, and her energy stirs deep emotion within me. I stand and smile as I allow the emotion of gratitude to move throughout my entire being...

... and I continue to smile as tears of emotion begin to fall... I feel gratitude for the joyful memories that bring a happy tearful smile... and I feel gratitude for the memories of sadness and pain that bring a quiet thoughtful, smile...

... for I am grateful for it all...

... and the emotion within me begins to expand... as the emotions of all people begin to flow into and through me... feelings of sadness, pain, and despair... blended with feelings of happiness, joy, compassion, and love...

... it all just moves and flows within me... and fills my entire being... until the stillness of the morning begins to sing... and the song becomes strong and loud... as my tears continue to flow...

"... find the voice within your heart... for it is wise and knowing, compassionate and true... and listen as this voice speaks... and *feel* all this voice so generously share with you...,

... and stand in the stillness that follows... and be sure you stay long enough to hear and feel it all... for just behind each raw and intense emotion... you will find a truth...,

… and the truth you find… is the wisdom of your heart… the compassion for another… the understanding… and even the path to forgiveness…,

… so stand with your Grandmother the Moon on this day… and give in to the emotions she draws up within you… and do not fight the pull this time… but allow the emotions to flow…,

… and allow yourself to feel and experience each and every emotion… all the way to the place of wisdom and compassion, understanding and forgiveness… until you reach a place of gratitude for each… until you find the truth that makes your heart sing and causes your face to smile…

… for this is a healing… a gift from above… and as you are bathed in the light of your Grandmother the Moon… you are also filled with her love…"

… a s qua di s di… and so it is good

I wake from dreams of being in the Ocean and the sound of my own heart beating loud within my ears… as I step out into the morning… I see Grandmother Moon sitting there above me… surrounded by the clear and dark blue of Father Sky… and it looks like she is a pearl just floating around in the Ocean

… I set ceremony in the South on this day… for I feel the need to be in the place of Water… and I sing the prayer songs for all people silently within… for I am certain I can hear the crashing of waves against a shore…

… I feel the protection of Mother Earth… and I see the light of Grandmother Moon… I hear the call of an ancient one… and I feel myself moving as I reach out and follow with my heart…

"… come now, child… come rest within the safety of this place… feel the water around you… and know it is your Mother's arms… quiet yourself now, Child… and settle into a deep and healing sleep… for the Sacred Waters are taking you back and back… through all of the life experiences of all of your life times… and cleansing away all of the negativity… so that you can know only the truths they came to tell you…,

… and the light of your Grandmother the Moon is gentle and soothing… and her light is wise and powerful too… and it reaches from high up in the Sky Place… to find you here, deep within the Ocean floor…,

… and you feel the love of these three… the most powerful and strong of the feminine… your Sister the Ocean, your Mother the Earth, and your Grandmother the Moon… and you know their love and compassion… for you feel it deep within your own heart… and they give you their wisdom as they hold you here… and they take away your pain and fear…,

… and feel yourself release now… from the place you have been held within… and feel yourself rising now… young and light and free as you follow the pull upward… and know this is your birth, dear child… and that you are good and strong and ready… and know that you are safe, dear child… in the hands of we four… your Sister the Ocean, your Mother the Earth, your Grandmother the Moon… and me, the eldest of the elder feminine…,

… and sing your song of gratitude, child… as you awaken now, ***anew…***"

… a s qua di s di… and so it is good

The Winds of Change have been blowing a lot lately, even though the Winter Solstice is almost a month away. I do realize that we can make changes in ourselves and in our lives anytime we want or need to, but the Winds of Change usually come as the seasons change, to provide us with the power and strength of both.

As I was standing with Grandfather Wind this morning, I asked about the energy of change that has been so strong lately… and he told me that so many people are calling for change now… it comes to him by way of their thoughts… their conversations with one another… in their prayers… and even in their actions…

… and Grandfather Wind is answering all of us now… in the only way he can… by blowing to each and every one of us… exactly what we need…

"… from my Wind gather strength and courage… for both are required in order to make a change… and if it is transformation you seek… then allow me to clear your mind as well… for you must set your mind to know and understand… that in order to transform… a change must be permanent… transformation requires you to commit to that change…,

… and allow me to blow out now… all that you must release in order to move forward… for you will be tempted to hold on to things that sabotage your effort to change… and true transformation cannot occur… if you keep hidden within you… those things that have created the need for change in the first place…,

… and know this is your choice, then… and trust in yourself to continue on… and have faith in me, your Grandfather the Wind… for I am the breath of your Creator… and we have heard you calling… we have heard your prayers… and we are here now… ready to assist… and all you have to do is breathe us in…everyday… as you reaffirm your intention to change…"

… a s qua di s di… and so it is good

The gathering has begun. I can feel the energy expanding, as thoughts of being together fill the hearts and minds of the people. My own heart sings with joy (too), for the knowing that my own family will gather soon.

We all become One in times like these, on holidays such as this one… for although we all gather and celebrate in our own individual ways, we are in fact all gathering and celebrating at the same time… and this is good… and this is **Oneness**…

"… stop for a moment… step away from the chaos of preparation and timing and such… and bring to mind the journey of your life… then look around and recognize… that everyone around you… is also making their way along their own journey of life…,

… and honor this… honor one another… for the struggles and challenges and discouraging moments each has and will face… and then rejoice with one another… for the accomplishment and victories and times of true happiness and joy… for each and every miracle… and for each grace and answered prayer…,

… and see then in each… yourself standing there… and feel then with compassion… for you have experienced the same… and though your journeys may not have all been exactly alike… you can understand the **Oneness**… and this is good… and this is something to celebrate…"

… a s qua di s di… and so it is good

Even though she is already waning, Grandmother Moon shines like a beacon on this cold and clear morning. I walk briskly out onto the prairie, wrapped up in two blankets, and knowing I will not stay out long (it is 5 degrees of cold).

The prairie is especially silent on this day, and I hear the song of the Old Woman as I walk. I see her as I near the ceremony place; she is sitting within the circle of stones that mark the place where the Tee Pee once stood. She faces West, which means she sits in the East, and she sings her song for all people with her arms open wide and reaching up toward our Creator…,

… I stop and stand quietly in honor and respect. I close my eyes as I listen to the Old Woman's song. I sway back and forth as I tighten my blanket around me…,

… and I hear the Old Woman whisper the message we are to know on this day…,

"… children of the Earth… open your hearts and let your spirits emerge… for it is the voice of your Higher Self that calls to you now… and you must not fear that your spirit will leave you if you allow it to expand and rise up… for it is connected securely to you… and it always will be …,

… your spirit is guiding you now… more than you have ever known… and your heart speaks with the highest of your being… more often now as well… and your Grandmother the Moon asks you to open your heart on this day… to provide an opening for your spirit to move through…,

… for you heart will understand what your spirit is showing you… in the truest and purest way… and your entire being will understand, then too… and there will be no need for words to explain… for you will just know…,

… and you will expand then… and feel a deeper relationship to all that is… and you will become a guide then… for all and any who have not yet found their light…"

… a s qua di s di… and so it is good

I am on the prairie early on this day, and I walk in gratitude for the many, many gifts and blessings in my life. I walk ceremony on this day, for it is very cold and better to keep moving. I sing the prayer songs for all people as I walk in and out of the prayer circles, and I hear the voice from the High Place whisper to me softly, as I stop at my altar to pray **Oneness**…

"… know yourselves as truly as you can… know your value and your worth… for each of you are created with a gift to share… and each of you will become more… by receiving the gift another would share with you…,… spend some time loving yourselves… and recognizing in yourselves how truly magnificent you are… discard judgment of any kind… and look only with eyes of love… for as you acknowledge and appreciate your own value and worth… you will begin to know peace within…,

… and that peace will touch all the world…,

… and you will begin to live differently then… peacefully and with trust… your relationships will become strong and smooth then… as you see the light in one another… more than you see the shadow…,

… and everything you thought you knew… about how to live in this life of yours… will shift and change… and spin completely around… until it becomes clear… and you will need to sit with this for a time… but soon you will know peace…,

… and that peace will touch all the world…"

… a s qua di s di… and so it is good

Grandmother Moon sits very high above me on this day, and her light is so bright that it illuminates the entire prairie. The prairie seems to be abuzz with sound on this day. It is an interesting sound that seems familiar, but that I cannot quite place.

I stand for a moment before I set ceremony, allowing myself to be drenched in the light of Grandmother Moon, and I ask for clarity about this sound that seems to be getting louder by the second…

"… you know this sound, Swan… it is the sound of energy… the energy of the people… it is the sound of worry and doubt and fear and concern… mixed with hope and prayers and faith and encouragement… it is the sound of the physical world…,

… and as you sing your prayer songs for all people… listen to the sound as it changes… listen to the buzz that is heavy and low… become a song that is light and musical… for that will be the sound of the High Place…,

… now stand for a moment and feel the pull of the energy… adjust your consciousness to connect with the physical world… and feel the pull of that heavy low buzzing energy…,

… and now adjust your consciousness to connect with the High Place… and feel the pull of enlightenment… of the song that calls out to your heart… feel the pull of that light and musical energy that is *Spirit*…,

… and this is the message you need to share at this time… that two-legged are attracted to energy because you are energy… you will respond to even the slightest energy shift… but when the energy becomes this strong and loud and heavy… it can pull you even if you do not want it to…,

… and so it is important to remember how to disconnect from that pull… and to reconnect with your higher self… and all you need to do… is to stop for a moment and make it your intention to go higher… make it your intention to disconnect from the pull of the physical place… and reconnect with the pull of the High Place…,

… then breathe in deep and blow out strong… until you feel the shift… and that low heavy buzz will leave your ears… and you will hear the song of your spirit… and your breathing will become easy… and your consciousness will rise…"

… a s qua di s di… and so it is good

I hear the Lions and Bears (from the Wild Cat Sanctuary across the road) roaring and growling as I walk out on this day. The air is fresh and cold, but not unbearable, it is a freshness I can smell and feel… and even taste.

I sing the prayer songs for all people, while the Lions and Bears continue their morning song, and there is a sense of something powerful moving in the air. It is like the Sun coming up, but not literally at this moment… and not just for one day… it is like the Sun coming up for all of us… and giving us a fresh new start…

"… if it is happiness you seek… begin to feel happiness within your entire being… if it is love… then feel love… if it is prosperity… then feel prosperous… for it is a time now… that each can bring into being their own desires and dreams… but you must trust that you can… and then *feel* it into being…,

… for you are given that which you call for… and *feeling* is the most powerful way of calling out…,

… and it is difficult to shift your feelings all at once… so begin with a little at a time… set a time each day to feel happiness and joy (or whatever it is you desire)… and really feel it within your being… remember a happier time… and allow that feeling to expand within you… and then keep it there as long as you can…,

… and use this practice for whatever it is you seek… feel the feeling as long as you can… and it will expand daily… in time and intensity… and you will begin to know this feeling well… and you will become one with this feeling… and you will be able to call up feelings of happiness (or whatever it is you desire)… whenever you want (or need) to…,

… and this is how you create a shift in your life experience… and this is how you call out for that which you need and desire…"

… a s qua di s di… and so it is good

And so it snowed… at last it snowed… and the beauty of the snow-dusted prairie is difficult to describe… and Father Sky is the perfect color blue… and the light of Grandmother Moon shines in such a way… that it casts a soft turquoise glow upon everything…

… and there is a certain kind of stillness on the prairie after a snow… like all of the grace of Heaven has come down to Earth… and this grace is now available to all of us two-legged… for it is contained in each and every snowflake… and this pure and perfect knowing is the wisdom of the spirit… and this knowing is now available to all of us two-legged… if we would only sit with it for a while… and listen… in the perfect stillness of an untouched morning… and allow it to speak out its wisdom…

"… kindness is what you seek… and kindness is the gift you should be exchanging with one another… but this is not an assignment… and this is not even a request… it is simply the truth from the High Place… for it is the answer to the many prayers and petitions for assistance… that have come to us… from the hearts of each of you…,

… and you may not understand this simple answer at first… and you may even shake your head and walk away… but if you will find a place to sit in stillness… and open your heart to the gift of kindness… you will begin to know its truth… and you will begin to live your life from a place of kindness…,

… and you may begin by showing kindness to the plants and animals… or to the land and the environment by respecting nature… or maybe you will show kindness to your loved ones and family… or maybe it is easier to offer kindness to strangers and shopkeepers and such…,

… and although this is good, two-legged… and how each should live and be… it is not right… for you must begin by showing kindness to yourself… and then by allowing others to offer kindness to you… and without demand…

or selfish entitlement… you simply receive the gift of kindness offered to you by another… and then what you offer to another becomes genuine and sincere and true…,

… and you are beautiful then… each and every one of you… just like the snowflakes that fall to you from us… for as you see the beauty in all people and all things… you will each reflect your beauty upon one another… and this is when you will know the wisdom of this answer we bring you today… and how you will realize it was the greatest kindness you have ever received…"

… a s qua di s di… and so it is good

DECEMBER 2010

It is my Owl Sister who shares the prairie with me on this day, and the air is comfortable as I walk out into the darkness. Grandfather Wind sleeps on this day and the stillness of the prairie is almost loud. I walk the Labyrinth as I whisper the prayers for all people, and I sing Oneness as I stand at the altar there within. I stand in Oneness for a time, and sing out the gratitude song before making my way out.

I set ceremony and move into stillness, just as *u gu gu* (my Owl sister) flies silently across the prairie and lands upon the fence post that is just to the right of where I sit…

"… as you begin this last month of your physical year… I offer my Medicine… for it is time for you (all)… to look into the shadows of your being… and seek out that which still hides there within…,

… you have raised your vibration over this year… and you have come to know and use many higher levels of insight, knowing, and wisdom… so it is time to look again… into the shadow places within… and see what you are now able to see…,

… and you have grown and developed to such a place and vibration… that you truly know and understand… that whatever hides within the shadows of your (or any other) being… is not necessarily intentional deception… but merely that which has not been uncovered, discovered, or realized yet…,

… and so… do not fear or go with dread… into the shadows within… but go with intention and purpose… and go with the Medicine of Owl… and know, too… with certainty and trust… that as you seek to know what is there within the shadows… and as you find whatever it is that is there… it will move quickly and easily away…,

… for as you have developed (throughout this year) the ability to see from a much higher perspective… you have also developed the ability to move and release… and to heal those things within yourself… that have escaped your vision until now…"

… a s qua di s di… and so it is good

I t is the Old Man who waits for me on this day… I smell the smoke from his fire as I tread across the prairie… and I hear his song as I near the place where he sits… and he stands as I arrive at his circle… and with his arms open wide… he welcomes me in… and we dance to the song the Old Man sings…

… and I bring to mind **all people** as we dance… so that each may be blessed with the sacredness of our dancing prayer… and the Old Man nods his head in agreement… and sings his song a little stronger… and our feet begin to move a little quicker…

"… sing your songs of hopes and wishes… expecting them to come true… dance your dance of appreciation and gratitude… for that which has been given… with every prayer a seed is planted… and with each expression of gratitude… they are watered and cared for… but every negative thought or notion regarding these seeds… is like a long hot day without water or shade…

… it is your happiness for what you have… that brings you more… and your negative emotions and fears… that keep you from receiving… so sing out your hopes and wishes each day… and know they will come forth… and dance your dance of appreciation and gratitude, too… for this dance is you… standing before the Universe… with your arms open wide and ready to receive…"

… a s qua di s di… and so it is good

T he energy of the prairie feels heavy to me on this day, even though it is not as cold as it has been. I walk out the gate to my ranch and up the hill to where a sacred Grandmother stands, and I feel the energy ease as I move from low ground to high ground.

I stand before the Standing One I know as Grandmother, and set ceremony here on this day. Everything feels different in this place, it always has. Each time I sit here with the Grandmother Standing One, it seems as if my mind becomes clear and all my senses activate to a higher vibration… it is like I move into my higher *Self* here… or is it the Grandmother who awakens this clarity within me…

"… you (all two-legged) may be sensing the energy becoming heavy and difficult to maneuver through now… like walking in waist-deep water… and that is just the energy that is created by the worries and fears of the people… and this last month of your calendar year is always this way…,

… but you (all two-legged) are ready now… to see from a higher perspective… and it will not be necessary for you to physically walk up a hill to do so… but it will require you to trust your intuition completely… and to engage all of your senses at once…,

… the days of this last month of your calendar year will be like a bridge now… and you will need to use your senses and intuition to cross it… for this bridge will take you from lower ground to higher ground… from heavy dense energy… to a light and airy place… where your mind will clear and your vibration will raise…,

… begin with the knowing that you are not merely imagining the heaviness you feel around you… for once you know it is real… you will take action to move above it… then, make it your intention to shift your awareness up higher… and this will be difficult for many of you… for you live or work in places where there is much heaviness (fear and worry)…,

… make time each day to find the highest, lightest vibration you can… and become accustom to that vibration… know it completely… and trust that you can attain it in an instant… for when you feel the heaviness set in around you… you will need to rise above it quickly… and this is how you cross the bridge… one experience at a time…"

… a s qua di s di… and so it is good

The Star People are brilliant on this morning. They call to me as I dance the prayer songs for all people. I watch them watching me as I move about the prairie, and I feel my heart expand with joy…

"... celebrate on this day... and acknowledge your growth and maturity... allow yourself to recognize how much you have grown and matured... by dancing in a child-like fashion...,

... for you (all people) have worked hard throughout this year... and you have achieved much... and you often fail to recognize your own growth and achievements... or do you hope another will acknowledge your advancement for you...,

... if you do not feel you have accomplished much throughout this year... make time now to look back and see where you were... and where you are now... then dance your celebration dance... while the Star People clap and cheer... for you must acknowledge how far you have come now... so that you can go forward from here..."

... a s qua di s di... and so it is good

I wake on this day from a faraway place, and with the words ... "speak your truth"... looping around and around in my head. But my throat feels funny, and as I open my mouth to sing the prayer songs for all people... it is the voice of a frog I hear sing out (or try to, anyway).

I quiet my voice and sing the prayer songs for all people silently... and I hear the voice of a strong and empowered Woman singing within me...

"... finding your voice is not something your do physically... although once you have found your voice... you will use it in the physical world...as well as in the spiritual world...,

... and in order to speak your truth... you must find and know your truth... and this happens through spending time in meditation, prayer, or journey... as your **highest Self**... and with the specific intention of seeking to know your truth...,

... and once you begin to know and understand your own personal truth... you will be more silent (at first) in the physical... but your conversations to and with the higher realms will increase... and you will become wiser, then... and you will come to know yourself more deeply... and you will know others more deeply as well...,

... and you will speak with compassion... and from your heart... in regard to yourself as well as in regard to others... and this is what it is to "speak you truth..."

... a s qua di s di... and so it is good

Standing on the prairie this morning, is like standing inside of a snow globe. Father Sky is black and clear, and the Star People begin at each horizon, creating a dome-like cover as they reach up, around, and above me.

I turn to each direction, honoring the Elders who live in each, and I sit upon Mother Earth as I open my heart and my arms up to Creator. I feel the joy pouring into my Crown chakra, through the vase-like channel I have created with my upstretched arms. I feel it move through my entire being, bringing warmth and energy as it seems to flow and pulse at the same time...

... and my face begins to smile now, as I hear the song of the High Place begin to play softly in my ears... and the joy I feel within me turns to a sense of beauty now, as I understand that all things and beings are joyous and beautiful... if you look at them with an open heart and spirit... and from the perspective of the High Place...

"... even in times of hardship and struggle... allow yourself to be joyous... to smile and laugh and sing... and to see the beauty in each being and experience... for the energy of joy is light... both in weight... and... as in brilliantly lit... and so it can maneuver quickly through any darkness (which is heavy)... and guide you to the place where healing resides...,

... this is your season of joy... but many are fearful and saddened by the experiences and struggles of this long and difficult year... and continuing to carry those feelings of sadness and fear (as well as feeling of anger and blame upon others)... only adds to the heaviness of the energy you are immersed in... when it is to be released from that heaviness that you cry out for...,

… so make good use of this season… no matter what it means to you (personally and by your own beliefs)… and connect with the joy that others are feeling… and find a way to remember joyous times of your own… and feel these within your being… as often as you can… for then you will feel yourself lift… up and away from the heaviness… and into a place that is light… and you will add to that light then, too… for you will become a part of it…,

… and look around now… from this High Place you have found your way to… for you will see the beauty here… beauty that you thought could never exist…"

… a s qua di s di… and so it is good

It is the song of my Owl Sister, (u gu gu), that accompanies me as I **walk** the prairie on this morning. She is perched on a fence post off in the distance to the North, and the morning is dark, but her song is clear and precise. I walk ceremony on this day as I listen to my Owl Sister sing, and I feel the prayers for all people within my being, as the spirit of Owl lifts me above the physical, and into to the place of Creator…

"… as you (each) make your way along your journey of physical life… you are realizing there is very little that is certain for you to hold onto… and this brings about the illusion that there is much to fear… but living in uncertain times is nothing new… and is in fact, a gift…,

… for uncertain times assist you in mastering the practice of living in the moment… and it is when you can consistently be present in each moment… living each day as it comes… that you begin to find trust within yourself… and it is by being present and experiencing life from a place of trust… that you rise to a higher knowing… and become a more developed version of yourself…,

… there is an issue of control that accompanies the need to know every detail of what will happen next… and this is not to say that it is wrong to plan and organize… but being prepared, willing, and able to move easily with each unexpected happening… is a valuable and powerful attribute…

… it is time to let go of the fear that stirs within when you cannot see what is just up ahead… and develop your own strengths and instincts… it is time to rely on that which comes from within to guide you along… rather than to become stagnant and paralyzed because you cannot see what your future holds…,

… there is really nothing to fear, dear two-legged… for just because you cannot see it… does not mean it is something bad that awaits… trust in the goodness of Creator… and in your ability to find the goodness that is yet to be in your life… awaken your greatest attribute… which is that of stepping up and living your life fully… and you will know the joy of becoming whole…"

… a s qua di s di… and so it is good

It is very common for me to see the Hawks who live in this valley, every day (even in Winter). But for the past several weeks, one particular Hawk has followed me along the dirt roads (both as I am leaving and as I am returning home), and makes certain I see him by choosing just the perfect time to fly across the road in front of me. He flew in front of me twice yesterday as I was leaving and then once again as I returned…

… and then he flew into my Dreamtime journey early this morning… so to guide me to what he wanted me to know…

"… today I am your messenger… I bring you the message from above… that you are being sent a vision… each and every one of you will receive a vision… that will assist you with your journey of life from here…,

… look for me… and call to me, also… stop when you see me… and acknowledge you have recognized me… and wait for me in the Dreamtime… or in your ceremony or meditation… for I will become your guide (if you will fly with me to the High Place)… and your vision will reveal itself to you there… in the highest, purest place you can reach…

… and know that when you receive your vision… while standing in the highest of all places… you shift, then too… your heart expands… and your mind opens… and your physical body releases that which would weigh it down… so that your spirit can expand within you…,

… and many of you will not receive your vision seriously… many will credit your imagination (or the last meal you ate) for that which you are given in vision… and that will just be so… but for those of you who recognize… the gift you have just received in this vision… you will also be given all that you need to follow it…,

… so remember me, (all) two-legged… and this message I bring… and look forward to the journey you will take with me… for if you agree to go… and if you choose to accept what you are shown in your vision… your life will change… and you will soar through it… in the same way that I glide upon the air…"

… a s qua di s di… and so it is good

It is the Wise Old Oak who calls me out on this day. I hear his leaves rustling in the Wind (even though Grandfather Wind sleeps on this morning). I follow the sound of rustling leaves across the prairie, until it becomes a whisper. I follow the whisper, until I hear the sound of a heart beating. I follow the heartbeat, until I feel the warmth of the Wise Old Oak. I walk slowly now, straight into the warmth of the Wise Old Oak… and straight into the Wisdom that he brings to us on this day…

"… you look to me for wisdom, (all) two-legged… but it is your own wisdom that you must call upon now… for that which is just up ahead on your path… will require you to make choices and decisions from your own knowing of life (from that which *you* have learned and experienced)…,

… it is time now for you to realize that you are wise… and to trust in your own ability to discern the answer, choice, and/or direction… from that which is uniquely you… and you do not begin this task with your mind, two-legged… but with your heart… as in following your heart… as in manifesting your heart's desire… as in seeing the world from a place of love and compassion… as in extending that love and compassion to others (all others, and yourself)…

… wisdom does not come through books, or classes, or any workings of the mind… but through being present in your life and experiencing it… and through drawing upon the lessons of every happening (both positive and negative)… to bring about an understanding within yourself…,

… it is from that understanding that your own wisdom begins to develop… and it is from that wisdom that you will move into your future… just remember to include the wisdom of your heart… for it will be through the union of body, mind, and heart… that you truly become wise…"

… a s qua di s di… and so it is good

Iopened my front door this morning and was greeted by a Shooting Star. I stood there for a moment, looking into the Star Place and tuning into the energy of my Star Relatives. I set ceremony just beneath the place where I saw my Star Brother shoot across, and I felt the Turquoise Rain fall down upon me as I began the prayer songs for all people…

"… the gift of our **Turquoise Rain**… is to be received by all… and should be given devoted attention… for it will bring to all people… many gifts and awareness's…,

… first allow the Turquoise mist to soothe your emotions… breathe out all tension and static… and breathe in that which is smooth and calm… and shift (then) from the harsh jarring to which you have become accustomed… to the sensation of floating and drifting here among us in the Star Place…,

… and step upon your Mother the Earth… with soft and quiet steps (then)… feel yourself blend into her as you walk… rather than to tread across her with heavy slamming thrusts… for when you walk softly upon your Mother… you receive all of her nourishment and wisdom… and you realize what it is to truly be grounded…,

… for being grounded does not mean that you anchor yourself to Mother Earth, so to never leave her… but that you connect yourself with her… by attuning your energy to hers… so to have the freedom to move about and experience all realms and vibrations of the Higher Places… and the ability to bring these into your physical world and being and daily life…,

… there is much to be explored and experienced in the Higher Realms now, two-legged… and it is time to bring these gifts and knowings into your physical world… and to do this you must be aware (and trust) that you can travel to the Higher Places… with the absolute knowing that you will return safely and at will…,

… so learn what it is to be completely grounded (connected) with your Mother the Earth… and then step into the **Turquoise Rain**… trust that you are safe and protected… as you take flight with your spirit as your guide… and notice as you return from the High Place each time… that the energy of the physical plane becomes more soft and supple (less harsh and jarring)… the more you blend Earth with Sky…,

… and notice, too… that you are able to move through your physical life with ease and grace (then)… rather than by always having to fight the static and the noise…"

… a s qua di s di… and so it is good

I feel the spin of the Medicine Wheel as I walk the Labyrinth on this morning. I have a very definite sense of the four directions as I stand in the center of these stones, as well as of the way they connect to and with the four aspects of our beings… East/Spirit… South/Emotion… West/Physical body… North/Mind and thought.

I set ceremony near my altar space now, and I search for my own center as I sing the prayer songs for all people…

"… yes, two-legged… it is good to find your center… for as you move into the next year… it will be essential for you to keep your balance… for you will experience the sense of being pulled in many directions at first… and it will be easy for you to neglect certain areas of your life and being… while you are tending to another…,

… keeping a strong center is a good thing to work toward now… for when you can maintain a strong center… it is easier to maintain your balance… and moving into the next year strong and steady… will serve you in ways you cannot know at this time…,

... then practice living in balance... once you have established it within you... be mindful each day of the balance in yourself and in your life... be sure to look in on your spirit, emotions, physical body, and mind each day... for as you move forward from here... you will move with ease and grace... if you can move centered and in balance..."

... a s qua di s di... and so it is good

The air smells fresh as I walk the prairie on the morning, like fresh-cut evergreens and juniper berries. I feel light upon me as I stand in the darkness, light that sings and has a heartbeat, light that is warm and makes me feel safe and protected, light that carries a higher knowing and seems to be permeating my entire being...

"... this time you spend in ceremony each morning... is more important than you realize, (all) two-legged... for as you expand the light of Spirit within you... and strengthen your connection with the Universe... you take in more and more of the wisdom and knowing of each...,

... it comes to you as light at first... and washes upon you... like a warm wave of heat... first you merely sense it... then you vaguely see it... you turn to look... and it seems to have moved... and then you chase this light... for as long as it takes you to realize... that the light must come to you... and it will... but only when you are ready...,

... and so you finally stop and wait for it to come... you continue with your daily practice of expanding your spirit... of awakening your higher knowing... of reaching up and out and in (deep within)... and as you do... your heart and mind and spirit open... and the hard shell that you have kept so tight around you begins to soften... and you realize that you can feel the light now...,

... and you open your eyes slowly... hoping to see the light that is so warm and comforting... the light that is so soft and kind... and yet is so powerful and protecting... but you hear it first... in that split second just before it reveals itself to you... it is the voice of the highest of all beings... and it is singing to you...,

... and you hear the heart-beat (then)... but this is a heart-beat like no other you have ever heard... for this is the heart-beat of all of humanity... it is yours... and all of those whom you love... it is God... and Mother Earth... and all of the Star people... and all who dwell deep within the Oceans... and all things (and beings) in between...,

... and you see the light (then)... and it is more brilliant than you have ever imagined... and you feel it, like a warm wave of heat... and you hear it, like the most beautiful song... and you realize that you know it too... and it permeates your entire being... and you are lifted higher (then)... higher than you have ever been before...,

... and this is why it is so important for you spend time in ceremony (prayer, meditation) each day... for as you reach for the light... it will reach for you... and as you connect with one another... you will become **One** with each other... and this is good..."

... a s qua di s di... and so it is good

I stand on the prairie breathing in the essence of our Creator, as a knowing comes over me. It is the knowing that the essence of our Creator is also the essence of me. It is the knowing that the essence of our Creator is also the essence of all things and all beings.

I am reminded, in this knowing, of our Oneness. I am taken through this knowing, to the place of our sameness, of our perfection as well as our imperfections, to the deepest desires that live within us each, and to the highest of our spirits that keep us moving along our journey of life... moving forward... always forward.

I sing the gratitude song now, and I feel gratitude within my entire being... for all that I have been given... all of everything I have and have experienced in my life. For whether good or bad, hard or easy... it has all been my life... and each has been a blessing that has led me to become me (to become more, better, higher... to try harder, to give more and to be generous).

The notion of forgiveness rises up now, and I know this is Creator speaking to me, reminding me that we are each spiritual beings trying to live in the physical world (in physical bodies and with physical limitations). We are all on our own journey of remembering our true spirit, and of finding our way back to the source of our origination… and if there is forgiveness to be given… we must begin with ourselves.

As spirit we can see from the highest perspective, but as human our vision is impaired by the limitations of our physical bodies and minds. Our hearts feel hurt and sadness, and pain and anger (as well as love and compassion and goodness), and when we try to work through all of these, our minds kick in with the best of what they have been given, and this is when we develop an understanding. And it does not matter whether that understanding is right or wrong, good or bad, it is simply the understanding we have come up with. And this understanding somehow becomes set within us… it becomes our own personal perspective.

I light the sacred herbs for ceremony, and watch as the smoke rises up. I release my physical being and allow my spirit to emerge. And that which has been pushing in on me eases away now, as the warm and loving embrace of our Creator moves in to hold me. ..

… and I realize in this moment… that there in nothing to forgive… only compassion to hold and offer… toward myself as well as toward all others… and it is from this place that I let go of that which I have held against myself (and others)… for I realize now… with complete certainty… that we are all simply trying to find our way… to that which is the highest and best of u

… and so we should nod our heads to one another now… and offer to one another (as well as to ourselves)… the acknowledgement of our accomplishments… as well as the support to continue on…

… a s qua di s di… and so it is good

Grandfather Elm beckons me up the hill and into the place of the sacred Standing Ones on this day. I find my way to where the council usually meets, and stop at the entrance to wait for permission to enter. Attending the sacred council of the Standing Ones is always magical… and a little different each time.

On this morning, the air turned warm as Grandfather Wind blew toward me, and from deep within the Standing Ones, a soft, gentle breeze catches my attention. I make my way through the long rows of Standing Ones now, and acknowledge my Owl Sister, u gu gu, who is perched high atop the last Standing Pine on my left.

I have come to the opening of the **sacred gathering place now,** and it is Grandfather Elm, himself, who invites me in…

"… you have set your intentions within your heart, dear child… and you have spoken them out loud in your prayers… now it is time to let nature run the course for you… it is time for you to step aside and trust that all will unfold just as it should…,

… for in order to expand and grow your senses… and to sharpen your own intuition… you must step back from the place of control… and allow what you have set in motion to move and flow…,

… it has always been so… that in order to truly trust… one must make their desires known… and then step back and allow them to become so… and this has always been difficult for two-legged to accomplish…,

… for two-legged are not willing to wait and allow their desires to come to them naturally… two-legged become impatient (quickly and easily)… and try to shift the winds and turn the paths… and fight against nature and force their wishes into being…,

… and this is the cause of most of the disappointments all two-legged experience…,

… so learn this now, dear child… and share this with your people… it is coming upon a time for you (all)… when it is imperative that you strengthen your trust and faith in the natural flow of all happenings... that you set your intentions (clearly and precisely)... and then allow them to become so, naturally...,

... for if you follow the natural course *with* your dreams and wishes... your trust and faith will become strong and solid... and you will have discovered a higher knowing... and you will actually begin living your dreams... for you will not be messing them up with your own meddling..."

... a s qua di s di... and so it is good

The prairie is uncommonly warm for December. I walk out to the sound of Owls singing in the distance. Their song is captivating, and I find myself walking in their direction without consciously realizing it.

I set ceremony as close to them as possible, and I sit quietly as I light the ceremony smoke. I sing the prayer songs for all people silently within as I breathe in the sacred smoke... and the Owls continue to sing their wisdom out into the morning...

"... the days are warmer than you are used to for this time of year... and it is easier for you to maneuver around and through your daily life and obligations... and this is but a simple shift... and one that is only so for your small portion of the world...,

... in other places they are dealing with more harsh conditions... and struggling to find ways to move about and live their lives around and through obstacles beyond their control... and yet in each situation... all will struggle to adapt...,

... it is a misconception among the two-legged... that adapting to easier times and conditions is less difficult... than adapting to harsher times and conditions... for change is change... and whether positive or negative... easy or hard... each will create the same discomfort within you (two-legged)... mentally and emotionally at first... and then physically...,

… keep this in mind as you move forward into your next calendar year… for as the energy shifts and the vibration rises… there will be many changes for you to adjust to… good and wonderful changes… and you may be surprised that your ability to adapt to all that is new and good and wonderful… is not as instant and sharp as you would like it to be…,

… begin now, two-legged… to prepare yourself for those things you have been dreaming and wishing for… begin by realizing that you do deserve good in your life… and by acknowledging the good in yourself… for as the good begins to show up… you must accept it… you must welcome and embrace it… you must receive it… and allow it to become a part of you and of your life… you must adapt to it in every way…,

… and do not fool yourself into thinking… that once the good begins to flow… your work will be done… for although you find it easier to maneuver through… you will still have work to do… otherwise it wouldn't be life…,

… adaptability begins in the mind, two-legged… and it is the power of your mind… that allows you to adjust to the changes of everyday life… but if you will allow your spirit to guide your mind… you will adapt more easily to that which is changing for you… and you will not only move forward with greater vision and foresight… but you will become self-reliant… and able to stand alone whenever you need to…

… a s qua di s di… and so it is good

There is snow on the prairie this morning, not as much as we had hoped for (we need the moisture), but enough… and I stand in gratitude with my arms open wide

I feel warmth coming from the circle of stones that mark the place where the Tee Pee once stood, and I hear the Old Woman's voice as I make my way across my ceremony area and enter the place where she sits…,

"… yes, child (children)… open your arms and let your heart sing out your gratitude… and stand for a time longer, too… for it is time for you (all) to open your arms and receive…,

… this is the most perfect ceremony one can make… the ceremony of giving and receiving equally from the heart… with open arms that both offer and receive… with open heart that extends out as well as welcomes in…,

… for this is Creator's prayer for you (all)… that you be loving beings who appreciate the gift of life… and who welcome and receive… all of what he provides for you…,

… and this is the circle, child (children)… and it is in constant motion… and you may know it as **the flow**… or as your connection to/with your Creator (the Universe)… but however you know it… become one with it… for all that you have been working towards and dreaming for… is making its way to you now…,

… and here is the question, dear child (children)… will you receive it or let it go by… have you found the confidence within yourself to know that you are worthy… or will you turn and look away…,

… ah, but the gift is for you, dear child (children)… and it is time for you to accept what you know in your heart to be true… and it is time for you to begin allowing all of your dreams to come into being… it is time for you to **step into the flow**…,

… so open your arms now… and let your heart sing out your gratitude… and stay then for a time longer… so to receive that which is so lovingly given to you from above…"

… a s qua di s di… and so it is good

My body feels tired on this day. I walk out onto the prairie wrapped in my shawl as well as my blanket, for although it is not really that cold, I can feel it to my bones. I set ceremony in the large circle of Grandfather Stones, and find that I am sitting with the Grandfather of the West on this day…,

… I sing the prayer songs for all people from a deep and silent place within…, and I feel the prayers of these old and sacred songs… encircle and surround me… before they rise up and out into the world… and I feel the Grandfather of the West emerge now… as my voice moves up through me… and sings out into the morning…

"… have you forgotten the importance of caring for your physical self, Swan… have you forgotten that your journey of physical life… relies upon you keeping yourself physically healthy…,

…clarity of mind… strength of body… and calm, smooth emotions… are essential now (for all two-legged)… for in order to receive (spiritually) that which is becoming available to you (all) from the High Place… your energy must be clear and strong and calm and smooth…,

… getting enough sleep and rest is difficult to achieve in your fast paced world… but when you make a commitment to tend to your health… it must include getting proper sleep and rest… and making a commitment to tend to your health is essential now (for all)…,

… for when your body is run down in any way… it requires more energy and focus (for the healing of it)… so by taking in proper nutrition… exercising in a good and healthy way… and making sure your body gets the rest and sleep it requires… it will vibrate higher… which will allow it (and you) access into the higher realms…

… a s qua di s di… and so it is good

The prairie sparkles and glimmers as I walk out on this day. The frost that covers it makes it look alive, but it also causes the grass to crunch beneath my feet as I walk. With each step I break the silence that is so sacred to me, and I find myself moving this way and that way, trying to create less sound.

I look back now and see I have been walking in a wild and crazy pattern (a crooked path). I have found my way to the place I wanted to set ceremony on this day, but in an effort to still the noise of my own movement, I walked farther and took longer… huh.

The smoke from my ceremony fire struggles to rise in the cold and icy air, and it seems as though my Star Relatives are moving closer to me now. I look up into the Sky Place and sing the prayer songs for all people, while my Star Relatives continue to gather around me...

"... at this time you must be mindful of your movement... for it is not only about moving forward... but equally about the grace and ease in which you move... as well as the paths you take and the directions you choose...,

... it is true that whether you walk a straight line or a crooked one... you will end up at the same place... and many will tell you that all you lose is time... but this is not true in regard to your movement forward now...,

... take a moment to stop for a time... and breathe in and out with strong deep breaths... draw together all of your senses... and move forward with focused intention... direct your attention on every step you take... for even if they are loud and disrupting... you must see and experience what each one has to show you...,

... and when you look back at the end of next year... you will find that the path you have walked was a perfect one... no matter how crooked it may seem to be... for you experienced everything it had to offer... you grew and shifted and changed with grace and ease... and you inspired others to do the same..."

... a s qua di s di... and so it is good

I sit quiet and still on this day, just offering my silence to all that surrounds me. "Feel the gratitude that flows out from my heart"... I say... as I begin to sing the gratitude song and turn my face up to Creator. My awareness expands (now) as I sing... and I feel like a tiny seed upon this great land we know as Earth.

I feel the spirits of all people... as my own spirit rises up to meet them... and our spirits dance upon our prayers... the prayers of all people who gather on this day to pray... and we know one another in this place... spirit to spirit... and we feel joy...,

… and we sing out our songs of joy now… as we dance and sing and move about… and we run to touch one another once more… as we begin to softly float down and back to our places upon the Earth… and we promise to remember that we are all one family… and in our hearts we do…

"… know that you (each) are a seed now… and that you are planted in rich and nourishing soil… and that you are fed by the waters of the Earth and Sky… and warmed by your Father the Sun…,

… and that to become a seed again… you must allow all illusion of physical restriction to fall away… and be for a time… only the purest of your true and original self (again)…,

… and during this time you emerge…,

… and you are protected by Moon each night… and nourished by Earth each day… and as you emerge… your spirit awakens (again)… and it is fresh and new and young and pure… and it remembers the family you have in spirit… all of them…,

… and you feel joy…,

… and your spirit expands within your physical body… and your heart awakens then, too… and you remember that place where you began… and you seek to find your way home…"

… a s qua di s di… and so it is good

It is the sound of the front-door screen slapping against the house that brings me back from the Dreamtime on this day, and I wake to find Grandfather Wind blowing fast and strong across the prairie. I wrap my blanket around me tight and hold my ceremony bundle close, as I take one last moment to ask for direction before walking out to set ceremony for today.

"Point me in the direction I am to go now"… I say out loud… but all I can feel is the need to go into the Earth… I stand for a moment longer now, waiting for a response… and again I feel the pull from deep within my Mother the Earth…

… I feel my hair whipping against my face now… and the strength of Grandfather Wind pushing me… but I remain steady, with my feet planted firmly upon the ground… and I listen now, to the voice of Grandfather Wind as he whistles and howls… his song is deep and low… and it brings my attention down (again)… it tells me (again) that my direction is within the Earth…

… and so I step out… into the full force of Grandfather Wind… and I walk with complete certainty… in the direction he is pushing me… and I follow the pull from beneath my feet… across the prairie and up the road… and I stop… as the energy from deep within my Mother the Earth… does not allow my feet to move any farther…

… and as I bend to set my ceremony bundle down, I see it… the Ant Hill… and I know what Grandfather Wind was telling me… and though my Ant relatives have all gone within… there is a small opening there… and I sing the prayer songs for all people… as I journey deep within my Mother… guided by my relatives, the Ants…

"… it is time to go within, Swan… for the Solstice is upon you and the year is coming to an end… it is time to consider your plans and options for that which will be your journey next… and it is time to reestablish your commitment to your own healing and growth…,

… trust in self is essential… for in order to accomplish all that you will set out to do… you must trust completely… not only in your own ability to achieve… but also that all of what you need… will be there and available to/for you when/as you need it…,

… from this place deep within your Mother… find the path to all that is your strength… and listen to the stillness here… as you traveled further and deeper within… center yourself with this, Swan… and remember how to return here… for just as you will return to the upper world now… you will need to return here as well…,

... and walk with complete certainty... placing your feet upon the solid foundation of your own trust and faith... as you find your way... by the strength and knowing of your own connection with earth and sky... and with the perfect balance of self and spirit..."

... a s qua di s di... and so it is good

I walk the prairie with my Grandmother the Moon on this day, for her light is brilliant and it lights the land exquisitely. I can feel her energy upon me as I walk; it is as if she were right here walking with me... just Grandmother and Granddaughter out for a mid-night stroll.

I make my way back to my ceremony place now, as I feel drawn to the circle of stones that mark the place where the Tee Pee once stood. My shadow is before me as I walk, and it almost looks like I am walking upon a mirror, for the way the bright light of Grandmother Moon shines upon me it casts a perfect (and solid) outline of my physical being. I see the shadow of a figure walking with me now, as I continue on my way to the ceremony place. It is similar in size to my own shadow, but is very faint (transparent compared to mine) and it seems to walk the way an old woman would...

.. is this the Old Woman of the Tee Pee?... is it my Grandmother?... is it Grandmother Moon come down to walk with me?... or could it be the shadow of my own self many years from now, come to offer me wisdoms from the years I have yet to explore?...

I stand for a moment before I enter the Tee Pee circle, and I see a channel of light stream down from the High Place into the center of the circle and down into Mother Earth. I feel the sacredness of this space expand around me now... and I hear the voice of the Old Woman call out for me to enter...

"... sweet child... sit here with me... do not move or think... but simply **Be** here in this light... allow your inner-sacred to awaken... and feel yourself expand outward...,

... do you feel yourself touching the prairie grass as it gently bends with the early morning breeze... can you feel the hot breath of the Buffalo as they walk along the fence-line… feel your sister the Owl, up there in that Cottonwood… and the bunnies that hide along the inner shadow of your barn…,

… this is what it is to sit in sacred space… and to simply Be… to connect with all that surrounds you… and to truly know that you are related to all and everything…,

… and stay for a while longer, child… breathe in and out, oh so slowly… and release and let go of your physical self a little more with each breath… and feel your Mother the Earth rise up through you… hear your Grandfather the Wind breathing… and allow yourself to become the spirit of all that is…,

… and take all of this with you… back into your conscious self… take all of the answers and knowing you have discovered in this time… for when you become the spirit of a thing… it tells you all that it knows… and this is why it is important to sit in sacred space as often as you can… for there is much the world has to tell you… and much that you need to learn…"

… a s qua di s di… and so it is good

It is the Old Woman of the Tee Pee who waits for me (again) on this frosty morning, and I walk straight to her with my blanket pulled snug around me. I hear her singing as I near the circle of stones that surround the place where she sits, and I stand for a time to honor her ceremony.

"… come, child (all children of the Earth)… we have much to do on this day… sit with me here… and I will teach you about the Medicine of your own being… come now… we will enter the place of Dreams… and your heart will tell you what it is you most desire…,

… quiet now, as I sing… still now, as your thoughts fade back and your dreams step forward… let go of your mind… let go of your body… and feel only with your spirit… feel that which is in your heart…,

… *you* are the Medicine you have been seeking… but it is your whole *Self* that makes your Medicine strong… and you must care for yourself as you would your most sacred Medicine Tool… and you must honor and respect the power that is held there within... and you must use this most precious **Tool** (your entire being)... in order to keep it strong and sharp and connected to Creator...

... for the time is upon you now... to become all that you were created to be... and as you do... you will naturally assist in the healing of all people... and this is what your heart has told me is your greatest desire...

... a s qua di s di... and so it is good

I hear the Old Ones chanting from deep within the Dreamtime, and I feel the power of their song as I travel deeper and deeper into the dream-place. Their song has no real words to it, but the meaning is very clear...

... "let go of the words now... and your heart will speak in tones... the language of the spirit world... which tells of truth that is your own... and locked within this perfect tongue... are the answers that you seek... as well as all that you desire... and the truth that you must speak" ...

... and so I choose to stay within the dream-place now... while the song of the Old Ones washes over me... and until I have lost all of my words... and my own truth emerges...

"... there is something that you search for... we can hear you calling out from a place deep within... but your thoughts are too strong... and cluttered with too many words... and you think you know what you are looking for... but you worry that you cannot see it...,

... so let go of your thoughts and words now... and sing out a simple chant... let your mind fade back and your spirit come forth... and do not expect to see anything at all... for when your truth is finally revealed... you will know it... even if you do not see it... "

... a s qua di s di... and so it is good

There is much static in the energy on this day. I feel chaos in the air (and frenzy), worry and concern. It feels like a runaway train, or like standing on the outer edge of a tornado.

I walk the prairie with my bowl of sacred smoke. I walk in a counter-Sun-wise circle and sing the song of release. I feel the energy shift as a quiet calm fills this space where I stand, and I walk the Sun-wise circle now, as I sing the song of gratitude…

"… settle now… and calm, dear children… for you are steady on your path… your direction is forward… and your path is clear… and your spirit knows the way from here…,

… and you can be within the chaos… or you can find the calm… but no matter on which side you choose to stand… to the light your spirit is drawn…,

… and your heart beats with the eternal Mother… and your light is fed by the unnamable **One**… and your Grandfather is the Wind, you know… and he whispers in your ear…,

… and your Grandmother the Moon, guides your nights… and Father Sun, your days… and as you walk, your path moves in to meet you… and sets you on your way…"

… a s qua di s di… and so it is good

It is the soft and kind spirit of Grandfather Elm who wakes me on this day, and I smile as I gather my bundle and make my way out to ceremony. The prairie is completely still and Father Sky provides the clear and deep-blue canvas for the brightest of the Star People who have gathered on this day.

I feel the calm as I walk, and the sweetness of the hopeful dreams of little children. I feel the peace as I set ceremony, and the faithful prayers of all people who set this day aside to be with family and friends and God. I say my own personal prayers now, and I feel the tears that fall for the memory of my Father… I have been missing him so much lately. I pull my blanket around me tight and feel my Father's arms around me.

"… today is about faith and trust… and about going beyond the worry and fear and stress and doubt… which is brought on by the happenings of everyday life… and living today (if only today) with the joyful trust that you are in good hands… (God's hands)… and with the faith that those hands will be there for you tomorrow (and the next day… and the day after that… and so on and on)…

… today let the running and hustling and last minute details be done… and simply be together… savor each moment of the time you have with one another… however that time comes to be… and for each of those moments… give thanks to your Creator… for giving you this life… and for all of the people who share this life with you…

… and sit for a moment if you can find one… and make time to find that moment… to sit in the background, out of the center… and watch your family, be a family… and feel your heart as it opens then… and your love for them that is so strong… and smile for the tears that well up in your eyes… and let those tears flow out…

… and remember how you got here… to this very moment, on this very day… for it was the faith and trust of a young child… that kept you moving forward… your Mothers heart and your Fathers strength… and the loving hand of your heavenly Father… always reaching out for yours…"

… a s qua di s di… and so it is good

Merry Christmas - da ni s ta yo hi hv

The clarity of this morning is stunning, and I walk with clarity of mind and thought as well. I follow a pattern set by my Star Relatives, and find myself standing at my altar. I look out to see the circles of stones that I have just woven myself around and through, and realize that I have unraveled and let go of yet another layer of doubt and fear.

I set ceremony at my altar for this day, and I see about a dozen Rabbits scampering around. Rabbit is the *Medicine* of renewal and new life (in my tradition), and so I set my intention for ceremony today on seeing with clarity… on remembering the new and endless potential that is within each of us… and for us each to embrace our infinite potential as we move forward from here…

"… yes, two legged… another journey has ended… and a new journey has begun… and if you choose to accept it… there is a new path for you to walk… it is waiting there (just up ahead)…,

… and it may seem to you… that new opportunities are finally showing up for you (at last)… but that is not completely so… for the opportunities have always been right there and waiting for you to choose them… you were simply not ready to see them…,

… and this is just the way it is, dear two-legged… and it is why you must always strive to expand and grow your mind… and why you must let go of thoughts and beliefs that hold you back… for there is always more for you to know and do… once you are able to finally see it…"

… a s qua di s di… and so it is good

I walk the path that leads to where the Buffalo stand on this morning. I see the White Owl fly off of her favorite fence post and onto a fence post just a bit farther away. I see the steamy breath of the Buffalo as they stand waiting to greet me, and I hear the White Owl hoot out her welcome as well.

The morning is alive with spirit, and I can feel the magical energy of the *nun ne hi* (little people - fairies) all around me. I set ceremony on the open prairie, right in the center of their ceremony circle, and I join them as they sing the prayer songs for all people…

"… you are strong and can stand alone… if life asks you to do so… and you can be among others without ever being seen… if you have a mind to do this, too… but that which you stand for… speaks loud and touches deep… and you make an impression where ever you go… and it is upon you… to choose your words and actions… with your spirit as your guide… for many are watching… and they will follow you… for they seek guidance now… and they need someone to show them which way to go…,

… there is a bridge that connects the higher worlds with the one that you walk upon… and there is a knowing deep within you (each)… that reminds you of the light that is there… and you seek this light because it is the light from which you were made… and you know this light… for it is your source of origination… and your light calls out to you as you walk your earth journey… and you know it is your purpose to find it…,

… and you remember… as you make your way toward that light you know as yours… that the light you seek is not far away, but deep within… and the path you have been searching for does not lead to some place out there (or even up there)… but to your very center… and the bridge is not a bridge at all… but it is a certain sound… and that sound is your own heartbeat… and it links all that is within you… to all that now surrounds you…,

… and you can see with great clarity, now… that all things are connected… and you wonder how you missed this… through all the years you have lived… but it does not matter really… for you can see it now… and you are strong when life asks you to be… because you are not alone… and it is not about being seen or not seen… when you walk among the people you know… for it is what they *feel* when you are near… that points the way to go…"

… a s qua di s di… and so it is good

Ismell the wet soil as I walk on this day. We have been watering a lot lately, due to the uncommonly warm weather. I walk the prairie by the guidance of spirit, rather than minding the places where the water has created puddles, and I find myself walking in the deep wet clay that is the foundation of this ranch. I set ceremony up on the North slope (above my altar) and breathe in the aroma of fresh wet earth.

I feel the quietness of the early morning prairie fill my entire being, and I sing the prayer songs for all people within, as my ceremony smoke rises and moves me into stillness…

"… find your own place of stillness now, (all people)… and from that place find your own passion… know that you are like the clay that is the earth here… and that you, as well as your life… can be shaped and formed in any way that you desire…,

… then allow your own passion and inherent creativity… to awaken and begin to breathe within you… and know then… that you can create (shape and form) whatever you desire your life and yourself to be…

… a s qua di s di… and so it is good

Grandfather Wind has come again to the prairie. I stand with my arms wide open as I face him, for he is my cleansing smoke on this day. I turn to each direction now, while keeping my arms open wide, and ask Grandfather Wind to cleanse my spirit, my heart, my physical body, and my mind…

… I turn to each direction again, and ask to be filled with whatever I may need, in spirit, heart, body, and mind… and I allow Grandfather Wind to blow through me in each direction until I am full…

… I reach down to touch my Mother the Earth and with both hands and feet connected to her, I sing the song of gratitude… I reach up my arms to my Creator and with arms open wide, I sing the gratitude song again…

… and I stand quiet and still now… for a longer time than I can even tell… and I just feel how I feel… for I have given away that which no longer serves me… my Grandfather the Wind has taken it for me… and he has filled that space inside me, too… with love and light and trust and faith… and with the knowing that I am connected to the flow… the flow that is fed by an infinite reservoir of love and light… and that infinite reservoir is our Creator

… and I set ceremony now… with Grandfather Wind still blowing hard against me… and I sing the prayer songs for all people… and I feel the flow of love and light moving in through my crown and out through my heart… to each and every *one* I know… and to all of those whom I don't even know… and I offer this incredible gift from above… to all people…,

"… and yes, dear children… you are all connected to the flow… and there is an abundant supply of everything and anything you could ever need or want for… just waiting for you to receive it…,

… and you have all that you need… to create your dreams and to achieve your goals… we see it all so clearly from our place up here above…,

… and it is you, dear children… who must see it now… and trust and believe… and make use of that which flows through you, every moment of every day… and feel the love… and trust the light… and step up to create that which you hold so close to your heart… and have kept buried so deep within you…"

… a s qua di s di… and so it is good

Ising the prayer songs for all people (loud and strong) as I stand upon the quiet prairie, and I feel myself expand upward. I feel my spirit and my heart align with the highest energy of the highest place I can reach… and then I reach up even farther…

"… align yourself with the light from above… and allow your spirit to connect with your heart… your mind and body will then fall in line… and the purest of your own truth will emerge…

… sit then, in this place of spirit… and embrace the solitude of your own being… and move about in this place… to explore all there is to know and be… until you realize, in full, all of who you are…,

… and know, then… the purpose of true alignment… for there are many feelings one experiences… as they consciously expand and align with the highest of their own spirit… and one of these is solitude… and it is in this place of solitude… that one becomes captivated by the sound of their own heart beating… and falls in love with the spirit of their own true *Self*…"

… a s qua di s di… and so it is good

As Grandfather Wind howls across the prairie, I feel the wisdom of the Old Ones gather. I feel the *nun ne hi* (fairies) gather around me, too, and their warmth is much appreciated

I sit within the ceremony smoke as I sing the prayer songs for all people, wrapped up snug in my blanket. I sway to the sound of ceremony drums, and I feel the spirits of the Old Ones gathering in closer… around me and the **nun ne hi** … and I let go of my thoughts completely… as I allow the spirit of the Old Ones to lead ceremony on this day…

"... the energy for transformation is very strong at this time, two-legged... so gather your hopes and wishes... and come with us to ceremony... release that which has held you... fastened tight to the lower place... where hopes and dreams must remain as such... and rise up now... into the place of all possibility...

... for just as quickly as your weather can changed from one extreme to the other... so to, can you create instant change that is just as dramatic... and transform any negative into a positive...,

... the energy of the new year... is that of balance... of moving forward giving equal attention to all aspects of yourself... and so set out now... to walk with the guidance of your spirit... and be certain that you feel within your heart... whether it is right action that you take... then engage your mind... and use your own intelligence and wisdom... to lay out your plan (to set your course)... before you set your body in motion..., ... for it is a time of all possibility, (all) two-legged... and it is time for you to shift your thoughts from fear and doubt... to trust and belief... for just as you can shift and transform any negative into positive... you can interfere with a positive... and make it negative...,

... so take the time now... on this day, before it ends... to consciously let go of that which you have been struggling with... and to call to you... all that you want your life to be...,

... be specific and be thorough... write it all down if you must... but trust completely that you can create that which you set out to create... and know for certain... that whatever you experience in this next year... you will have created... and that you can shift and change any experience at any time..."

... a s qua di s di... and so it is good

JANUARY 2011

There is a peaceful calm on the prairie this morning. Grandfather Wind has finally gone back into the North and there is a completely different feel to the land as I set ceremony today.

The Old Ones who followed me into the Dreamtime last night, told me that Grandfather Wind brought a storm to mark the end of the old and the beginning of the new… so to help us make the shift within our own personal beings… and to help us to let go of all things negative and confining, so to make way for all things positive and healing…

… it is like a great cleansing has occurred… even my *Aura* feels clean…

"… and it will take some adjusting now, children… and you will need to focus on adapting to the new… and remember that ***the new*** is a gift… for it is the answer you have been waiting for…,

… feel the lighter energy that surrounds you now… and know that the heaviness has lifted… the healing has begun… and you can move about in a positive atmosphere now… where you are supported and assisted by others who look to create that which is new and more… better, best…,

… and you will find now… that many share your same intentions and desires… and so you gather into communities of like-minded people… who work together for the greater good… and assist one another in creating a better place for all to live… one that will support all people… as well as all future generations…,

… and you will see then… that all you could ever need… is (and has been) right there and available to you… and you will know… why you could not see it before… and you will know, too… the value in each relationship… and you will respect and honor each ***one***… for what they have taught you… as well as for what they have learned…,

… and this is your gift for the New Year…"

… a s qua di s di… and so it is good

… a li he li s di   i tse   u de ti yv sa di sv i - Happy New Year

And so it begins…

… the first day of the New Year has passed and it was amazing… well at least the energy of it was amazing.

I wake early today… ready to walk the prairie and anxious to begin ceremony… I feel warm and comfortable out here in the light of a new morning… and I feel that same amazing energy I felt yesterday…

"… watch the smoke from your ceremony fire, Swan… see it rise up and move like waves upon the air… feel the winds of change move deep within you… and make peace with the idea of change… here… now… in the sacred space of ceremony…,

… it is all about choice, Swan… and no matter what choice is made… it cannot be wrong… for it is more about realizing that every experience of your life is a choice… (and that you get to make each one)… rather than worrying about which choice to make…,

… so move about with grace and ease… and let your heart speak loud and clear… and listen with your spirit… and decide with your heart… and rest your body and your mind for a while… for all is well and you are safe… and time is yours to spend… and life is yours to live…"

… a s qua di s di… and so it is good

I find myself sitting in the West on this day. I set ceremony beneath my wool blanket, and I hear the Old Man who lives there (in the place of journey and introspection) calling to me… and he seems very close…

"… consider the place in time where you are… that you are beginning a new year… and then consider the **Medicine** of this place in the West… for it is all perfect, you see… for today you sit in the place of end… which will be also the place of begin… as soon as you recognize that you are in the place of **choice**... and that all you have to do is **Dream...** in order to know what your heart really desires...,

... the Bear has been sleeping there in that cave for a while now... and it is only now... that the **Dreams of Future** have begun... for the journey within is much like the journey without... there are many roads with many options... and certainty is elusive... and you must get to the place where you will make the time... to sit and reflect... to open your eyes and to truly see... rather than just speeding along with eyes closed (and screaming all the way)...,

... it is the deep, deep sleep you must find now... because you must get past the wishes of the mind... and get to the place where the wishes of the heart are kept... and then you must go deep within the heart... to the very center... for there are many layers there in the place of the heart... and the wishes on the outer edges... will be the newest and are usually connected to the wishes of the mind... so you must get to the center of your heart... if you seek to know that which your Spirit has dreamed for you...,

... ah... now you have found the place of **sacred dreams**... and now you will be given your vision... and now you will hear the voice from within you speak... and you will know the true meaning of death and rebirth... for there is no space of time between them here in the place of the West... as you let go of an old (issue, thought pattern, belief, or the like)... and welcome in anew... it is quick and instant... and the healing is pure and it is perfect...,

... and Father Sun will find you then... and shine his light upon you... and out from the shadow you will walk... transformed and new... reborn and complete..."

... a s qua di s di... and so it is good

I see light on the horizon as I walk out on this day, just a slight glow that highlights the line where Mother Earth meets Father Sky. I hear the ancient song of our ancestors, and the primal drums that beat along with the loving heartbeat of our Mother the Earth.

I am captivated as I stand listening… as the song of the Old Ones hold me spellbound… and I feel myself move into another space… a higher space… and I feel as though I am in a trance… as the song and the drums become louder… and stronger… so strong that I can feel movement beneath my feet… movement that moves within my entire body… and I feel as though I am dancing… yet I know I am not moving at all… for I am just standing here… with my eyes fixed on the horizon

… and I see them now… the ancestors… the Old Ones… dancing their Ghost Dance… just there on the horizon… and I hear them, too… as they sing the old and ancient chant… and I see their energy… as it moves across the prairie… and I feel it… as it moves within me too…

"… we dance for the return of the old ways… we dance for the return of joy and happiness… we sing for simple times… and for all people to love and respect the land, and one another… and we feel the healing of this… as we dance and sing…,

… and this is what you would call our prayer… but it is more than what you know as prayer… for what you know as prayer… is what we call a wish…,

… for to us, your Old Ones and ancestors… a prayer is when you connect with all that is… through movement and song… and make the feeling of your desire move throughout your whole being… and it is your spirit that moves within you… and makes the journey outward… and as it (your spirit) moves out into the world… it touches everyone and everything… and it rises high, then… and communes with the Creator… and there is no mistaking what you are requesting… and the answer requires you to take action as well…"

… a s qua di s di… and so it is good

There is a violet glow on the prairie today. I look all around to see where it may be coming from, but I cannot find the source. So I close my eyes and *feel,* and that is when I know, that the spirit beings from the High Place have all come down to sit with us today… and it is their light that creates the violet glow…

"… there is much you (all) have learned through the experiences of your lives so far… your awareness has expanded many times… and your senses have all become more sharp and keen… more accurate and intense…,

… it is time, now… to focus on your own personal growth… how much you have grown and in what ways, yes… but you must also look to your growth from here… and at what you will focus on now… at how you will grow from here… as well as at what you must let fall away… in order to truly grow *"up"*…,

… and the secret to your own personal growth from here on… (as well as the growth and health of your Star, Earth)… is held within your heart… for your heart is your center… it is fluid and flowing… alive and beating… and so it is the place from which you feel… and feeling is the original way of communicating…,

… and all things (knowledge and knowing… wisdom and truth… the way to love and to live) were given to you (each) through your hearts… and theses were meant to flow in and through and out… in order to be shared and used… in order to create growth…,

… the heart was meant to channel in (the positive as well as the negative)… to feel as it gathers the learning… and then to let it go… so to allow the flow… so that more can come through… and pain does not stay…but knowing does…,

… feeling creates the experience… and experiencing something is the most thorough way to learn anything… and so you began to *hold* within your hearts… fearing that you will lose the lesson… and also because *feeling* is so active and so real…,

... but then holding inhibits the flow... and creates a block... it keeps more from coming in... and makes that which is there to go stagnate...,

... so now it is time to learn and grow... by reconnecting to and with the flow... and by allowing all that has been hold-up in your heart to flow out... and by trusting that you will keep the knowing and the lessons... and the love and the joy, too... but that you will also share this with others... and be able to receive more...,

... and this will enhance your growth... and you will grow at a more rapid rate... and you will grow more completely... you will grow and rise up... and your life will flow... and you will become a source of the violet light for others to see... and they will be guided by that light... and you will have become a part of the flow..."

... a s qua di s di... and so it is good

I am tired on this day as I wake, and the Cowboy tells me that Thursday is the hardest day of the week for him, and I try not to think about how... *there was a time... not so long ago... that I would just bound out of bed... no matter how much or how little sleep I had... or how hard I worked the day before... and never even notice the difference...*

... I stand on the prairie now... wrapped in my blanket... older... wiser... achy, but strong... tired, but alert... and I feel someone coming toward me... and I know before I see him... that it is the Old Man, come to share our ceremony for today... and I never hear him complain about his tired old body... and so I decide not to complain about mine...

"... young one... it is a good time in your life... and it is right that you will feel your body call out to you for care and consideration... and it is time for you to honor and respect that body of yours... especially when it speaks to you... for it must take you a longer way... than even you have thought about going...,

... and it is time to consider this, too... you (each) must honor your future... by caring for your *self* and your *life*... now... and here... in this time... today and tomorrow... and to be mindful of how much you work... and then balance that work with rest… and to be sure to notice how much time you spend in spirit as well… and how you balance what you eat with how much you move about…,

… and notice, too… that you may not have had much time… during the young time of your life… to truly get to know yourself spiritually… but now you do… for your own body will tell you settle down now… and sit for a while longer… and sort through all of what you have picked up along your Earth Journey…,

… and as you do this… you will find that which is no longer of service to you… and that which you will want to examine further… and your Earth Journey will begin to shift… and your Earth Journey will become a Spiritual Journey… and you will see then… why you must care for yourself now…"

… a s qua di s di… and so it is good

It is a clear morning as I walk on this day (and fairly warm). I walk a bit before I set ceremony, bringing to mind all of the people who have requested specific prayers. I stand on top of the knoll in the Northwest corner of this ranch, and sing out the prayer songs for each, as I see their faces in the black-blue of Father Sky

… and I stand for a while longer… in silence… and I look into the black-blue of Father Sky… and I ask for peace… for light to pour into our hearts… and for love to pour out… and I ask for the return of common decency among one another… and then I feel the warmth… as it moves in and through my entire body…

… and I stand for a while longer… in silence… and I look into the black-blue of Father Sky… and I sing the gratitude song for all people… and then I sing **gratitude** again… for all the people I have just made specific prayers… and I see the faces of each again now… in the black-blue of Father Sky… and their faces smile…

… and I feel the light pour in now… and I feel the love pour out… and I feel the joy and the relief and the gratitude… for all of the goodness that occurs each day… and I feel the despair and the anguish, too… and the panic and the fear and the stress… as if the breath is being held… like when you just do not want to exhale… for fear *"it"* will all fall apart…

… and I stand for a while longer now… in silence… and I look into the black-blue of Father Sky… and I ask about this…

"… dear child (children)… this is the most complex thing you could ask about… for you ask about **life**… and once **life** begins… it moves and flows and dips and rises… guided by the one who is living it… and affected by all who touch it… and each life is its own…

… and it is because there is difficulty… that one can know ease… and it because there is ugliness… that one can know beauty… it is because there is a negative… that one knows there is a positive…

… and it is because there is despair and anguish… and panic and fear and stress… that one looks up in prayer… and opens the door for the light to pour in… and for the love to pour out… and remembers that each and every other… is their brother or their sister… and then begins to treat one another in a good and decent manner…,

… and so one will always experience both… the positive and the negative… in this thing called life… for in order to truly live it… one must truly live it…"

… a s qua di s di… and so it is good

I step out on this cold morning and find the Medicine Woman waiting for me. We walk along the sacred paths and trails here on the ranch, until we come to stand before the **Praying Tree.** She is stark and bare right now, but is still as powerful and generous as always…

"… come, child… walk in close to this **sacred standing one**… and empty your mind for a while… sway and breathe with the spirit of this **Medicine Being**… and release that which has captured your own spirit… for it is a crooked path that you have asked your spirit to travel lately… in order for it to slip by the blocks and hot spots created by your own worry…,

… your body will experience a natural purging then… as it lets go of built-up toxins that have the potential to make you very ill… and so you must listen to your body… and give it the time and rest that it needs…,

… but do not forget about your mind, child… for your mind has much more to do with the way you feel, than you give it credit for… step back now… and look again at this *sacred standing one*… see that she has three distinct parts to her… even though she is the same tree…,

… see her center… standing straight and tall and reaching right for Creator… this part stands in the South… and carries the medicine of action (with the excitement and innocence of a child)… here, her connection to/with Creator is ever flowing… and you can see… when spirit flows in… it goes straight to her heart…,

… and see the side of her that reaches East… bending to catch the warmth of Father Sun as he rises… this is the place of balance… for this is the place of male meeting female… strength and wisdom perfectly blended with compassion and love… here is where all things are determined and sorted through… where you are given the piece (or pieces) you need… in order to recognize an issue…,

… and see the side of this *sacred standing one* that reaches West… bending now to follow Father Sun as he escapes into the horizon… reaching over and down and into the place of healing… see how she goes into the darkness and works through every question and issue… until it is done…,

… and she stands deeply rooted in your Mother the Earth… where she is continually fed and nourished in every physical way necessary… and she reaches up, straight and tall… continually being fed and nourished in every spiritual way necessary… and she faces the North… where she can access the wisdom of the Elders at any time… and this is you, child… and this is all people, too… and sit with this for a while now… and allow the *Medicine* of this *sacred standing one* to awaken within you… and be well now, child… be well…"

… a s qua di s di… and so it is good

I feel the changing of a season as I walk on this day, but it is not the changing from Fall to Winter that I feel, it is the changing of my own *season*… like I am moving into something (or someone) new.

I make my way to the Praying Tree again, hoping that the Old Medicine Woman will come again, but I know as I stand here… she won't…

… I wait anyway… just sitting in silence… just waiting for words to come… just being still and hoping that if I don't move… I won't have to move… but I know that is wrong, too…

"… and why are you so afraid of this change, child… when all who stand in the High Place honor you for your journey…,

… do you know how much we honor *all* of you there… for the journeys you have chosen… and for continuing to move forward… and for going on and on…,

… and change is always present… it is what drives you forward… it is what brings you to the next place… and it is why you are still excited to see what tomorrow will bring…,

… so why does this next change frighten you, child… when all that is behind it is good and more and better… and when all that you have experienced throughout the whole of your Earth Life… has prepared you for each step forward… and specifically… for this next step forward…,

… so relax now, child (children)… and welcome-in that which is waiting there for you… and trust the place where you are now… and honor your own *self*… as we honor you… and see what comes to you next… for you are ready… and life is waiting…"

… a s qua di s di… and so it is good

Istand in deep snow on this day, and Grandfather Wind still blows. The wind chill is 15 below zero, so I set ceremony inside.

I sit in my ceremony space (inside my classroom area), and feel the presence of all who have come here for classes over the years. I see their faces and I hear their sweet voices, and I feel the warmth of everything that each one has given to me over the years.

… such generosity… such wisdom… such love and compassion… such beauty and grace…

… and within each of these… is a story… and I feel the story of each… as I sing the prayer songs for all people…

… and I sing the **old medicine song** now… the one that honors life… for each life is sacred…

… and I sing for those we have lost over the years… and for those who have passed on recently… and I sing for those who are still deciding whether to go or stay…

… and I feel the Medicine that is Creator… as it expands right here in this space… right here where I sit… and I quiet my mind… and I feel with my heart

"… children… look after one another… give more than you ask for… give more than you receive…,

… reset your understanding of success… for it is much greater than any small one could ever claim…,

… true success is when all are cared for… and none are left without… and so set out each day… to be successful by assisting another… and then you may smile at your success…,

… when all are cared for… and no one is left without…"

… a s qua di s di… and so it is good

The floor is cold as I step out of bed on this morning, and I feel the cold air all around me, too. There is nothing wrong with our room heaters… it is just very cold out here on the eastern plains of Colorado today.

I set ceremony inside (again) on this day, and I am grateful for this sacred place inside. I sit close to my ceremony fire as I sing the prayer songs for all people, and I find myself moving deep within… or is it far away?… or back to some place long ago?… or maybe out to some place up ahead?… to a time that is yet to come.

I stand just inside a large open cave, now… and there is light here… I look around to see there is a fire burning… and I can see the back wall of this cave from where I stand… and there seems to be a face there within it… a face in the back wall of the cave… and she is looking at me… it is as if the whole of the cave is a being… and I just stand quiet and still… to honor and respect.

I can feel the warm sand beneath my feet, now… and I hear water just outside… (ocean waves)… I smell the fresh sea air… and I can even taste the salt… I feel myself moving into the place of journey, now… as the shrill cry of the Sea Gulls mix with the sound of waves crashing against the rocks… and this becomes like music to me… and the song takes me deep within… it creates a bridge for me to walk upon… and I cross that bridge as I go deep within the Dreamtime…

"… find your place of comfort, children… and seek to be at ease… place your feet upon your **Mother**… and let the madness cease… for it is time to come back to your own… and to center now, and ground… and it is time for you to know your **home**… and to listen to its sound…,

… feel your feet upon the land… and the pulse of all who breathe… and remember where you came from, now… as you feel it in the breeze… and does your heart beat loud and strong… and does it reach for another one… and do you ache to know the way… to find your **Self** and come home to stay…,

… then sit here now, my darling one… and feel the earth and the shining sun… and listen to the stillness here… for she speaks the wisdom of all the years… and do not think or even move… for there is nothing here, that you are called to prove…,

… and when it is time, you will stand again… and walk out there and look ahead… and walk your talk and lend your hand… and be connected to the land… and know your Father is the Sun… and be in love with every **One**…"

… a s qua di s di… and so it is good

It is the Snowy Owl who calls to me on this day, and it is to a place back and far away that we fly. I remember this flight from many years ago, and the way it felt to walk upon our Mother the Earth when she was young and fresh, and when there was far more open space to explore.

It is to a gathering of Elders that we fly on this day, and it is the small round hut where the Old Men sit that we seek. The Old Men sit in silence as they await our arrival, and it is the beating of their hearts that we listen for as we make our way to their lodge.

… and it is Snowy Owl who shows me the way… and we stand silent as we wait at the doorway… until the Old Men invite us in… and we stand in the center of their council… as we offer tobacco (our greeting) to each… and we sit then… the Snowy Owl and I… right there in the center… as the Old Men speak their wisdom for us to hear…

"… self-deception can be blinding… and will cause permanent damage if one stays in the place of shadow too long… it is sometimes comforting to hide within that darkened place… to offer yourself time to settle or reflect… but be aware of the time spent there… for it can be deceiving…,

… we have sent Snowy Owl to be your guide for a while… for she sees perfectly in the darkened places… and because she is white… she will be easy for you to follow… Snowy Owl will take you anywhere you wish to go… however deep into the darkness you need to go… and you can be sure that you are safe with her… and you can be certain that you will not become lost… for she can bring you out at any time… all you have to do is follow the white light of Snowy Owl in flight…,

… so take this gift, dear one… and go into the darkened place to explore… find what you are hiding from… and see how small it has become… once the light is shone upon it… and get on with your life then, dear one… and walk out of that shadow you have been hiding in…,

… for there is much for you to do, now… and nothing for you to fear… and the shadow is nothing but uncertainty… and the light… it is your own…"

… a s qua di s di… and so it is good

It is the Grandfather Stones who call to me on this day, and the soft voices of all of the Stone People who make up the prayer circles here. Their voices are soft and sweet as I walk around and through each circle… and they speak in song and verse as they remind me of dreams I have let fade and memories I have so needed to remember…

"… bring Heaven and Earth together… as you bring your spirit-self together **as one** with your physical being… for it is time to bring a change to this life you live… and you will need to use all of that which resides in the High Place… to bring about this change…,

… you (all people)… have been living a double life for far too long now… for you have kept your **spiritual-Self** and your **physical-Self** separate from one another… and though you have seemed to function well in this state of being… it is time to go beyond functioning… and get to the place of truly living… and in order to do that… you must bring yourself to wholeness…,

… the path ahead has much to show you… but you will see only part of it with your human eyes… and can only walk on part of it with your physical feet… which means you will live only half a life… until you decide to keep your spiritual-Self awake and active at all times… and blended as one with your physical-being…,

… there are many doorways and windows of opportunity open for you (at all times)… and you feel them (we know you do)… but you believe they are just beyond your reach… when they are really just out of your physical vision…

… and if you focus your vision by opening your **spiritual-eye**… you will see the whole picture… and all will be revealed to you (then)…"

… a s qua di s di… and so it is good

It is a dark morning here on the prairie. The Cloud People have settled in above me, and I feel as though I am wrapped in a blanket. Safe and protected, I sing the prayer songs for all people, and I feel the embrace of all who reside in the High Place now, as I move into stillness…

"… this is **your** blanket of protection, Swan… not ours… and it is good that you know how to find this place… but it is we who must tell you… that you cannot stay here long… for you seek this place of safety and comfort… whenever you are faced with a decision that you feel is beyond you… but even you know that the choices are yours… and that it is you who must make them…,

… so come to this place of quiet and still… and wrap yourself in the wisdom and peace that resides here… but use this time and this place to dispel all and any negative and un-serving thoughts… for it is only the positive that you need now… so that you can see with clarity, the choices that are before you… and so that you can make your choices with certainty…,

… and if you feel heavy as you walk… come and wrap yourself in us… for we can draw the negative energy up and away… just as if you were sitting in the **"sweat"** … we can help you sweat out the negative… and once the negative is removed… the positive rises up… and when the positive rises up… you will attract all the good that you have been seeking… and then you will know that all is right and good…"

… a s qua di s di… and so it is good

The Star People guide my walk on this day, and I stand beneath them as the humble child that I am. I have been called to stand up and be wise, and to lead and to guide from my own wisdom and experience so much lately… and doing so has made me feel large and important…

… but here… now… out on the wide-open prairie… with the whole of Father Sky above me… and all of the Star Nation looking down upon me… I find again, perspective… and I am again, *just me*… simple and small and young (in comparison)… and old, too (by earthly years)…

… and I know that I am important… but in a different way than my human-ego-self had been feeling… for I am important simply because *I Am*… just the same as each one of us two-legged… (and winged, and crawly, and four-legged, and standing one, and plant, and stone, and so on and on)… are important…

"… look up now, (all) two-legged… and find the largest of us… and can you see the smallest of us, too… and do you think that any one of us… is any less important than another…,

… you have (all) lived long and learned much… and you have much to share… this is true and valuable and important… but each day you begin again… fresh and new… and so you must find your way to a place of new… each day... and be like a child again… ready and eager and willing to learn more…,

… and this is the true wisdom of an Elder… and this is the true experience of life… to wake each day and live it fully… to share of yourself and of your experience… if that is what is asked of you… but to take in all that you can as well… as if you were a child again…,

… for when you see the world (and your life) in this way… you live in a place of renewal… and you find more to experience… and then even more will show-up for you to see and know and do… and you will not stay in just one place… but you will grow and expand… and be ever-changing… ever-growing…,

… and each day you will feel large and important… and each day you will know… that you are small and young and new… and both will be true at once… and you will continue on and on and on… and this is good, dear children…"

… a s qua di s di… and so it is good

As I drove out yesterday, Hawk sat on the high pole, watching me as I drove by. I stopped for a moment then, to give respect and to listen, and as I began to drive away, Hawk flew beside me until I reached the road where I turn.

I felt the message Hawk brought to me as we traveled along together (I felt it in my heart), and I then said a prayer for my family, and I said a prayer for you and yours, too.

Hawk is here again today, he sits out on the fence as I sing the ceremony song. I asked him if he brings the message for today… and he flew around in a circle above me as he spoke this message…

"… count the blessings of your life… and appreciate all the gifts you have received… be grateful for each moment you have been given… with each and every loved one and friend… and appreciate something of your life each day…,

… for it is through recognizing each good… that brings about more good… and it is by giving… that you receive… give of yourself in any way you can… and you will receive in abundant ways…"

… a s qua di s di… and so it is good

Last night as I drove home, the White Owl was waiting for me. She flew off of a short fence post and alongside of my car for a few minutes. I saw her again just before I turned into our ranch, and I heard her calling as I woke this morning.

I walked out to see Grandmother Moon setting in the West, and even though there was no sign of the White Owl, I could feel her presence. The morning is warm for this time of year… and so I set ceremony out on the prairie… where I am joined by the White Owl… and Grandmother Moon…

"… you are infinite, children… and you have the ability to create anything at any time… but you question how… so come here now, children… and listen…,

… all things begin with an idea… an idea that becomes a seed… and if you plant that seed… and tend to it daily… that seed will begin to grow and become…,

… but remember, children… sometimes you need to lay out a plan… and set yourself goals… or draw a picture or visualize the outcome… and remember, too… that once you have planted your seed… you will need to nourish it… and don't forget to prepare and tend to that soil…,

… and each day… as you tend to your seed of creation… actively call out to all of the power and energy of the Universe… and ask it to be a part of your growth (your plan, your creation)…,

… and each night… as you sleep… know that the Universe is still watching over you and your creation… and this is most powerful, children… for you have the ability to create anything at any time… and when you invite the Universe to join you… your creation is certain to become…"

… a s qua di s di… and so it is good

As Grandmother Moon sits high above me on this day, I honor the lives of two dear friends. Both passed away unexpectedly (one Sunday morning, one yesterday), leaving the Cowboy and I with thoughts and feelings that make us question our own lives… and the way we have lived them.

"… honor your life… and live it in a good way… honor your future… by planning for it today…,

… honor the lives of each and every **other**… by respecting the path they have chosen to walk… and know that *"living your life in a good way"*… means something different to each and every **one**…,

… think of your life in the way of a circle… and look in on that circle when you feel burdened and **off**… and notice then… if what you take in… is balanced with what you give out… and find a way to make that right in your own circle… for your balance will be different… than it is for each and every **other**…

… and if you honor your life as you live it… you will have lived your life in a good way…"

… a s qua di s di… and so it is good

The fullness of Grandmother Moon provides the perfect light for me as I walk the prairie on this day. It is like walking in the Dreamtime, for there seems to be a misty-glow all around me… and I can feel Mother Earth beneath my feet… but I cannot see her.

I hear the whispers and tiny voices of the *nun ne hi* as I make my way to my altar. I walk up the slope to the Purple Smoke Bush (which is where they stay most of the time), and I set ceremony here on this day…

"… listen to the earth… and listen to the animals, too… connect with all of nature… by becoming still as you stand out in it…,

… close your eyes… and relax your tightened muscles… release your breath, expand your heart… and feel your spirit rise…,

… now stand there upon the land… as the spirit that you be… and let your mind just drift away… and let your spirit breathe…,

… then feel your spirit come alive… and feel yourself expand… and take a step outside yourself… as you walk upon the land…,

… and you don't have to listen now… or wait for thoughts to form… for everything you need to know… came through when you were born…,

… the rhythms of the earth are shifting now… and you must shift as well… but your spirit knows just what to do… if you give it a chance to tell…"

… a s qua di s di… and so it is good

It is the Star People I hear calling, and I come from a place deep within. I lay still for a moment, as I need time to awaken completely. I walk out now, to the light of Grandmother Moon (who is big and round and close), and ribbons of Cloud People (who are woven across Father Sky)…

… and as I stand looking up… I hear my Star Relatives call out again…

"… you must look beyond now, sweet dear… and allow your spirit to find us here… look past the blocks and locks and doors… and know for certain that there is more…,

… look with eyes that do not deceive… and what you need, you will receive… and listen from the place within… and your will know your-*Self* again… and stepping away makes your sight so clear… that you can trust what you see and hear…,

… and you have blended with your Mother the Earth… and you have learned your value and worth… and you are part of your Father the Sky… and yet you continue to question… why?…,

… why am I here?… and what is my path?… and will you show me now, at last?… and how will I know?… and what if I don't?… for I so want my life to count…,

… ah, there, sweet dear… it is all there before you… and it is all there within you… it is all around you… all the time… and everywhere…

… for your feet are awake as they walk upon your Mother… and your mind steps back as you call upon your Father… it is the balance of Earth and Sky… that you have finally found… it is the balance of body and spirit… of man and woman… of what you can touch and see… with what you feel and know…,

… and this is how to go forward, sweet dear… and this why you cannot miss it… because it is all there before you… and it is all there within you… it is all around you… all the time… and everywhere…"

… a s qua di s di… and so it is good

As Grandfather Wind whips and whistles around me, I feel the need for solitude. I make my way to the quiet stillness of my ceremony space, here inside the classroom area of our barn, and set ceremony for today.

With the sacred smoke rising… I breathe in deep…. I cleanse this space and my entire being in the sacred smoke… and I allow my physical self to rest… as my spirit rises up…,

… I pull the stillness in around me now… as my heart sings silent prayers for all people… and my spirit moves even higher… as it gathers the message for today…,

"… much can be found in the stillness… healing can occur there… and clarity will come, too… but you must allow your Grandfather the Wind to blow through you first… and take away the chaos… so that you can move into the stillness…,

… and if you practice this each day… you will no longer need your Grandfather's assistance… for you will be able to find the stillness *within* the chaos… at any time and in any place you find yourself to be…,

… and it is *Life t*hat you come to look in on now… and you wonder how you have done… and you ask yourself… "how have I treated (my life) the greatest of all gifts" … and you look behind you… at the long road traveled… and speculate on how you could have done better…,

… but, dear child… if you look for imperfections… you will certainly find them… and as you see these… you will notice patterns that you can adjust… and then you can set about to make changes… as you turn to go forward from here… but this is only part of what the stillness has to offer you… and this is only part of the healing that happens deep within this place…,

… for you must also look to see your goodness… and feel it move within you… and if you look behind you… at that long road traveled… then you must look ahead as well… to see the patterns that brought you joy… and those that mark your goodness… and then you must bring these along with you… as you turn to go forward from here…,

… and move deeper into the stillness, now… and find a way to simply ***"Be"*** … and sit with your Creator… sit quiet and still… sit without thought or plan… without question or opinion… without limitation or expectation…,

… and… well… then… you will see…"

… a s qua di s di… and so it is good

The healing energy is strong on this day. I walk out onto the sleeping prairie, and feel the presence of many guardians from above. I walk to each of the sacred guardians who live upon this ranch with me (the standing ones, the stone people, the animals, and such), and offer my gratitude for their presence in my life…

… and they speak to me about becoming more whole and balanced in my life… and they tell me of the healing this brings…

"… and so, two-legged… you know it is time to find your community again… it is time to expand your life… by connecting with others around you…,

… for as you experience others… you will learn more about yourself… and this will provide you with another way of honoring your life… for as you honor the differences in others… you will begin to understand and honor your own…,

… there is great healing in this simple commitment, two-legged… for as long as you keep yourself separate and alone… you have only your own thoughts and experiences to teach you… and there is no balance…,

… but as you move about within the community… you have all of the experiences of everything and everyone to teach you… and so you find balance… and balance is the key to healing in every way…"

… a s qua di s di… and so it is good

The morning is crisp and cold and bright. I walk the prairie in my usual way, but I feel a difference about this particular morning. My mind has had much to think about over this last week, and I feel a *nudge* to release all of that... and to look to things more basic and easy...

"... *simplicity* is the word we speak to you on this day... so seek to find that which is simple... in all that you have made complicated...,

... think of that which is most important... and let the rest fall into place around that... for life is moving faster for you now... and time is something you should not waste... for much can be left behind... when you live your life in haste...,

... you are in a place of choice now... and this may be a new concept for you... but it really *is* time for you to know (and understand)... that your life will be what you make it to be... and your path... well, you can choose that too...,

... and you don't have to throw it all away and start over... even if you feel you want (or need) to start over... you can simply begin with one little change at a time... one thought... one commitment... one deep breath... and one step forward..."

... a s qua di s di... and so it is good

I hear Grandfather Wind calling to me as I wake on this day... he is whistling and blowing so hard against our house... that is sounds like waves crashing against the shore...

... I walk out wrapped in my blanket... and I struggle to stand, with the force of Grandfather Wind crashing against me... I look up at our Grandmother the Moon... who is struggling to shine through the foggy mist that is between us...,

... and I sing the gratitude song for all that I see and feel and hear and know and have... as well as for all that I do not know and do not have...

I recognize the beauty of life… in all of its perfection… and I see that perfection… by comparing **Life** with a **Rose**…

… for to truly enjoy the Rose… you must also deal with the thorns… and in living life… you will enjoy the good times… and endure the hard times…

… but whether a moment is a good time or a hard time… it will bring you something of value… something you will hold dear… something that will inspire you… or something that will challenge…

… and you may look upon these… as the beauty and the thorns of life… for some will make you smile… and some will make you cry…

… but I just stand here and smile… because both are so very worth it… (**Life** and the Rose)… and because I cannot say for certain… which I value more… the **beauty** or the **thorns**…

"… look in on your lives, dear children… and see that it is perfect… but make the improvements that you need to make… for this is just part of life…,

… and work through the challenges… as you grow and strive to become… and enjoy the good times… for all that they are… and be the child… and the grown-up, too… and honor the teen-aged youth within you… when nothing else seems to fit…,

… then spend some time… with the **elder** within… especially when you struggle to see the beauty among the thorns… and you will see the perfection of it all… and find the will to do it all again…"

… a s qua di s di… and so it is good

When we begin to create something new in our lives... we naturally become rocked to the core... and no matter how much we want or love this new creation... be it a living breathing being... or something that inspires us to live and breathe...

... our life changes... and we find ourselves outside of our comfort zone... and then we begin to change... and that brings about growth, and transformation... and in many ways we are re-born as well...

... I mention this today... because the energy that is here for us now... is that of creating... of birthing something new... and of re-birthing our own *selves*... and this energy has the potential to stir us up... to shake us to our cores... and we will begin to experience great changes, now... we will think new thoughts... and feel new feelings... and our bodies will change... and our spirits will expand...

... and this will be good... even though we may struggle at times...

"... children... your dreams are *becoming* now... and you are changing now, too... and as you work to bring about the *new*... you must take time to step away as well... to play awhile... to step back a while... and to rest your mind... so to nourish your spirit...,

... for the energy of creation can become intense... it will cloud your vision... and disrupt your thoughts... it can challenge you physically... and bring about unexpected emotions... it will bring you to you knees... and reacquaint you with your faith...,

... and all of this is simply the process of creating... and it is good (and okay) to be in the process... for soon you will experience the joy and happiness of creating something new... whether it be a child... or a business... or a new product to be used... or a new way of living and/or healing... or even a new you..."

... a s qua di s di... and so it is good

I can feel the wisdom of an Elder waiting for me as I walk through the snow on this morning… wisdom that seems to hang in the air.

I do not see the Elder as I begin ceremony on this day, but I feel the presence of many who are old and wise. I hear Wolves howling as I sing the prayer songs for all people, and I find myself standing in the *Cave of the Seven Wolves* as I move into stillness and begin to receive the message for today…

… here in the Cave of the Seven Wolves… they all are here… the Seven Wolves… the seven wise ones… the seven elders… and they are all waiting for me… they each sit upon their own ledge… and they watch me… as I watch them…

… they are Seven who are teachers… and I know I am their student… so I quiet and listen… for I can feel the wisdom in the air begin to move… as it settles in around me…

"… (all) two-legged… we come on this day to present you with a challenge… a challenge that is as difficult, as it will be healing… for we ask you on this day to look into the disappointments of your life… and recognize where these disappointments have become blocks and barriers for you…,

… begin with your childhood… and follow the path to where you are now… recognize the places where you lack trust or have fear… note these issues within your relationships… and the places along the way where you have held back or not even tried… (due to lack of self-value and worth)…,

… for each of these will be connected to a disappointment… and along with that disappointment there will be an emotion… from broken promises to abandonment… from sadness to devastation… and you will begin to measure the impact each disappointment has had on you… and on how you have lived your life… as well as which negative emotion is connected to or with each disappointment…,

… and once you have discovered all of these… you will understand more of who you are… and how you arrived at the place you are today… and you may even see how some of these have served you over the years… or at a specific time in your life…,

… but the knowing you are given today… is not to be an excuse or an entitlement for remaining stuck or small… you are to use this information to release yourself from old patterns and restrictions… so that you can move and expand and grow…,

… so know this as a calling… and accept it as a challenge… to bring about a healing within your own *Self*… for your own healing will affect all who are around you… and through each of these… your healing will affect the world…"

… a s qua di s di… and so it is good

I stand in gratitude a little while longer as I begin ceremony on this day, and I make it my intention to reestablish my connection to/with all that surrounds me. I sing the prayer songs for all people as I bathe in the sacred smoke… and I ask that all people find their own peace within…

"… peace is a good thing to pray for… but peace will not look or be the same for each… and even throughout one's lifetime… the peace one prays for will change in meaning… depending on their own personal experience and need at the time…,

… communication is essential… but it will not be the words one uses… that brings about the clarity and connection one seeks… it will be one's own ability to communicate with *Spirit*… through their own spirit… that will make the communication strong and clear…,

… this is true of earthly relationships and how one communicates with others, too… for when the words one speaks are different than the thoughts they are thinking and the way they are feeling… the connection is weak and the communication is all but lost…,

… and many are asking now… for the return of their inner-guidance… but this is not something they have lost… it is only that they have lost the ability to trust the guidance they have been receiving… due to a weakened line of communication…,

… it is a new year for you, (all) two-legged… and along with the new challenges you will encounter… there is new energy for you to make use of as well… old behaviors and beliefs must be reexamined now… and a new connection to all that *"is"* must be established…,

… so collect your thoughts… and take time to get in touch with your feelings… and this could be more difficult than you expect… for you need to find the thoughts that are your own (vs. those of others)… and emotion is powerful… and there will be many feelings that you have not completely worked through… but take the time to work on these now…

… for once you do… your connection to/with your own spirit will become strong and clear… and you will begin to trust your inner-guidance again… and the communication between your own spirit and your Creator (Spirit and the Universe) will become strong and clear as well… and you will know peace…"

… a s qua di s di… and so it is good

The weather has been more like Spring than Winter lately, which could explain the playful energy I feel as I walk out on this day. I feel the ***woman energy*** on this day as well, and the understanding of why we need the release of play when things get a bit too serious…

"… finding the balance in your lives may be a greater challenge than you expect… for you live in a time where the demands of physical life will always take the lead… and necessity always wins out over desire…,

… and it is good to be mature and responsible… by making sure that everything is done… it is something that makes you feel good… but do remember… that making time for rest and play is how you achieve the balance… and if you are not working-in time for rest and play each day… you have not found the balance…,

… in order to be at your best… especially during stressful times… you must make sure you are ***at your best***… so make some choices now… set some goals… and balance your work with your play… your play with rest… your seriousness with your playfulness… and remember to nourish yourself properly as well…,

… for as you smooth out your own lives with balance in this way… you will set an example for the children to follow…"

… a s qua di s di… and so it is good

I am aware of the waning of Grandmother Moon as I stand in ceremony on this day (for emotion is strong and rising within me). Father Sky is dark and black at first look, and my Star Relatives appear one by one, as I continue to gaze into my Father's eyes.

I hear the sound of Ocean as I stand in the silence of this morning, but not like waves crashing against a shore, more like being deep within the Ocean …

… and it is the Dolphins who come to me now…

"… breathe… and draw in your breath with intention… call upon whatever healing it is you require… and direct the healing that you desire… with each breath you take…,

… breathe out then… whatever negativity has caused your dis-ease, illness, or unrest… and continue this until you feel relief… and then practice this daily to maintain good health…,

… use this ***medicine*** in any way you need it… and with all aspects of your being (spiritual, mental, physical, or emotional) as well… to bring about good health throughout your entire being…,

… and remember (too)… that you can use this ***medicine*** to shift the consciousness of the world… by breathing in pure and unconditional love from the High Place… and breathing out any and all negativity that would contaminate that purity and grace…"

… a s qua di s di… and so it is good

The prairie is very dark and quiet as I set ceremony on this day. I sit in the center of the Grandfathers Prayer Circle (of stones), for I am in need of their compassionate wisdom. I sit in stillness as I prepare the sacred smoke, and I sing the prayer songs for all people silently within… as the **Grandfathers** beginning to stir…

… I hear their voices now… like an ancient whisper… they offer me their greetings… and I feel the air around me warm now, too… as the Grandfathers begin to sing… and it is an old chant that comes up in my ears… and I sit oh so quiet and still… for the Grandfathers are preparing to speak…

"… you have come looking for our wisdom on this day, Grandchild… but it is the pure and simple connection to your Mother (the Earth) that your spirit seeks… for you have been moved off your center recently… and it is simply grounding that you need at this time…,

… that is why you have found your way here to the place where we sit on this day… for here among the Elder Stones… you can settle down and find your center again…

… so we will sing the **old songs** for you now, Grandchild… and you will sit here among your stone relatives while we do… and you will feel yourself reconnect to your Mother (the Earth) then, Grandchild… as you rest your mind from the details of life…,

… think of family and friends now, Grandchild… for it is the time you spend with the ones you love… that you need most… (and your spirit knows this all too well)…,

… so find time to walk upon the Earth, (all) Grandchildren… and to sit with the Elder Stones… for it is essential that you find your center and keep yourselves grounded (especially now, in these times)… and remember, too… that it is equally important (now, in these times)… that you make time to spend with your family and friends…,

… for you need more than being grounded and centered now, Grandchildren…
you need the support and compassion… the trust and connection of being
unconditionally loved… and in order to receive that unconditional love…
you must give it as well…"

… a s qua di s di… and so it is good

I saw the *White Owl* as I drove in last night. She caught my eye just as I
came around a bend in the road, and as she flew off into the darkness,
she spoke our message for today…

… so I sat in ceremony last night, as I was told by my friend White Owl…
"the prairie will be too cold and foggy in the morning"…

… and as I stepped out this morning… I saw the fog that White Owl had
spoken of… heavy thick frozen fog covered the prairie… and I could not
see even two steps in front of me…

"… expand your vision now, two-legged… widen your horizons… and look
beyond that which is right there before your eyes… for there is so much
more to see and experience…,

… expand your minds now, two-legged… and keep your minds open to
embrace all others… then look with eyes that seek adventure… and break
out of your old comfortable habits and mundane patterns…,

… live this year by experiencing life… in every way you can… for your quest
to change and transform… to heal and awaken… begins with a commit-
ment to step out of the old and into the new… and now is the time for you…"

… a s qua di s di… and so it is good

FEBRUARY
2011

I set ceremony inside on this day, for it is too cold to be outside. I set ceremony wrapped in my blanket and breathe in the smoke from my ceremony herbs, as it rises slowly before me… and Grandfather Wind whistles just outside.

I sing the prayer songs for all people now, and the energy in the room expands higher and higher. I hear the voices of the Old Ones now too, as they struggle to be heard over the whistling of Grandfather Wind…

"… it is a good time to look in on that which you keep deep within, (all) two-legged… for emotion that is pushed down inside can become toxic if left for too long… emotional cleansing is very challenging… but it can also brings about the most profound healing…,

… take some time and go within… go with the intention of clearing out old emotions… look in on that which causes negative action and reaction… and go with the intention of understanding yourself more completely…,

… too much truth is hidden deep within you, (all) two-legged… buried beneath those old and un-serving emotions… it is time now to release that which you carry around unnecessarily… and make room for that which is **truth**… as well as for that which is fresh and clear and new and valuable…,

… and then… just as this deeply cold air moves out… and the warm air and light return… so too, will you experience the warmth and light rise up within you again…"

… a s qua di s di… and so it is good

Grandfather Wind moved out early last evening, giving us a much appreciated break from the "wind-chill factor".

I step outside for just a moment on this morning, and then set ceremony inside again. As the sacred smoke fills the room I feel the familiar and comforting heartbeat of our Mother the Earth rise up… and she begins to speak…

"… all people and all beings are in great need of nurturing at this time… and many of you (two-legged) do not know what this means… for it has been too long since caring for one's own-**Self**… has been considered a proper and acceptable practice…,

… but you must recognize now, all people… that in order to understand the needs of others… one must understand their own needs first… and in order to truly nurture one another… each must become acquainted with the practice of nurturing one's own-**Self**…,

… the message (now) is to get past the idea… that just because your body (your life) is functioning… that this is all there is (all that is required, all one can do)… for to simply function is the very least of what you (your body, your life) can achieve…,

… but this is not to say that one should over-indulge and over-extend oneself in order to do more… to the contrary… the message is to nurture and care for your-Self in every way… that is mentally and emotionally, spiritually, and especially physically…,

… this means finding and maintaining balance in every way… and to truly "get back in touch" with your own (and whole) being… know your body… know your limits… listen to what your body is telling you… and then follow those instructions…,

… this is also true for knowing the importance of kindness, caring, comforting, and nurturing… for once you truly "get in touch" with your own being… you will understand how essential caring for one's self is to each and every human life…,

… and once you begin to live your life in this way… you will naturally move from merely functioning… to living your life fully… to being at your maximum… in a way that replenishes you daily… rather than depleting you moment by moment…,

… and you will have more compassion for one another… and more tolerance and patience, too… and unconditional love will be something known and felt by all (for all)… rather than something one would only dare to dream of…"

… a s qua di s di… and so it is good

The words that came to me as I woke on this day, are… growth, health, the path you walk, and step into the light…

… words that may seem to be simple enough… and almost self-explanatory at first… but when given just the small amount of time that it took me to prepare for ceremony… stirred around within me… poking and whispering… until they developed into many thoughts and questions… thoughts and questions that I could not push away…

… and so… as I sit in ceremony on this day… silently singing the prayer songs for all people… I include these questions… for all people as well as for myself… and as I quietly move into stillness… I ask for clarity and understanding in regard to these words…

… and then… in the deep and sacred stillness of a very deep and powerful ceremony… I was given glimpses and fragments of knowings and understandings… pieces to my puzzle of life… pieces I have been diligently searching for… throughout the *awakened* portion of my Earth Walk…

… and I know that my answers are personal to me… just as your answers will be personal to you… and so the message is not to share with you my answers… but to invite you to take this journey…

… so take the time… when it is right for you… to go in search of that which dwells deep within… and seek to know the words that are meant to stir around within you… the words that are simple enough at first… but then begin to provoke deep thought and contemplation…

… and follow the path as it is shown to you then… and keep yourself steady on this path… for your answers and knowings… and your own understandings… and all of the pieces to your puzzle… are waiting for you to seek them out…

… and I can only tell you now… that my own experience has been one of great expansion… and that one must be in the process of expanding… to truly appreciate the tiny glimpses and fragments of what you will discover… once you embark upon this journey…

… for this is not a journey that begins and ends… like a ride at an amusement park… no, this is a journey that began so long ago… and one that will go on and on… until… well… who knows… for it is like day turning to night… or a song, or a book…

… because even though it may seem that you are beginning at the beginning… you know that no matter where it starts (the day, the song, the book)… there was something that came before… and there will most certainly be something that comes after…

… a s qua di s di… and so it is good

The extreme cold seems to have passed… and I feel like I am emerging from a cave (in oh so many ways)… there seems to be darkness behind me… heavy and un-serving darkness… nothing like evil or such… but like there was something I needed to let go of… and it was time to release that something…

… or maybe like scraping off a scab… for that which I have let go now… had served me at one time… it had served me for a long time… covering me, protecting me… allowing me to grow and mend and heal and renew…

… and now its job is done… its purpose has been served… and the scab must fall away… to reveal that which is clean and fresh and strong and new… yes, this is how I feel… and I am somewhat surprised… for I feel a bit apprehensive… but I am ready…

… for I took advantage of the extreme cold that pushed me inside for the last several days… and I spent some time in solitude… contemplating my life… and things that cannot be addressed in and around the detains of everyday life…

… and so (in oh so many ways) I really am walking out of a cave… and I stand with my arms outstretched now… and with my face turned up to my Creator… I sing out the gratitude song… loud and clear and strong… and I speak out loud to my Creator… *"I am ready now… and I am open to receive all the good that you have to give me… and thank you for my life"*…

"... and so you have call forth the powers of the Universe... and you have increased your ability to draw to you all that you desire... but you must remain open to receive... and stay strong and courageous, too...,

... for that which you have called out for... brings change... and you must understand that change is *c h a n g e*... and in order to receive a *new*... you must let go of an *old*... and though this can be scary and uncomfortable and even sad and difficult... it is the path that is before you...,

... and just beyond the place where you begin this walk... you will step into the flow... and there, within that flow... you must open to receive... for that which you have set in motion... is waiting there for you..."

... a s qua di s di... and so it is good

I stand at my Altar on this morning, looking at the blanket of snow that covers the prairie. It is so perfect and pristine; it reminds me of a freshly frosted cake you see at the bakery. The tracks of my footsteps stand out so clearly that I appear to be one solitary being... but I know that I am many.

I set ceremony here on this day, and I breathe in the sacred smoke as I sing the gratitude song. I feel the presence of many from the Spirit World as I call to the Elders... and to the Grandmothers and Grandfathers... and the Holy People and Shamans...

... I call them all now... and ask for them to gather here... and join our ceremony for today...,

"... what is your village, children... where is your community... do you draw together with those who walk the same path as you... or do you believe that you must walk your path alone...,

... there is much that you must do and experience personally and in quiet solitude... but be aware, too... that many walk the same path as you... and as you each share and contribute your own awakenings and experiences... all will gain and grow and expand... in fact even those who do not walk *"the path"* will benefit as well...,

… seek one another now… and be open to all that is offered through these encounters and relationships… discern that which resonates with you… and honor the rest by accepting it as another's truth…,

… move into this with the intention of sharing and learning and growing and receiving… rather than with the idea that you know it all and are the designated teacher… offer what you have been shown (through your own experiences)… and take time to contemplate that which another has to share…,

… for though you may feel that you are one solitary being… you are in fact **many**… because each encounter and experience… and every connection and relationship to and with one another… has influenced your growth and expansion… and has assisted in making you who you are…"

… a s qua di s di… and so it is good

I wake on this day with an overwhelming certainty that life is about choice, and I consider this as I gather my sacred bundle and prepare for ceremony…

… "we can certainly choose to stress and fret over every detail of our existence… or we can choose to trust in a natural flow of life… we can choose to be happy… choose to accept the challenges we are met with… choose to attract more good than bad… and choose to see each and every experience as part of the excitement and joy of living… no matter what" …

I walk past the one "Lone Pine" at the bottom of the steps, and I pause, for he is whispering to me (with the assistance of Grandfather Wind). And so I set ceremony here, close to the barn and protected from the elements…

"… time has the power to transform anything… and through time you will come to understand this more completely… you already know how effective time is in helping you to remember joy, when sadness has overcome you… and in the healing of broken hearts… and in restoring hope, when hope has been lost…,

… but consider your partnership with time for a moment… and if you were to combine the power of time with your directed intention… what you could accomplish… for time can (and will) transform anything (everything)… but left unattended… the transformation could be to a negative (weakening, lessening)… rather than to a positive (strengthening, healing, making better)…,

… and the air is filled with love and happiness now… and with the positive energy for creating something new and good… and you can choose to work **with** time now… as partners who create… and you will **need** time now, as well… time to plan and to prepare… time to consider each and every detail… time to adjust your mind so you can move with and accept that which you have set in motion… and most of all… time to actually choose… to consider every option… and to really make a choice…"

… a s qua di s di… and so it is good

Grandfather Wind whispers to me as I prepare for ceremony. I sit in stillness honoring Grandfather Wind and the wisdom he has come to share with us on this day…

"… it is natural to feel insecure and unsteady during times of conscious change… and when all that surrounds you… changes radically and in ways that are beyond your control… well, even the ground you walk upon (the foundation of your life and being) can seem even less solid and steady…,

… and this is one explanation to why it is so difficult to manage change (of any kind, in any way)… for that which is out of your control… stirs fear within… and you naturally avoid that which makes you feel unstable and insecure… this is simply basic human nature…,

… but do not dwell on these facts, children… but consider all of the changes you have consciously made throughout your lives… as well as all of the changes that have just happened around you… and see that you have survived and endured through them all…,

… and that, dear children… is your own strength and fortitude… that is your own faith and trust… that is your own will and **Warrior Spirit**… that is you… bracing yourself against whatever seeks to challenge you… and finding a way to prevail…,

… and I am here to tell you… that all of your victories are deserved victories… and each of these are measured by the size and shape and degree of the obstacles that you have overcome (conquered)… and that you are each fine and strong **Warriors** (fine and strong **Warriors of life**)…,

… and I assure you each… that for whatever is challenging you now… you are supported and protected… from here above (in the spirit world)… as well as by those who are there in your physical world… and know this, dear children… as your solid foundation… and use this knowing as the solid ground you need to walk upon…

… and know this too, children… that it would serve you well… to secure a solid foundation in many areas of your lives… rather than to build upon just a single foundation… for as you move through (and conquer) each challenge and change… you will need to stand more solid and strong… you will need your ground to be more stable…,

… and as you secure each foundation around you (and within your life)… you create (as well as embrace and accept)… all of (more of) the support that is there to assist you…"

… a s qua di s di… and so it is good

Last night I drove home during the strongest part of a storm. The winds were estimated at 45 to 50 miles per hour, and I could feel them as they pushed against my car. The blowing snow was so heavy and thick that I could not see the road (at all).

It was a slow and stressful (white-knuckle) drive, but when the truck I was following went straight at the place I had to turn, I felt a chill of fear run up my spine. I took a deep breath, spoke to Creator, and turned into a wall of white that was surrounded by nothing but black.

I came to a dead stop then, for this is a steep hill with drastic curves and a huge drop off. No cell service and no one on the road… hum… I spoke to Creator again…

… and then I saw her… Raven… somewhere in that heavy wall of blowing snow, I thought I saw the black wings of Raven. I began to move again… ever so slowly… and I followed that black bird right down the center of that steep and curving road… I could not see her clearly… but I could feel her… *"thank you Raven for guiding me safely home"*…

… Raven is here now… waiting for me to begin ceremony… and she sings with me the prayer songs for all people… and she follows me into the stillness… and again she becomes my guide… and she offers us a message for today…

"… to many I create a feeling of uncertainty… I bring up unsettling feelings from deep within… and this makes the two-legged turn away and try to hide… but I only come when I am called… and so if you see me… know that some part of you called out for my assistance…,

… and I am not evil… nor do I bring about dark and wicked happenings… but I do know the darkness very well… for going into the darkness to retrieve the answers you seek… is your greatest request of me… and it is your own fear and distorted concept of light and dark that creates the illusion of wicked and evil…,

… life is an incredible experience… which can be scary at times… and darkness is nothing to fear… but rather something to be explored… for darkness is simply that which is unknown… and if you refuse to explore it… you will never know what gifts lie within…,

… but once you turn to face it… once you step into it… your light reveals it… the dark becomes light… and you become more… for all that you seek to know and be… waits for you within the dark…,

… and your fear becomes less… and your courage returns… as you seek out the darkness… and discover who you are…"

… a s qua di s di… and so it is good

Iwake from a faraway place on this cold morning. I was someplace warm, and it was a time long ago. I was with the Old Woman there, and we were in her garden…

"… big changes are happening for you now, young ones… as a result of the personal work you have done throughout your life… this is called growth in my world, young ones… and though it can scare you… and even intimidate you… the realization that you have grown and expanded… should be exciting and exhilarating…,

… see here… sit with me in my garden… and watch as I tend to these plants… see, you are like these plants… see that one there… off in the corner and away from the light… it is not as full and strong as this one who stands where the light shines all day long…,

… and this one here is surrounded by many others… they support and protect one another… they share the light and the water, the nourishment of the soil… while that one in the corner there, is left to be on its own… and I did not plant that one over there… it just shot up out of the ground on its own…,

… and see these over here… they stand where the water leaks out of my trough… and I did not plat them here… they just migrated over here to drink up the water that is so plentiful… but they are growing out of control now… and though there growth is faster and fuller than the others… it is not appropriate… it is not necessarily better… so I must cut them back and thin them out… I must take away some parts of them… in order to bring about their best growth… and to make them strong and full and vibrant…,

… today we will move this one from the shadowy corner, over here… and we will be very careful as we release it from the soil where it has been… and we will be very careful to bring some of that soil with us as we move it… we will prepare this new place just right… and we will tend to this one very closely… and we will see if it is willing to accept the new place we have planted it…,

… for change is drastic… it can shock the system… and it will take some time for this plant to adjust… and this is true for us humans, too… and so you will have to adjust to the changes that you are experiencing now…,

… but if you tend to yourselves… nourish yourselves… and give yourselves attention… and if you are willing to accept the new place where you stand now… you will grow and flourish and become strong and sturdy and whole… just like the plants in my garden…"

… a s qua di s di… and so it is good

I smell the sacred smoke of ceremony as I wake on this day, and I do not have to travel far to find the Old One who has come. It is zero degrees outside today, and so I set ceremony in the open space of my living room.

I sit wrapped in my blanket on the cold, bare floor, slowly rocking forward and back as I sing the prayer songs for all people… while the Old One sings his healing chant in the background…

… and I am saturated in the purity created by his song… and I feel myself move into stillness… as the Old One begins to speak…

"… the greatest work that you do, dear children… is the work to overcome inner conflict… for it is by healing all that has been hidden deep within… that you are truly healed without…,

… and you have been looking for the "quick fix" for so long… and you seem to find what you are seeking at the time… and these offer some relief for a short time… but it is only when you go deep within… and take the time to really see what is there… and face the fear… and accept the truth… that you can truly heal…,

… and so it comes again… to a choice for you to make… but first you must see that it is a choice… and that you are the one who must make this choice… and so I ask you now…

… do you want to continue searching for the "quick fix"… and spend all of your time and energy doing and redoing this… or are you ready for the true and real healing… so that you can get on with that which you came to do…"

… a s qua di s di… and so it is good

Father Sky is clear on this morning. My Star Relatives are close and embracing. I walk quickly to my ceremony space, and in the quiet moments that follow, I hear their song…

"… children… we see you… and we see all that is around you as well… but our view has no limits… no boundaries, no obstacles… and **you** must strive (at all times) to see past (above and beyond) many limits, boundaries, and obstacles…,

… so look to us now… and look to us often… for we can help you to find the clarity you seek… we can help you see the full picture… and we can show you what you are missing (when you know that you are missing something)…,

… and at this time… we see prosperity and abundance before you each… and you will meet with this opportunity… your hard work will come to fruition… sometime between your Spring and Summer…,

… and you must be diligent in your work (whatever that particular work may be)… and you must be receptive to all that you are creating (or desire to create)… and you must begin now… healing the part of you that does not believe that you deserve (or could ever create) prosperity and abundance…,

… for there is prosperity and abundance around you at all times… and there is more than enough for each of you… and if you will open yourselves to receive it… you could stop worrying about it… and get on with that which is really important… "

… a s qua di s di… and so it is good

The prairie is calm and still as I walk out on this morning, and warm enough to stay out for a while. I **walk** ceremony on this day, and I sing the gratitude song as I go.

I stand at my Altar now, looking out across the moon-lit prairie, appreciating the beauty and grandeur of this land. I feel peace within my entire being and gratitude for my life (for all life and for all people).

I sing the prayer songs for all people now, and I feel a **deeper stronger peace** flow through me… **a peace** that is accompanied by a sense of relief… **a** *peace* that is filled with tears of joy and hope… a peace that comes with a long awaited exhale… a peace that is enriched by the knowing that all is right and good…

"… step back for a moment, children… and evaluate your present situation… feel gratitude for that which you have… and feel gratitude for that which you have never had to endure…,

… send love now, children… with sincerity and from your heart… to all people… for all people… send love that offers strength and support, compassion and acceptance…,

… for all people (including you and yours)… are fighting a battle of some kind… and each of these are personal and significant… and these are not to be measured or judged by any *one*… but to be honored and respected by *all*…,

… believe in the power of your good thoughts and prayers, children… and of the love and compassion that you send out simply by feeling it within your own being… and know this too, dear children… each time any one finds peace within… it is a gift that is received by *all*…"

… a s qua di s di… and so it is good

Father Sun wakes me on this day; it seems my old tired body needed to sleep a while longer than usual. The prairie is beautiful with the soft light of dawn illuminating every bit of it. I walk out and stand in the center of the path that leads to where the Buffalo are grazing, and they begin to run as I turn to greet and welcome each direction.

It is a beautiful sight. Buffalo are so graceful when they run. I feel their energy wafting across the prairie as Grandfather Wind blows in to say good morning. I turn to offer him my greeting in return… and I hear him whisper… "Listen now, as my Winds tell you what you came to know on this day" …

"… close your eyes now, child… and release the tension that restricts your perfect flow… rest your mind from all its worry… and just breathe in the freshness of this day…,

… allow the graceful movement of the Buffalo to permeate your entire being… and *feel* what it is they have come to share with you… for you cannot receive and comprehend their gift fully through words alone…,

… with each breath out, release your thoughts… and with each breath in, simply feel what you are to receive on this day… and as you stand there… with Father Sun slowly rising behind you… feel the energy and renewal of your soul and spirit…,

… and when you open your eyes… look again at the prairie around you… and see that all you have been seeking… is closer than you think… see all the resources that are right here… within and around you…

… and even though you must look ahead to the future… do not look to far away… for that which you seek… is already here… present and available…"

… a s qua di s di… and so it is good

The notion that great changes are upon us has been occupying my mind for several days, and I walk out on this day as if I am walking in on someone's private conversation. I stop for a moment with the intention of turning around, but my body will not move… and then I hear the voices of Grandmother Moon and Grandfather Wind call me to join in their council.

"… it is positive verses negative that has called us to council on this day, Swan… and how two-legged manifest their life experience… by thinking and speaking with either positive or negative attitudes… for we act as guardians of your physical world… and our task at hand is to assist you (all)… to shift from negative thinking and speaking… to positive thinking and speaking…,

… so we come on this day to remind you… that your thoughts and words create your reality… and this is true for each individual… as well as for that which has become a collective consciousness… that all or many lend their thoughts and words to…,

… so hear this, children… and mind your thoughts and words… for all and any negative thoughts and words you think and say… and every negative feeling that you feel... will be reflected in the happenings that surround you... just as all and any positive thoughts and words you think and say... and every positive feeling that you feel... will be reflected in the experiences of your life...,

... and as each *one* shifts from concentrating on the negative to the positive... their life experience will reflect this... and whatever each *one* creates for themselves... will affect those around them... and this is big, Swan... for it is time for all to take responsibility for the happenings of their own lives... and to participate in bringing goodness into the lives of others... for now and for the future..."

... a s qua di s di... and so it is good

I feel as if I am spinning as I wake on this day, not spinning that makes you dizzy, but rather spinning that takes you higher. It is as if I am connected to the ***upward spinning spiral***, and my body is trying to catch up with my spirit, while my heart and my mind are working to even make a connection at all.

I am not in love with this feeling, but I know that it perfectly describes the way I have been feeling lately...

... not every minute of every day... but in those quiet times just after you wake... and in the silent space between a certain moment or breath... I feel this sense of disarray and disconnection... and then I pull myself together quickly and ground myself... I find my balance and locate my center... and then make it my intention to look in on this... and I am told now... that today is the day to do just that...

"... everything is moving faster now, Swan... not just for you, but for all people... and during times of accelerated growth and change... it is natural to feel unstable and out of balance... disconnected or out of sync...,

... and it is good that you can pull yourself together quickly... and that you know how to find your center... that you can ground yourself quickly... and that you know how to maintain balance... yes, this is good and it will get you through the day...,

… but there is something unsettled deep within you, Swan… which is why you are not just traveling freely… upon the upward moving current of energy… upon that upward *spinning spiral*… which is flowing and available to and for all people at this time… some place within you, Swan… there is resistance… and wherever there is resistance… there is an unresolved issue that must be tended to…,

… and this is true for many at this time, Swan… and the sense of being unsettled and out of sync that many are feeling now… is beginning to collect and become an energy all its own… and these two energies are like magnets that push against one another… making it even more difficult to connect with the *upward spinning spiral*… and to take advantage of the opportunity for accelerated growth and change…,

… now, more than ever… it is essential for all people to look in on what may be unsettled deep within… it is time to resolve any issues that come into your view or sense of knowing… so that you can disconnect from the lower, more negative energy… and connect with the energy that is drawing you upward…,

… and once you do… your entire being will align with the perfection of the High Place… and the positive energy will strengthen and become more accessible to all… and the negative energy will dissipate and dissolve… and you will be free to travel forward, and upward with ease and grace…"

… a s qua di s di… and so it is good

It is the warm and compassionate energy of Grandmother Moon that wakes me on this day. She is there in the West as I walk out, sitting just above the place where the Buffalo stand… and I stand face to face with her as I sing the prayers songs for all people.

I feel great emotion welling up within me as I continue with my morning ceremony, and the urge to dance the old traditional dance of life brings me to my feet. I begin to step in rhythm with the sound that is in my ears now… and this song I dance to, is magnificent…

… it began softly… with the sound of my own heart beating… and then our Mother the Earth joined in… and then the distinct and beautiful heartbeat of Grandmother Moon blended in… then the buffalo… and all of the animal life… and then… as if a it were a choir coming up from out of everywhere… the collective heartbeats of all people… and the song became full… and the energy became strong…

… and so I dance the old traditional *dance of life*… for all people and for all life… and I hear the song of Grandmother Moon so clearly as I dance… and within her song is our message for today…

"… it is your emotions that you must tend to now, dear children… for it is your emotions that empower your thoughts… and much of what you feel, and how you react to any situation or event in your life… is merely an automatic response… driven by emotions that were developed from the time you were born into the physical…,

… and these emotions can be a good thing… and these emotions can also create challenges and consequences for you…,

… it is coming on Spring for you now… and there is great energy for *creating* available to you in the Spring… and however it is that you make your plans… first in thought… then on paper… or spoken out loud… you need emotion to give those plans life…,

… and because emotions provide the power to all of your thoughts… you must look in on how you feel and react to that which is happening in your life… and you must sort out how you think and feel about your ability to create… about your ability to make the changes you seek to make… you need to know where your emotions go automatically… when you begin to think about and plan that which you wish to change or create…,

… it is time to consider how powerful your emotions are… and to seek out the emotions that have the power to sabotage your good wishes, desires, and plans… then simply begin to *consciously* feel love and gratitude… whenever you recognize a negative emotion rise up… and soon you will notice a shift… and you will begin to change…"

… a s qua di s di… and so it is good

I t is the Grandmothers and Grandfathers who sit in council on this day, and it is my Grandmother the Moon and my Grandfather the Wind, who come to accompany me to this gathering.

There are many reasons that a council would be called, as many to celebrate the good as there are to discuss a problem or situation that has the potential to cause harm… and especially in regard to anything that may imposes real and lasting danger.

The council that I am attending on this day seems to be discussing **the great awakening of all people**… and I sit quiet and still as the Grandmothers and Grandfathers speak…

"… within each and every two-legged… there is a divine heart… a place within that holds the most sacred of their being… and in this place… each **one** will find their true purpose for being… and once **one** finds this place… they will know inner peace… and then their own world will begin to blossom and grow…,

… and it is the search for this place of inner peace… that occupies the minds of the two-legged… whether they know it or not… and drives each in a different way… and can even drive some to madness… for they know they are so close to finding their truth… and yet they are still so far away…,

… for deep within… each **one** knows… that once they find the place of their divine heart… they will truly awaken… and they will have a second chance… a new and fresh start… a renewal… a new beginning… and deep within their innermost knowing… they each know… that by finding this place… they will know fulfillment…,

… but it is not in the locating of **one's** divine truth that brings about the peace and fulfillment… it is the accepting of that truth… and the following of it… that brings about their true awakening… and there is always a choice to make at this moment… and a commitment, too… and these can be difficult decisions for many…,

… and so it is that the divine heart is located deep within… and that just as each are given the absolute knowing of it… each must set out with intention to find it… for the journey that leads each **one** to their own divine heart… provides great lessons, growth, and maturity… it is the journey itself that helps to bring about the clarity and insight… each **one** will need at the time of discovery…"

… a s qua di s di… and so it is good

It was after midnight when I arrived home last night, and so I took some time to sit with our Grandmother the Moon. She is full and bright now, and it was good just to be there with her.

I quieted my mind in the time I sat with our Grandmother the Moon, and I opened my heart to all that is good and right and waiting for me…

… and it was my heart who spoke to our dear Grandmother last night… and it is my heart who brings you this message from her today…

"… dear children… open your hearts… let all that is sad and painful out… so all that is healing and loving can pour in… for you are supported and assisted from above in everyway… and you would know this… if you would only open to receive that which is waiting to become a part of you… a part of your life experience…,

… it has been too long… this fascination you have with the sad and the painful.. with being hurt and wounded… with being a victim at every turn… for you are not… but all of what you draw to you will remain these lower energy concessions… until and unless you open your heart to release all that makes you feel this is all that you deserve… and make room for all that is waiting for you… all that is so rightfully yours…,

… for in order to shift the vibration on your Star (earth)… from the place of want and lack, sickness and despair… to the place of abundance and prosperity, health and joy… each must release the belief that **"there is nothing you can do"**… and realize that you (each, all) can do anything… everything… and that you have everything to do with the vibration that effects the whole…

… and this shift will happen quickly (instantly)… as each releases their connection to the negative… and begins to accept the gifts of the positive… and for many this will not be easy… so begin with just one issue, thought, belief, emotion… and release it from your being on every level… heart, body, and mind (especially your mind)… and then with directed intention… open to receive the positive and the good… the healing and the joy…

… and do this every day with anything that creates the sadness and the pain… with anything that connects you to the lower (victim) energy… and you will begin to rise above then… and you will feel the shift in your own vibration… as well as in the vibration around you… and this will be good… for you and for all people…"

… a s qua di s di… and so it is good

It is a voice from the High Place that I hear calling as I wake on this day, and I walk out to find Grandmother Moon waiting for me. She is round and bright, and her light pours into my crown as I stand in gratitude and begin ceremony for today.

The prairie is illuminated in her light on this morning, and it is quiet and still. I stand in silence for a time before I sing the prayer songs for all people, and I feel the love and grace of Creator move through me and out into the world…

"… stand in this light, children… and allow your highest spirit to emerge… for here in the purity of this light… your true and perfect *Self* will be revealed…,

… and as you become acquainted with the highest aspect of your *Self*… you will see and know that you travel a path that is truly yours…,

… and you will see your life journey for all that it is… for all that it has been… and for all that it has the potential to be…,

… and there will be no question within you… of where you are going or what you are meant to do… for here in this moment… you will feel it within you…,

... and you will breathe out then... and set one foot in front of the other... and continue on your path...,

... and you will feel your soul begin to smile... and your spirit will become even brighter... and you will feel yourself connect with the highest of all places...,

... and this is how you will travel... as you move along from here..."

... a s qua di s di... and so it is good

This morning smells fresh and clean, after our unexpected rain. It is still and quiet, and there is a feeling of sweetness all around me. I had intended to walk out near the Buffalo for ceremony on this day, but I am beckoned to my altar space instead... and it is my Grandmother (in spirit) who has called me here.

The fragrance of Sweet Almond Oil floods my senses and I see that Grandmother is preparing for a healing ceremony... a healing ceremony for all people...

"... come, child... you will assist me on this day... and together we will work to relieve the bitterness that has been seeping into the souls of the people... for a hard layer (a shell) has formed around the souls of many... and this healing will assist them to remove that shell... layer by layer... so to feel the power of Creator within them...,

... this sacred oil is perfect for this work, child... for it will penetrate the hard shell... slowly and thoroughly... and because it is sweet... it takes away the bitterness... allowing there trust and hope to return... and reminding each to seek out and acknowledge... the sweetness of life that is present at all times...,

... and we will take our time, child... for this work cannot be done in haste... and we must allow each **one** all the time they need... first, to accept the healing... and then, to allow it to become complete (permanent)..."

... a s qua di s di... and so it is good

The Cloud People have gathered today. I saw them last night as I drove home around midnight. They lay in ribbons across the eastern plains, and I realized they were telling me something of my life.

As I drove into their misty fog and back out into the clarity of the moon-lit night, I realized that this is how our lives can be (or have been) at times. We have moments of clarity, followed by spaces of fogginess, mystery, uncertainty, and illusion… or is it that the clarity follows the mist?…

… no matter… what is important… is that we work through the fogginess, mystery, uncertainty, and illusion… to find the truth and clarity we seek… that we pay attention and learn all we can from each experience… so that we come to live in the clarity… more than we live in the mist…

"… there are many ways to understand the message of emerging from the fog… (or walking into it)… for some will tell you that your earth-life and your physical being are the illusion… and the High Place and your spirit are the reality… it is simply all in the way you look at it…,

… but our message for you today… is about exploring all that you can from *within* the foggy, mysterious, uncertain place of illusion… until you begin to see with great clarity *within* that space… until you understand all it has to teach you… and you realize there is no foggy-mist anymore… only new adventures to embark upon and new experiences to explore…,

… and though you seek the clarity… for you are comfortable there… and you can see all there is to see within it (or so you think)… you must embrace the foggy-mist… for it is when you are there, within that foggy-mist… that you rely on your higher knowing (rather than believing that you have all of the information, simply because you can see clearly)…,

… yes, deep within the foggy-mist… is when you reach for and connect with your intuition and spirit… and call upon your Creator… and stretch beyond your normal limits…,

… it is during times like these… when you are deep within the fog… that you reach out, expand, and become more…"

… a s qua di s di… and so it is good

I sing the prayer songs for all people on this day, with the assistance of the four directions. I feel them each step into my ceremony circle as I turn to face their direction.

I feel my spirit awaken as East steps in… I feel my heart awaken as I turn to the South… I feel energy begin to pulse throughout my entire physical body as I face the West… and my mind engages with all that surrounds me as I turn to stand in the North…

… I walk to the center of my ceremony circle… and become aware of perfect balance… I feel it within me… I feel it all around me… and it is here… within the perfection and purity of this place… that I receive our message for today…

"… to stand in balance is one thing… to find balance in your life is another… and to be balanced in spirit, body, heart, and mind is yet another… but we come on this day… to awaken you to another knowing of where balance is essential…,

… as you work toward your own healing… it is important that you realize… your entire being has been affected by whatever experience, situation, trauma, or even your own actions… which have caused you to require healing…,

… it is in your memories… it has stained your heart and soul… your physical body even has a place to (and a way of) recording these traumas…,

… and so as you work to heal and release each imposition… remember to work in a balanced way… check in with each aspect of your being as you begin your healing… that is your spirit, heart, body, and your mind… and be sure that you have discovered how each has been affected by the experience, trauma, situation, or any action of your own…,

... for if you have not considered these... as you work through each healing... your balance will be off... and you will need to go back and correct these... in order to truly find and maintain perfect balance... within and without..."

... a s qua di s di... and so it is good

I can hear the Wild Cats from across the road roaring as I step out on this day. I feel a deep and tribal energy stir within. I stand with the light of Grandmother Moon pouring through my crown, and I feel her light move all the way down to my toes.

I feel a connection to and with the whole of this Star we know as Earth. I feel the peace that is in some places, and I feel the unrest that has consumed others. I begin to sing the prayer songs for all people now... and as I do... I am taken to a ceremony for peace and healing...

... and this ceremony is attended by the spirits of all who feel the need for peace and healing within them... whether it be for their own personal life and needs... or to assist in bringing about peace and healing to the whole of our world and all of its people...

... and the roaring of the Lions and Bears from across the road... provide a vibration that is perfect and necessary for the work we are doing in ceremony on this day... and as we all stand in ceremony... we use this vibration... to draw out whatever may be there within us... whatever holds us captive in our own lives... whatever keeps us each in a place of unrest... and keeps us each from truly knowing peace...

... and it is compassion that fills our beings... as we release the anger and fear that darkens our light... it is forgiveness of self and others... that relaxes our tension and softens our hearts... and the static that had once been pulsing within and around us each... begins to dissolve... as a brilliant glow of light is now emerging from within us each...

... and as the Lions and Bears end their morning song... the prairie becomes silent... and it is my own heart beating that I hear now... as well as the collective heartbeats of all people... and deep within the sound of our spirits as they sing... I feel the grace of Creator wash over our world and all people...

... and I speak out now... onto the gentle wind that blows around me... *"may we all know peace on this day"* ...

... a s qua di s di... and so it is good

Flashes of light wake me on this day, flashes of light mixed with brilliant colors that sparkle and flash. I feel the light and the colors before I see them, and I recognize the energy that is pulsing within me. It is that energy that comes when it is time to get going, to get up and get out, and to set your intentions into motion...

... and the colors are amazing as they begin to appear one by one... and the light becomes more brilliant as the energy becomes more intense...

"... and so it is time for action now, children... it is time to set the goals and make the commitments... it is time to stand up and step up... and to spend some energy on your own selves... your own healing... your own happiness... your own security...,

... for complaining about the lack of these... only brings about more lack of these... and as each one regains their own personal power... healing... happiness... and security... others begin to seek their own as well...,

... and the circle begins (then)... and the lack becomes abundance... and this is the power of you, dear children... this is the power of you..."

... a s qua di s di... and so it is good

I hear water as I wake on this day, like a stream or a brook in the deep of a secluded place, and the movement of this water calls out to a place deep within me. But I stand on the open prairie today, and I can feel that Snow is getting ready to fall… and the sound of water flowing just continues to move steady in my head…

… and I look up now… and see with great clarity… the Universal flow of energy, of life… it calls out for my own life force to connect with it… and it moves closer to me now… and tells me it is available to us all…

"… your lives are in constant motion, children… always moving… always changing… and just as with each Moonset and Sunrise… you know you are one day closer to the changing of the season… know that with each Moonset and Sunrise… you are one day closer to your goal…,

… and once you connect with the Universal-flow… you will feel as if a button has been pushed… a button that engages your own *action mechanism*… for you will begin to move and flow with great focus and determination… and then you will move steadily toward your goal…"

… a s qua di s di… and so it is good

Grandfather Wind woke me at 2:38 this morning. And when I stepped out onto the prairie, I felt the two a.m. cold as if it were poured upon me. I followed a voice that whispered from within the force of Grandfather Wind… and stood upon a path I did not know was there…

"… it is the shift in your own perspective that allows you to see this path, Swan… and the more you transform your own limitations (worries and fears) into possibilities (thoughts and beliefs)… the more you will live your own truth… and the more access you will have to the higher realms…,

… and you will walk in *oneness* with Creator then… and all that has confounded you about the physical world will become clear… and you will understand the mystery of physical life… and you will see (too) how physical life serves the greater good…,

… but you must remember, Swan… it is all about the journey… the journey to begin so pure and perfect… and to live the experience life with all of its challenges and imperfections… understanding it is your goal to find your way back to that place of purity and perfection…,

… for along the way… from one place to the other… from beginning to end… each will discover and create… and each of these discoveries and creations… will assist in the expansion of all things… even that which resides in the place of spirit…"

… a s qua di s di… and so it is good

I walk ceremony on this day. I walk in the in-between space of the Medicine People, and here in this place I find myself gazing upon the sacred *Tree of Life.* I quiet myself in every way as I stand before this sacred **Old One**, for even my thoughts can disrupt the serenity and peace this **Old One** brings forth.

I stand in silent meditation, connected to the wisdom that has been gathered for more years than anyone could ever count… and I feel the message begin to flow out… as the ***oldest of the old ones*** begins to speak…

"… use your strength now, (all) two-legged… your will and your intention… command yourself well, prosperous, intuitive, and safe… for all that you struggle with… could be gone in a heartbeat… if you would only trust in your own truth… and realize that all the power is held within you…,

… then use your positive influence… to assist others to take charge of their own will… and let the healing of all people… be the epidemic that takes hold of your world…"

… a s qua di s di… and so it is good

We walked the prairie yesterday, the Cowboy and I, we corralled the Buffalo for the day and walked the land that they walk every day. It was a beautiful morning, quiet and clear, and as I stood upon a high place there, I felt a moment of freedom…

… not freedom *from* anything… but freedom to move and create and grow and expand…

… I received lifetimes of information as I stood in that place… understandings and validations… insights and wisdoms… that lit up places within me… I never knew were there…

… and in that moment… I stood present and aware of only that moment… and all of the emotions that link me to past traumas… just fell away… and I breathed in the feeling of just that moment… and felt the feeling of freedom again…

… only this time… it *was* freedom from something… freedom from all that I had held so tightly to… hurts and betrayals… meanness's and cruelties… those which were imposed upon me… as well as those that I myself had imposed upon another…

… and I felt myself become lighter, then… and the air I breathed became sweet…

… and it is my spirit who stands (now)… upon that same ground… in the dark of this cold and silent morning… and the Buffalo roam all around me… and I can feel their warmth from where I sit… and I hear their message call out… from within the deep and quiet stillness of my morning ceremony…

"… know this, two-legged… that you can choose to fill yourself with love and light and gratitude and compassion… and as you do… you will find peace and joy… and the air you breathe will become sweet…,

… and we know this is your greatest struggle… for it requires trust and courage to step up higher… to live in the present moment… and disconnect from the negativities of your past… for your past made you who you are… and how can you be you… without remembering and honoring your past…,

… but this is where trust is essential, dear two-legged… for you will not forget who you are… you will simply be free to become more… as you will be guided by your spirit then… rather than by hurts and pains and grudges and excuses…,

… so call to us now, dear two-legged… and trust in our strength… let us offer you the added courage you require… to forgive and let be… to choose to step into a higher place… where the heaviness of your past can fall away… so you can begin the next part of your journey… ”

… a s qua di s di… and so it is good

MARCH
2011

I hear the Lions roaring as I walk out on this day, and I stop for a while to pick up their message. I hear the Coyotes answer back to the Lions, and then they all sing out a strange sort of call… seven short growls by the Lions… followed by seven short yaps from the Coyotes.

I am captivated by this sacred morning **chant** of the Wild Beings… and I feel myself snap into alignment as I began our morning ceremony today…

"… alignment is part of the message we bring to you on this day, two-legged… and communication is another… but it is the maturity that occurs within you… when you draw your whole being together as one… that is the greatest lesson we share on this day…,

… it is essential that you walk in alignment… *spirit, heart, body, and mind*… all working together as one… and you may think this is how you live already… (for how could you survive if these were not working together)… but look in on this, two-legged… and you may find… that these four aspects of your being… are not always in alignment (or even connected)… and further, may not even be communicating with one another…,

… are there times when you feel a certain way, but think another… and then go on to act in even a different way from these… or is it that you must choose which one to follow… your mind or your heart… and where is your spirit in all of this, two-legged…,

… make it a daily practice… to consciously connect and align your spirit, heart, body, and mind… feel these come together within you… and then allow yourself to stay in this alignment as long as you can… before going on with your day…,

… and once you feel confident that your alignment is secure… look in on how your spirit, heart, body, and mind communicate with one another… and then notice… how much your life changes… for the better…"

… a s qua di s di… and so it is good

Father Sky is close on this day. I feel like I can actually touch the Star People. I see generation after generation of my Star Relatives moving forward, as I sit looking into the face of Father Sky.

I sit within the circle of Grandfather Stones now, still gazing up at my Star Relatives, and wishing I were there (home with my Star Family).

… an Old Grandfather speaks to me now… as I turn my attention back to the ceremony I am making for today… and as I listen to this Old One speak about the power of Turquoise… I see a small nugget of Turquoise on the ground right where I sit…

"… and your struggle to awaken your spirit in the physical, goes on… and I have come to tell you… this is a life long task… and you feel as though you have found your way back to the beginning… that you are somehow beginning again… and this is just the way life is… but know this, child… with each new beginning… you become more… you see more… you feel more… you know more… you do more… *you are more*…,

… it is like the Stars that come in from behind… those that you have never seen before… who fill in the spaces behind and in-between… that bring the Sky close to you… and make the darkness light… and you believe that the Sky has moved closer to you… but I ask you to consider this… that you have moved higher and closer to the Sky…,

… and this is a difficult time of transition for you, child… which is why your *old friend* has come to be with you now… you know this *old friend* as the Turquoise Star who watches and protects… and you know this *old friend* as the Turquoise Stone that you hold in you hand…,

… Turquoise began in the High Place (as spirit, as light)… pure and perfect and part of Creator… Turquoise chose to become physical and live upon the Earth… and so was planted deep within the soil… which is how Turquoise brought Earth and Sky together… and why Turquoise carries the knowing of both Earth and Sky… of Body and Spirit… and now Turquoise comes to share this knowing with you…,

… so sit with your ***old friend*** a while, child… and trust that you are moving in the right direction… take some time to look around… and see that when everything looks different… it is because you have grown and expanded… because you have reached a higher place… and because you actually see from a higher perspective…,

… and remember, too… all those generations of Star Beings that you can see now… have always been there… just as your spirit has always been a part of you… and the more you awaken, acknowledge, and expand your spirit within you… the more whole you become… for when your spirit awakens… it fills in the places that you thought were empty… and this is when you realize… you have always been whole…"

… a s qua di s di… and so it is good

I heard the Wolves howling last night, it was just before midnight. I looked out across the prairie hoping to see the Wolves, and heard the Coyotes yapping as well. I stood silent for a while, listening to the Big Dogs sing and gazing up at Father Sky.

Father Sky looked like water to me… dark and black and deep and mysterious… and the Stars looked like glistening reflections of light… and the whole of the Sky Place seemed to be moving… like water in a pool… and the Wolves told me to listen to this teaching… and then I heard the Coyotes say…

"… close your eyes and feel… for your eyes can trick you… and if it is the fluid feeling of emotion that stirs within you… then dive into the Sky… and feel those emotions that beg for your attention…,

… do not think… and do not look… but only feel… and feel as you have never felt before… feel without hesitation… without fear… and without concern of consequence… for there is no consequence when you swim in the mysterious waters of the Sky Place… only healing… there is only healing there…"

… and I felt like Otter… as I swan in the mystical pool of the High Place… I felt the release of many emotions that had been swimming around within me… and I felt joy again… the kind of joy I thought could only belong to a child… and then the Coyotes called out to me again… just before they ran off to a place far away…

"… you are all children… and you are all worthy of the simple and unspoiled joy of just **Being**… joy, without fear and without worry… joy, without pain and without obligation…,

… and your soul needs to remember this kind of joy… and your spirit needs to play with this kind of freedom… so come out now… come out and play for a time… in the joyful mystical waters of this place that is so pure and perfect…,

… refresh your spirit… and nourish your soul… become joyful again… and the world around you will respond in a joyful way…"

a s qua di s di… and so it is good

I could feel the sacredness of this day the moment I woke, for it was the song of my Owl relatives who sang me awake. I sat for a moment when I heard them singing, for they seemed to be singing the old traditional song that calls the village to sweat.

I moved swiftly as I gathered my ceremony bundle, and when I stepped out into the morning, I saw that the Cloud People had come, too. They were just finishing their task of covering the prairie and creating the sacred lodge that I am to sit within on this day…

… and so I spoke out loud… the sacred prayer we say when entering the sweat…

… (gu s di i da da dv hni)… for all my relations…

… and the sweat began… and all became sacred… and I found myself deep within it… as the Owls continued to sing the sacred songs… and I moved deeper and deeper into the blackness of the sweat… and in an instant… the entire Universe surrounded me…

… and I felt the heat from the sacred stones… and I heard them sizzle as the water poured upon them… and when the steam rose up… I felt myself become spirit…

"… as you step into the tiny lodge… you are small, too… and you feel your humanness completely… as the heat surrounds you… for you are immersed in the heat… and you are held within the lodge…,

… but as the sacred water awakens the **spirit of the Grandfathers** (the stones)… and they move about within the lodge… they fill the space… and they call your spirit out… and once your own spirit emerges… you find that you are not small anymore… and that you are not held within that tiny lodge… but you are infinite, endless… and you are free and moving within the whole of the Universe…,

… and the steam pushes its way into your physical body… and it pushes out all toxins and impurities… all hurts and wounds and grudges and regrets… and the heat transmutes each of theses on contact… and as your spirit dances free and joyful in the place of its true home… your body is cleansed and purified…,

… and the door opens then… and you are instantly reunited - body and spirit… and as you breathe in the fresh clean air… you accept the healing of this sweat… and you know the prayers you wish to speak… and you speak them out into the night…,

… and you offer your gratitude to all who came… and to the Old Ones you met along the way… to all who came before you… and to the whole of the Universe, too… for you know now… that it is by their lives and the grace of God… that you are here…"

… a s qua di s di… and so it is good

I pull my blanket around me tight as I walk the prairie on this day, for though it is still and quiet, it is very cold. It is the time of the New Moon as some would say, and yet I feel my **Grandmother's presence** close and strong as I walk.

I see the Old Man there in the darkness, he is standing in the center of the path that leads to where to the Buffalo stand. I nod to him as I begin walking his way, and we seem to be walking above the physical plain. The Old Man tells me there is a fork up ahead on this road we walk… a place where the road splits and we must choose which way to go… but I know this road, and I know that it does not split…

… and so it is that I am accompanied by both a Grandmother and a Grandfather on this day… and they have come to tell me something of great importance… so I listen attentively to what they have to say… and I hear the teachings of the **old ways** sing out in the words they speak…

"… yes, there are choices to be made now… and it will take your full attention to come to a decision about these… and you must be clear and focused with your intention… as you reach to find the assistance you need… and you must do more than put all of your attention into the choices ahead… you must become fully attentive to them as well…,

… and you must do more than make sure you are watching and listening with great thought and care… to find the insight and guidance you need… you must also realize that choices made now… must be made with affection and respect… for these choices are the kind that will have a lasting effect on the quality of your life… as well as on the lives of others…,

… and so as you step up a little bit higher… and see from this expanded perspective… be sure to acknowledge that you must set a course for yourself soon… and that you must lay out your plans with great detail… and you must commit to follow through with your plan… for the benefits and rewards of that which you begin now… will be like a ripple in still water… for they will go on and on and on…"

… a s qua di s di… and so it is good

I set ceremony at my altar on this day. I walk in and around the stone prayer circles as I sing the prayer songs for all people, and I hear the Old Woman singing from inside the Tee Pee circle. I stop to honor her song…

"… come in, child… sit with me now… and listen closely… for you must be sure to hear… exactly what I have come to say…,

… as the spirits of the people begin to awaken and expand… they will need to pay more attention to the health of their physical bodies…,

… for as the spirit rises and reaches the higher vibrations… their physical beings must be able to lift and rise to meet this vibration…,

… and it is as simple as it has always been, child… and it is as difficult as it has always been, too…,

… for all that is required to keep the physical body in good and healthy condition… is to feed it properly…. (whatever that is for each individual)… give it the proper amount of work, play, and rest… (also according to each individual)… and to keep the spirit nourished and clean…,

… and this may sound simple and easy enough… but it will be a challenge for most…,

… but it is a challenge that each must consider and choose as they will… *by their own will…,*

… for you are well on the way to creating the future of your Star (your planet Earth)… and it will take all of you to do this… and your physical bodies must be strong and healthy and ready to complete this task…"

… a s qua di s di… and so it is good

My mind has been filled with details for the past few days, and I can feel that old familiar pressure begin to build within me…

… when we take on so many projects (over and above our normal daily obligations)… that we have no time to think, or sit, or breathe… it seems to be at this particularly fragile time… that something big happens… and our entire house of cards begins to fall… (or more likely, our body and our health take the hit).

I walk out onto the prairie… and I breathe in the fresh clean air… I stand for a moment… and just *be* in the quiet stillness here… but I feel those details begin to creep back into my thoughts again… and so I walk…

… I walk the first path I come to… and I find myself noticing every detail of this path… I notice the prairie around me with great detail… and then I stop for a moment… for it is as if there is some reason I am to be aware of *the details* on this day…

… I set ceremony near the barn now… for I am sheltered from the cold here… and I sing the prayer songs for all people… with all confidence that I will release my physical stress and lift into spirit… but as my heart and spirit sing… my mind is looking in on the details…

"… it is not the details, as much as it is the overload… and it is not the overload, as much as it is that one must be prepared for all that is coming… (spiritually and from the High Place)…,

… for there is so much to grasp now… and it is coming so fast… that many are feeling quite overwhelmed… and confusion has taken the place of certainty… and *"how about some clarity here, and maybe we can find our own way to certainty"*, is the message we receive most often…,

… but it is taking on too much, too soon that is causing your confusion… for the idea of going step by step has everyone in a panic… but there is a process that each must follow… and the process is unique to each individual… and no matter who you are… the process requires each one to follow each step… for there are details along the way that each must tend to on their own…,

… and so relax a bit now… step back from time to time… and go about your daily life… trust that you are right on track… and set the time and place for your spiritual expansion… take it one step at a time… for following a path that is clear and certain… is much more efficient… than stumbling along a path that is dim and cluttered, confusing and vague…"

… a s qua di s di… and so it is good

I wake from a sleep that seemed to be light and shallow… but in reality was heavy and deep… and I walk out onto the prairie expecting to see bright Stars and a blanket of snow… but walk into the blackest morning I have seen in a long time… and the sound of this morning is unexpected… for it is the sound of being in a tunnel… rather than of being on the open prairie…

… and I see the Old Shaman standing there now… he is far away… at the other end of the tunnel… but as he begins to speak… I hear his words close and clear… as if he is standing right here… right here next to me…

"… within each being are many seeds… seeds of happiness… seeds of creation… seeds of gifts and abilities and dreams and desires… seeds of knowledge… seeds of wisdom… and seeds of spiritual awakenings… even seeds of wealth and abundance and prosperity…,

… and as you grow and live… theses seeds grow and become… but each seed must be nourished and nurtured and tended to and cared for…,

… and for some of these seeds… this will happened naturally and without much attention on your part… just as the grass and trees and animals in the natural (open) lands… live and grow by the earth and the rain and the wind and the sun…,

… but some of these seeds need your attention… and even your *intention*… for they must be nourished and nurtured like a garden you have planted… or like the animals you have taken in and accepted the responsibility for… these rely on you to care for them…,

… and I can tell you… that I see Father Sun rising upon you… and I see the seeds that are there, deep within you… I see them reaching up to meet their Father… and to live upon their Mother… and I hear them calling out for life…,

… and it is you who must listen… here in the place that is supposed to be light, but instead is dark… and it is you who must set an intention for each seed that lives within… and it is you who must set about to nourish and nurture, tend to and care for each of these…,

… for it is you who gets to choose what will grow in your garden… and what you will do with that which is harvested from within it… and only you can choose whether you will share any of this with others… or keep it to nourish only yourself…"

… a s qua di s di… and so it is good

The morning frost gives voice to my steps as I walk the prairie on this day. I find my way to the dirt path that leads to where the Buffalo stand, so to walk in silence to the place I have chosen for ceremony today.

The Buffalo gather near to me as I sing the prayer songs for all people, and I feel the double heartbeat of the two heifers that will calf in May. I feel the young heartbeat of our little calf from last year, and now the elder heartbeat of OB our bull brings in the strong, loud, deep, and booming heartbeat that completes this morning song…

… it is like the sacred drums of the old villages… the ones we are told about by the Grandfathers… who were told by their Grandfathers… who were told by their Grandfathers… who were there…

I move into my own place of stillness now… and the Buffalo stay close and still… and I sing to them a gratitude song… for lending me their spirits as I pray for all people on this day…

"… and it is between you and your Creator, (all) two-legged… as it has always been… and it is time for you to seek this truth now… for your sacred path is waiting to be seen…,

… and you can hear yourself walking… as you journey along your way… and never mind the path that others take… for they (too) must go their own way…,

… and soon your steps will be silent… as your spirit takes the lead… and you will hesitate to go any further… for there is no sound for you to heed…,

… but continue on, dear children… and follow with your heart… and trust your spirit and quiet your mind… for this is your new start…,

… and let go of that which restricts you… and that which dims the light… and move along within the flow… and believe with all your might…,

… for your spiritual path is yours, dear children… and it is up to you… to follow it to the very end… and see there is (still) more to choose…"

… a s qua di s di… and so it is good

I am greeted by the *nun ne hi* (fairies, little people) as I walk out on this day. There is a lightness in the air which rises up to meet a thick layer of fog that is acting as our ceiling today. The space between the earth and the fog creates an amazing acoustic on the prairie, and the *nun ne hi* take full advantage of this.

I am surround by song as I walk to the purple smoke bush, and I set my ceremony here today, while the *nun ne hi* provide us with music and song to carry our spirits higher…

"… we see the goodness that surrounds you each… and the **new** which is waiting to be born… and it is up to you to call in your own goodness… and give life to that which is forming there within you…,

… and it is time for you to declare your plan… and to speak out loud you dreams (and goals and desires)… but you must affirm that you can bring them forth… by attracting what you need and trusting that you can…,

… and be sure to affirm that you are worthy and deserving… of all that you dream and hope to create… and don't forget that to make it so… you must make your commitment and set your goals… and lay out your disciplines and follow them through…,

… and once you can do this… you will know for yourself… the power of your own will… and the sacredness of your (own) connection to all that is of the High Place…"

… a s qua di s di… and so it is good

I walk with my *staff* on this day. I saw it there when I was gathering my ceremony bundle, and it spoke out to me. I see my staff standing there every day, but on this day, as I called out for support and guidance, it was the voice of my *staff* that called back.

Like an old friend who has sensed that you need support and just shows up at your door, my staff stepped up on this day to assist me, and it feels like I am holding the hand of my good friend now… and we walk the prairie and set ceremony together…

"… if you feel the need for assistance, support, or guidance (love, compassion, understanding or the like)… call for it… and it will come…,

… and if you wait too long to call out… your heart and spirit will do it for you… but then you must be able to recognize the assistance when it shows up…,

… it is a time of great change now, two-legged… and the energy is very different and intense… and you are being called to reach up higher… to expand and to awaken… and all of this makes you just want to plant your feet firmly into what you already know and are comfortable with… and stay put…,

… but you know that everything is changing… and each day you become one step closer to the new… and one step further away from that which seems comfortable and familiar… and change is hard enough… when it is just you and you have a cushion of time… but when everything is changing at once… and the pace is set by the *all* rather than by you alone… well, it is expected that you would need assistance…,

… and it is a measure of wisdom, maturity, self-respect, and expansion… when one feels the need for assistance… and then follows through by calling out… especially now, two-legged…,

… for the changes that are happening now… require the coming together of all people… and the sharing of wisdoms and insights and experiences… and as you enlist the assistance and support of one another… you awaken the voice of communication… and once communication is achieved… your mind(s) will expand to greater knowing and understandings… and you each will go on to create the new… both individually and together…"

… a s qua di s di… and so it is good

I feel the changing of the season coming on now, and although the official first day of Spring is still more than a week away, it is very present here on the prairie. I startle the *bunnies* as I walk out on this crisp and clear morning, and they run quickly to their hollow for safety... all except for one... who sits at the center *Altar Stone* inside the Labyrinth... staring at me... waiting for me... as if he has something to say...

Rabbit carries the Medicine of renewal in my tradition, and although I see them often, it is on this day that one decides to see me...

"... I see the energy of the space around you, (all) two-legged... and it is filled with colors... like a rainbow, the energy that surrounds you is filled with life and potential and promise... and I see that you (all) walk taller than before now, too... with more confidence and closer to Creator...,

... and this is good, two-legged... for you have much to accomplish now... for you are called to bring about great changes (for all of our good)... and we (all plant and animal life) are counting on you... but we are all here to support and assist you as well...,

... in fact... the entire Universe (and everything held within it) is alert and ready to assist all/any who are ready and willing to take action now... to step up and to rise above... to trust their connection to/with all that is... and to become a part of the renewal of this Star we know as Earth...,

... the only thing holding (any of) you back... are negative thoughts and limiting beliefs that cloud your vision and confuse your mind... and it is the light that comes in from the High Place... that is meant to give you direction... and it is that same light that gets in your eyes and sends you running for cover... (like we Rabbits do when we see the lights of your cars and flashlights)...,

... and you know the light is pure and good... and you know that you can trust it... but it comes in so quick and so bright now... that you are startled by it...,

... so close your eyes... and feel the light... let it speak to you from above and from within... *feel* the clarity and purity of the light... and let it expose and burn away all of the negativity within you… and let it burn away all limiting beliefs as well…,

… for it is coming on Spring now… and it is time for growth and movement… and the energy of change is strong and present… and you can draw upon this energy… and ask it to assist you… as you move with direction and purpose… and this is powerful, (all) two-legged… this is powerful…"

… a s qua di s di… and so it is good

A PRAYER FOR ALL PEOPLE

… I smelled the rain late last night as I stepped out to check the ranch. The night was quiet and the air felt heavy and damp, and even a bit warm… everything was still and silent…

… I prayed for all people then… and all of my senses seemed to expand… and I felt the people all around me… and I cried as my physical being began to move and expand… and I felt myself rising up and up…

… and I know it was my spirit rising… for my physical body just stood silent and still… and I don't know why… but I called the night air to me… and I felt it as it wrapped around me… and I just kept quiet and still… until I was completely immersed within it… and I breathed it into my body… (that mysterious night air)… and I became **Rain**…

… and all of the prayers that I think and feel every day… as I encounter the hardships (and the blessings) that I see and hear and know about… just rose up within me, then… and I felt them as they made their way out… and I watched them as they rose up even higher…

… and the air around me began to breathe then… and there was a heartbeat within it, too… and I could feel the peace of the High Place… and a knowing that all is well…

… and the rain began to fall… and I did not move at all… but I just stood there, quiet and still… and I knew that in that moment… if only for that moment… that I was a part of it all…

… and I heard a song begin, then… and it seemed to be falling down from the Sky Place… it was soft and warm, and sweet and beautiful… and it fill every bit of the space around me… and then it came in closer… and I could feel it within my body… and just as I began to know the meaning of this song… the rain turned into snow…

… and in that perfect stillness… as big soft puffs of snow fell down from the Sky Place… I knew peace within me… and I whispered *"for all people"*… as I stood there, quiet and still…"

… a s qua di s di… and so it is good

I sat with the Grandfathers (stones) when I got home last night. It was warm enough to sit without a blanket, but I wrapped up in one anyway, for my blanket brings me comfort and has the power to shield me from the noise of the world.

I sat with the Grandfathers again this morning, and then I walked the prairie and sang the prayer songs for all people… and as I returned to the Grandfathers for ceremony… I heard them whisper…

"… children… your sacred space is there within you… and you only need to call to it… for it to surround you at any time… you create an obstacle for yourself… when you believe that you must stand in (or go to) a certain place in order to converse with your spirit (or with any who live in the High Place)… you keep your spirit locked within you then… (or separate from you)… and your relationship with the greatest part of you becomes formal and restricted… rather than easy and flowing…,

… it is a time for becoming whole now, children… and getting acquainted with your spirit is a big part of becoming whole… so look to see if you have been keeping your spirit separate or held within… only allowing it to come out at certain times… or when you are in need… ***and know this is not right***…,

… awaken your spirit now, children… and know that you are the sacred space that you have been seeking… become accustomed to calling to your higher ***Self*** at any time and in any place you want (or need) to… and your spirit will show you that it has been there all along…"

… a s qua di s di… and so it is good

The prairie is beautiful on this morning as I walk out. It is fresh and there is a feeling of purity in the air. The idea of cleaning comes to mind (like Spring cleaning), and the need for inner-cleansing comes up as well.

I smell the aroma of fresh Bay leaves for some reason, and I walk the prairie in search of them (or whatever it is that smells like them). I find myself at the Praying Tree. This is where the smell of fresh Bay leaves is the strongest, and I can tell now, that it is this sacred Standing One who has called me here, by using the smell of Bay leaves…

"… two-legged… inner-cleansing is not something you do once and then you are done… but it is an ongoing practice… just as your home requires regular cleaning… so does your physical body, mind, and emotions… and your spirit needs regular attention as well…,

… and you (each) are **like** in many ways… but you (each) are individual as well… for your cycles (or personal seasons) are all unique to you… and this is where you become confused and out of sync with your own rhythm of life…,

… have you noticed that every plant and tree has its own growing cycle/season… and that some come in early, while some come in later… some stay green and growing all the time… and some go completely asleep (or even die away) in Winter… before coming back in Spring…,

… well you, **two-legged,** are no different than we plant life in this way… except that instead of being trusted to know your own cycles/seasons… or even honored for being one who has figured this out for yourself… you are expected to follow a along with another's idea of what cycle/season you should be in at any time…,

… find your own natural rhythm of life, two-legged… and honor this within yourself… then trust others to discover their own natural rhythm of life… and honor them as well…reconnect with your own being… in every way (on every level)… and discern for yourself what your body, mind, emotions, and spirit are telling you (or have too much of, or are in need of)… for it will be different for each of you…,

… just as we Standing People will require more or less water, light, nourishment, or warmth than another… you (each) will require different nourishment, attention, rest, and activity as well…,

… and it is important now, two-legged… for you (each) to become in tune with your own **Self** in every way… to be able to sense for yourself what your own needs are… and to honor these needs within you… and to take responsibility for caring for your own needs… and to honor one another as unique and individual… and to trust that others will honor you for who you are as well…"

… a s qua di s di… and so it is good

Grandmother Moon glows a soft orange as she sets in the West, and I set ceremony out on the open prairie so I can see her clearly. With my back in the East and my heart to the West, I sing the prayer songs for all people, and I sit watching our Grandmother the Moon as I sing…

… she moves quickly as she sinks into the Western Sky on this day… and she calls to me… her heart to mine… I can feel her pulling something through me… as she disappears from my sight… and I feel the strength of Father Sun fill my entire being now… even though he has not yet shown even a glimmer of himself on this day…

… his spirit has come in ahead of him today… and it is the spirit of Father Sun who fills me now… and I stand in gratitude and honor… as I acknowledge and receive this precious gift…

"… your direction is straight and true, children… but you cannot perceive this…and your spirit is strong enough to last throughout time… for it has already brought you to this time and place… and will carry you on from here… but you do not trust this…,

… and so you struggle… or you feel as though you do… and you carry around your burdens… as if someone told you that you must… but theses burdens are simply steps… and they are not meant to be carried… but are meant to lead you forward… to step upon and walk away from…,

… for as you acknowledge each one… and learn from its teaching… you must also accept the growth or healing or wisdom it brings… and then you are to put it down… and step up on it… for it will lead you to another… and then to another… and before you know it… you will have gotten high enough to see…,

… that your direction is straight and true… and that your spirit is strong enough to last throughout time…"

… a s qua di s di… and so it is good

I see the flow of prayers on this day… the prayer and the answer… as spoken and received by each… I see the energy and feel the emotion… I see the light and feel the presence of God within it… and I see them unite… as they flow one into the other…

… guided by the light of Grandmother Moon… I walk the Labyrinth… I stand at the center *altar stone* looking up… and I see the energy of emotion… as the prayers all rise up and up…

… I see the light from the High Place, too… soft and glimmering… strong and certain… like the warmest embrace… like the truest heart… as the most trusted of all beings… sends out his love…

… and the love he sends is instant… and without hesitation… and within it is the answer… the acknowledgement… the direction… and the promise… as well as a word of assurance… and a knowing of being loved…,

… and as each flows… one into the other… the power is great and the feeling is intense… and I wonder how anyone… including myself… could ever miss this… the answer to our prayers…

"… there is usually a layer of fear that surrounds you when you call out your prayers… and fear creates a barrier which can block you from receiving… your emotions are strong a pulsing… and can prevent you from receiving a clear response… and your mind also has this power… for you mind is the last one to trust…,

… but this is simply how it is to be human… and it is part of the journey of being human… to expand your consciousness… to get to know your spirit… to connect with all that is of the High Place… and to trust that when you call out for guidance, assistance, answers, direction (or anything)… that you will receive them…,

… and so it is that you are encouraged now… to get to know your spirit… and to connect securely with all that *is* the High Place… everyday… in the quiet times… when there is no great need or fear or urgency… so that you can feel the flow of **prayer and answer**… so that you will know it… so that you will trust it…,

... for once you feel the vibration of this truth within your own being... you will never doubt again... and when you call out your prayers then... nothing will ever block or disguise them again... not fear, not emotion, not even your own mind..."

... a s qua di s di... and so it is good

Deep within the Dreamtime, I am deep within the flow. I feel my heart beating with the whole of the Universe, and I hear my own breath as it takes in all that it can to awaken and support my journey to wholeness... and I hold it within me for a time.

I hear my own breath again, as it blows out all toxins and fears and negativities, as it cleanses me from the inside-out... and prepares me for my next breath...

... the one that will expand within me even more than the last one... the one that will awaken me to even more than I had glimpsed once in a journey through the Dreamtime... the one that connects me to all things and all people... the one that is the purity of spirit and the grace of our Creator...

"... as you journey throughout your Earth Walk... be aware of your breath... and use the power of your breath... to assist you to live in harmony with all life... for all things that live... breathe in and out... just as you do...,

... and as you become aware of your breath... become aware of the natural flow of life... and discover within this natural flow... the patterns of how you live your life...,

... for once you have discovered your own pattern of life... you will understand yourself more completely... and through the understanding of your own self in this way... you will understand others more deeply...,

… and it is through this kind of understanding… that you begin to pick-up the unspoken message from others around you… as well as the messages from everything that surrounds you… and then living in harmony with all of life… becomes a natural thing for you… as natural as breathing in and back out again…"

… a s qua di s di… and so it is good

California is always beautiful, but it is the house of my youth that soothes me as I wake on this day.

I wake to the song of the Old Ones, and the words of their song speak to me as I translate their old language into the one we speak today…

"… all is not always as it seems, children… and it is time for you to find order (in your own lives, but in the world around you as well)… listen closely as you go about your days… listen with your ears… and then translate with your highest spirit… but listen with all your senses, too… for when you listen with your whole being… there is no need for translation… there is only knowing…,

… be mindful of your relationship to and with all things… (your imprint upon the Earth)… and be mindful of your relationship to and with one another (most importantly)… for it is time for you to recognize one another as your family… and to honor the relationship you have with one another… by building it together…,

… and you begin this honoring of all life as your own… by simply showing one another kindness… and soon you will know respect for one another… and you will begin to honor the life of one another as well… deeply and sincerely…,

… but more than that… you will begin to honor your own life… and this is when the greatest healing of the world begins… when you begin to honor and respect your own life…"

… a s qua di s di… and so it is good

Grandmother Moon has been a celebrity for the last few days… and setting aside time to sit out and watch… *"the rising of the biggest Moon in eighteen years"* … was the agenda for many folks (and I was one of them).

Now the cloud cover here in Southern California inhibited the spectacular view that some folks got (the photos are just breathtaking), but I was more than happy to just *feel* our Grandmother so close to me (us)…

… I sit in ceremony for all people now… drawing in the magnificent healing energy of Grandmother Moon for us all… I called to our dear Grandmother… and ask her to drench every inch of our home (this Star we know as Earth) with her healing light… and I ask for that light to assist us (all) to cleanse and purify ourselves in whatever way we need… even if we cannot name that need…

"… and so… as you bring to mind those things that are not in line with the harmony and joy you wish to create in your lives… feel them burn away in the purity of my powerful light…,

… and there is no need to let go on this day… but only to allow all and any thoughts or feelings that bring about disharmony within you (or in your life)… to rise up…,

… and then sit within my light… with the intention that these thoughts and feelings be burned away… transmuted completely… and you will feel the heaviness leave as the light pours in… as all that is new and good and pure and joyous… fills in the space that has opened there within you…,

… and you will be filled with joy and hope and promise…and you will attract only that which is in harmony with your dreams and goals and desires… and you will receive this goodness each and every day… and live the joyful life of your dreams… the life that you desire to live…"

… a s qua di s di… and so it is good

I went out early this morning and stood in the rain for a while... I did not stand there long though... because I heard our message for today very clearly... the voice of the Rain Keeper is unmistakable... and his words were just what I needed to hear on this day...

"... it is time for solitude, children... and so make some time to retreat for a while... to pull back and become still... and to call forth your own healing...,

... if you have been holding something (and pushed it deep) within you for too long... let it go now... if you have been holding onto anger, grief, hurt, or even guilt... let it go...,

... for any emotion that does not serve your greatest good... will only cause illness, unrest, pain, or *dis*ease... if you hold onto to it for too long...,

... and something about (any kind of) emotions you must know, too... it does not take long for emotions to become a part of you... any kind of emotion... positive or negative...,

... of course you want to keep the positive emotions... and let them grow and heal and strengthen you... but the negative emotions are sometimes elusive... and good at finding places deep within to hide and stick...,

... and these become difficult to find over time... and even more difficult let go of as time goes on... and so they will become a part of you... just as any positive emotion will... and it will be so natural and easy... that you may not even notice...,

... for you will adjust quickly to the heaviness, sadness, anger, edge, despair (and such) that you carry within... and you may think you are the one who controls these feelings within you... but you will be wrong...,

... so take some time now to become still... to go into the silence and to call out all of the negative emotions that rule you... and as they emerge... let the rain wash them away...,

… and as the rain washes them away… know that all of the goodness that lives there within you… will rise up and expand… and happiness will grow within you then… and the healing will be instant and natural and easy…"

… a s qua di s di… and so it is good

There is a sense of healing within and around me (as I wake from a deep sleep) here in the house of my childhood. I felt a flickering of this healing begin when I made the flight plans for this visit… and I felt that flickering grow as the days all fell away, one by one, until it was time to fly…

… and the absolute joy I feel to see my Sister waiting for me, causes this healing flame to grow… and the overwhelming peace of stepping into my Mother's house for the first time (in however long it has been) expands the healing flame even more …

… and laughing like little girls again… and playing with the new puppy… and making plans and helping out… and being stuck inside because the rain is so heavy…

… and then going out… and taking in that first deep breath… and just being held by all of these moments… expands this healing flame even more…

… and I miss my Father… oh, how I miss my Father… but he is here… all around and everywhere… and his voice is in my head… and there is peace in this knowing… and healing, too…

"… mind your inner-child now, children… and assist in your own healing… for it is you who knows (best) what you need… and you who can make sure you receive it…,

… and decide to receive your healing now, children… for you know there are times you resist it… bound by some reason that is long past now… you hold tight to what has been…,

… but there is a door there before you now, children… and it has been there all along… and it leads you into the present… and allows the past to fall away…,

… and it is just one step for you now, children… one brave courageous leap… one decision to step forward… one choice for you to make…,

… for with each of these you grow stronger, dear children… and you find your wisdom, too… and you begin to trust that you are the one… who watches over you…"

… a s qua di s di… and so it is good

I woke early this morning (2:14 am). I stood outside with our Grandmother the Moon for a while, and sang the prayer songs for all people (silently within). The ceremony for today begins then… and I attended it in quiet solitude…

"… listen now… for you (all) have connected to a higher part of your being… opened to a fuller understanding of physical life… and awakened more of your spirit… and so you must quiet now, and listen… for much of what has been a mystery to you… will now become clear…,

… and you will need to spend time in stillness now… more than ever… for once you begin to receive the knowing from a higher place within… your understanding of life will expand… and the way you live your life will change (naturally and automatically)…,

… you will begin to make different choices… and you will understand with greater clarity… (and from a place of compassion)… you will know how and why you came to make the choices you have made so far… and you will see the divinity in the choices you made… and you will know this same clarity, understanding, and compassion toward others for the choices they have made…,

… and then you will align… within each time of stillness… more purely and completely with your Creator… and with the whole of the Universe… and with the great **all that is**…and you will become empowered then… and be guided by your own higher wisdom… and you will begin to live to your fullest potential…,

… and you will seek the stillness more and more (then)… for you will know… that truth is found there… deep within the stillness… and that you are given more truth and clarity… more wisdom and understanding… in just one moment of stillness… than could ever be written in any book… or spoken in any amount of words…"

… a s qua di s di… and so it is good

I fell asleep to the sound of rain (pouring rain that came early in the day and lasted through the night)… and it was the Dream-keeper who came then… and guided me to the place in the Dreamtime where we can see what lies ahead…

…this is the place in the Dreamtime where we are given a glimpse into our future… details about where we are headed… insights about choices we have made… we are assured of our participation in our own lives here in this place… and without judgment or opinion… we are offered time to discern for ourselves… what (and if there are) adjustments we want to make in our present course…

"… and do not spend time worrying, dear children… about whether a choice you have made was the right one or not… for there are no wrong choices… just as the choice you make now will be right and correct…,

… for each choice offers an experience… and each experience offers an opportunity to learn and grow… and you worry now… that you have wasted your life or let opportunities go by… but the only way to do that… would be to spend all your time worrying about that very thing… rather than actually living…,

… so do not enter this place in the Dreamtime… with the expectation of finding the answer… do not look for the mistake or the place where you went wrong… for you will not see anything like that here…,

… here you will see yourself in a very different way… here you will see how you attract what comes to you… and you will know that it is not punishment or reward… that determines the experiences you attract… but it is simply where you are on your path…,

… and once you find your way to the place on your path… where you understand that you are to participate in how (and where) your life goes… your path will open wide… and you will open wide, too…,

… and everything that you need will gravitate toward you (then)… and all that you do not need will move away… and you will see your life in the way of a circle (then)… and you will understand each and every experience of your life with gratitude and grace…,

… and as you make your way forward from here… you will move with certainty and trust… with patience and wisdom… and with the knowing that you can decide your own direction now… ***and so you will…***"

… a s qua di s di… and so it is good

The sound of **Rain**… it is the sound that sang me to sleep last night… and it is the sound that awakens me early on this day…. rain falling… graceful and constant… is also the sound that guided my dreams deep into the place of spirit… and to the place where our message for today spoke out loud and clear…

"… be aware of the signs around you now, two-legged… and reacquaint yourselves with the Animal Kingdom… for your Mother the Earth is talking… and she wants you to listen…,

… as two-legged… you will always seek guidance… from within and from without… (and without even thinking, asking, or knowing it) from the books you read, the programs you watch on television, the music you listen to, and especially from advertisements (for these are so repetitive, they connect to you on a very deep level)…,

… you are overwhelmed everyday by the constant flow of guidance you receive without even asking for it… and so you must consciously make time to go within… you must seek out the stillness… and you must go deep within that stillness… in order to disconnect from the loud and constant chatter of the physical world…,

… for your Mother the Earth is talking to you now… and she wants you to listen… (and she speaks to you through the rain and the wind, and the way she moves and shakes)… and she will raise her voice if she must… but she would rather know that you will find a way to come and listen on your own…,

… so call upon the stillness now, two-legged… and call upon, we, your animal guides… for we are close to the Mother and are not distracted by the loud and constant chatter of the physical world… let us assist you to find the stillness… and help you to hear what the Mother is saying…,

… for once you can hear above the **white noise** of your physical world… you will be connected to the true nature of your physical world… and guided by your own ability to read the signs of nature… which are all around you, all the time…"

… a s qua di s di… and so it is good

It is so quiet and still as I set ceremony on this day, that I decide not to disturb it and sing my gratitude song silently within. I sit in the quiet, as I sing the prayer songs for all people (with my heart rather than my voice)… and I *become* the quiet, as the sound of my own heartbeat becomes a mantra for this morning's ceremony…

… like a circle of Elders chanting in the distance… the sound of my own heart beating fills in the space around me… and it seems that many more are joining in now… as I move into stillness and listen for what message I am (we are) to receive on this day…

"… there is a story in your heart, dear children… and if you know to listen for it… you will begin to know this story… and if you believe that your heart holds your truth… it will reveal **your truth** to you in the song it sings… (but then you must be prepared to live that truth)…,

… and they tell you that you can change your life… by changing the words you speak… and so you decide to sit down and write out the words you wish to speak now… you write down the truth you wish to live… and you learn these words and speak them out like a chant… and this chant becomes your mantra… and so it is good…,

… but there is a truth within the story that is there within your heart, dear children… and this truth is **your truth**… and it speaks to you every day… (and sings to you each night)… just as it has spoken to you every day since the day it began to beat… and there is no chant to learn, when you listen to your heart… for the mantra of your own heartbeat… is one you know **by heart**…,

… so, listen to your own heartbeat, dear children… (especially when you are lost, confused, overwhelmed, or under-inspired)… and find a truth that you can write down and follow… listen to your own truth… as it sings out your own perfect mantra… and follow this mantra, this truth… as you live each day from your own perfect truth…,

… and you will know (then), dear children… what it is to speak your truth… and how it feels to actually live it… and this will be good, dear children…"

… a s qua di s di… and so it is good

No matter how many times I return to the place where I grew up, I am surprised by the memories and emotions that rise up within me. Some come on quick and fast like a flood, some are more subtle like a *slow moving river*, some lurk around and taunt me to seek them out, and others just come from out of nowhere and hit me head on.

Memories and emotions go hand in hand, and whether we label these *good memories or bad memories*, I have come to believe that they are all good, for each one offers us a place to heal, let go, gain wisdom, or simply enjoy a wonderful happy time again. Memories take us to times and places in our lives that have gone by, and give us a chance (as the person we are today) to experience, learn from, and even evaluate *each* from a whole new perspective.

I believe that no matter who we are, how old we grow to be, or how happy our lives were, are, have been, etc… we can all be surprised by memories that come from out of nowhere, catch us off guard, and make us say… "Wow"…

"… come to know this now, children… you acquire great power when you bring your mind and heart together as one… for you have experienced the power of a memory… you have relived past joys by them… been taken to your knees by them… returned to a child through them… been frightened down to your soul by them…,

… but it is time now for you to stand steady and strong… to see and feel beyond the initial impact of past experiences… and realize that each experience (memory) of your life has had a purpose… let go of that which can only keep you wounded and small… and take in the wisdom that each can provide…,

… then understand the power of bringing thought and feeling together as one… by realizing the power of a memory… and know this now, too… when you bring thought and emotion together with focused intention… you can (and will) accomplish anything…,

… so it is not only that you must set your mind on something… but you must be clear about your intention… and set your heart on that something as well… ”

… a s qua di s di… and so it is good

Ceremony comes early this morning, as Mother Earth has much to say. It is the feminine voice I hear calling to me as I make my way out into the early morning, and it is the feminine aspect of all two-legged that gather (now) to listen…

“… the fruits of your future are planted by you… here and now… and that which you care for and tend to… will flourish and grow (survive) throughout time…,

… and life will become rich and beautiful for you… as you become more and more attentive to it… and you will see beauty in all things… as you join in the circle of life… and participate in protecting the life of all things (beings)…,

… and your spirit reaches higher now… as your roots grow deeper into the land upon which you walk… and as you hold the balance between these two… you hold steady the light for all who seek to know it…”

… a s qua di s di… and so it is good

The Dreamtime took me deep into the Ocean last night, and offered me an amazing journey. It is always a wondrous adventure anytime we have the opportunity to explore places beyond our normal living space, and for me, these adventures always awaken me to a deeper/greater knowing of my *Self*...

... there are no boundaries when we travel about in the Dreamtime... just as there are no boundaries deep within the Ocean, high up in the Sky Place, or out among the Planets and Stars.

"... you spend much of your time, (all) two-legged... confined within... whether the confines be a job, a place, a relationship, a way of life, or a belief... you do spend much of your time, confined within...,

... and this is not a bad thing... and this is not a good thing... this is just so... an observation of how two-legged go about the journey of life...,

... but your world is changing, two-legged... and you must change with it... and you will be offered plenty of opportunities (now)... to discover a greater/deeper knowing of your *Self*... and as you journey through these adventures and experiences... you must trust in who you are... and you will discover who you are along the way...,

... for each of you are strong and courageous... and each of you are kind and compassionate... and each of you will step forward and assist... even though each of you know there is fear deep within you...,

... it is a time for experience now, two-legged... a time to put to use all of what you have learned from books and through the accounts of others... (and from places deep within your own Dreamtime)... it is time to expand yourselves now, two-legged... and to call out everything that lives deep within you... it is time to break free from the confines of your minds... and trust that there is more for you to live and know and experience...,

… and you will find the one who lives deep within you (then)… and you will awaken your own wisdom and strengths… and you will get to know things about yourselves… that you only dreamed could be true… and you will find there are no boundaries for you, two-legged… and a new adventure will call out for you then…"

… a s qua di s di… and so it is good

The prairie smells fresh and the ground smells sweet. I walk out into the morning and my spirit stretches out, and then runs on before me like a child. I stretch out my arms to embrace this wide-open space, and breathe in the cold morning air. It is always so good to be home.

The Cowboy finished the cross fencing while I was away, and moved the Buffalo up to the front pasture for the Spring. I walk quietly now, and with respect, as the Buffalo are still getting used to being so close to us.

I walk the stone prayer circles now, and set ceremony at my altar. I sing the prayer songs for all people, and the Buffalo gather near…

"… let your spirit guide you now… as you reach into your soul… and breathe a sigh of forgiveness… for all hurts and wounds untold…,

… and as you reach out and up… feel yourself expand… and understand with compassionate love… the innocent heart of man…,

… listen, two-legged… for it is important that you let go of those things that you hold deep within… (things like anger and pain and hurt and sadness)… and know that it is these that hold you back… these that keep you from living in harmony with one another…,

… understand now, two-legged… that most of what you hold in contempt… as wrongs imposed upon you… or that you acted upon another… are simply the struggles of (you) each… trying to make sense of living as human…,

… and when you can live with this understanding… you will become stronger and healthier and happier… and you will live more as spirit than as human (then)… and there will be harmony among you all…"

… a s qua di s di… and so it is good

"The best thing anyone can do for the world… is to become the become the healthiest person they can (in every way… spiritually, emotionally, physically, and mentally)"** …

… the message I received this morning in ceremony… was about **transmuting*** our negative thoughts and energy… and focusing on the positive aspects of our lives and beings… it was about setting positive goals and seeing them with our inner-eyes… reaching for them with our whole being (beginning with our spirit)… and achieving them because we drew them to us… purely, and without the static of negative thoughts or words or worries or energy getting in the way…

… and it occurred to me as I felt this message pour into my being… (first through my spirit, then my heart, then into my mind, and last throughout my entire body)… that I get it… I really get it… but I also realized (instantly)… that it wasn't so long ago that didn't get it (or at least not so clearly)…

… and what I have to say on this day is this…

… set out to be the healthiest person you can… spiritually, emotionally, physically, and mentally… take it a little at a time… in great big chunks… one aspect of yourself at a time… or however it happens to come to/for you… find the positive in everything every day… and make it your intention to **transmute** the negative whenever it tries to move in…

… for as long as we are striving for these things… we **are** being the healthiest person we can be…

… a s qua di s di… and so it is good

*TRANSMUTE VERSES TRANSFORM
(my own analogy):

To transform is to change... but we could (in fact) transform into something lesser, lower, or not necessarily better... and not necessarily removing the negative.

To transmute is to change... completely and most usually to a higher more perfect version... and most usually removing the negative.

As always intention has everything to do with it.

APRIL 2011

It is my Star Relatives who greet me on this day, and Grandfather Wind has quieted some. I stand surrounded by the Sky Place on this very dark morning, and with the Star People so close and bright, I feel safe and protected….

"… children, as your vibrations raise… they will each raise at their own pace… and each of you will experience these shifts in different ways… and though these changes will happen gradually… you will feel them come on "all of a sudden"…,

… like suddenly seeing something with great clarity… suddenly understanding (more) completely… suddenly *knowing* that which has confounded you… suddenly being able to fit certain pieces together… suddenly "getting it"…,

… and whenever there is change… there is fear… it is simply a natural human characteristic… and when there is fear… there is need for protection…,

… the kind of protection that assures you… like the trusted voice of a parent or grandparent or loved one… like the feeling of being supported with a nod of approval… like the hand that touches yours and tells you… "even though things are changing around you… even though things are changing within you… you are okay… everything will be okay"…,

… and so it is time for you to understand about protection now… for as you raise in vibration… your ability to sense will expand… you will become more open… and you will remain open for much of the time… for there is so much for you to take in now… and you will know this (instinctively)…,

… and as you experience this shift… you will need to protect yourselves… not from any harm or injury, mind you… but from contaminating the purity of what you are receiving… for there is an in-between place that you will go through… on your way to a higher consciousness… and all of your fear, doubt, worry, self-doubt, and notions of sabotage will be present there (and strong)…,

… and you know how it is to be human… and how once you finally get what you have been dreaming of, working toward, hoping for, even praying for…

you tend to push it away… you use excuses such as not deserving, too good to be true, this was too easy (and the like)… and you begin the process of pushing away (or sabotaging) that which you have worked so hard to achieve (or acquire)…,

… so understand this, children… and develop ways of protecting your spirit as it expands and awakens within you… like putting on a jacket and warm boots when it is cold… call out for protection now… with the intention of preserving the clarity and purity of all that is awakening within you… and so not to contaminate, block, or turn away from all that you have come so far to know (be)…"

… a s qua di s di… and so it is good

On this morning before the New Moon, I walk the prairie seeking perspective. The prairie is dark and Father Sky is black. The Star People are here, but they remain high and distant. I feel heavy as I walk on this day, heavy and low, and I know that it is a higher perspective that I must find.

I walk out our front gate and up the road to the little knoll. And as I make my way to the top, I feel the heaviness within me fall away, I feel myself become lighter. I stand at the top of the knoll, and in the darkness of this morning, I look out across the prairie. I see with my physical eyes only a vague outline of what I know is there, and so I close my eyes and look with my spirit…

… and Hawk cries out… from deep within the darkness… I hear Hawk cry out… and I see light now… even with my eyes closed… I see light… and my vision becomes clear… and my perspective expands… and I offer gratitude to Hawk… for bringing me the perspective I seek on this day…

"… there is much to consider when strong feelings rise up within you… especially when those feelings are brought on by the words or actions of another… for you know what you are feeling (hurt, angry, sad, confused, afraid, worried, troubled, and so on)… but you also know there is more to the story…,

... it is essential that you honor yourself and feel the emotion... respect yourself and the emotion that is running through you... and respect the other as well... evaluate the feeling and seek within yourself for reason, explanation... and even though you know most emotional encounters have no logic... know that they have reason... there is always a reason...,

... do not look for or place blame (on the other or yourself)... but look in truth... seek out a higher perspective then... and you will see more... for each of you have your own perspective... which has been developed through the personal experiences of your own life journeys... and so each will always see from their own perspective... but each can come to understand the perspective of the other... if you look with sincerity and truth...,

... and so it is not that you must deny your feelings... or that you must deny the feelings of another... it is that you seek to understand... and in order to understand you must get to a higher perspective... and from that higher perspective you will be shown a story... and within that story you will find understanding... and it is the understanding (then) that defuses the emotion...,

... and once there is understanding... there is light... and you can see clearly in that light... your perspective expands and you can see truth... and from that place of truth... you can go on to deal with the situation... whatever it may be...”

... a s qua di s di... and so it is good

It is difficult to keep my balance as I walk out into the power and strength of Grandfather Wind on this morning, for he is moving fast and with great force today. A storm is coming, and Grandfather Wind always comes around first to prepare us (or is it that he is the reason for the storm?).

These are definitely **Winds of Change** that greet me on this day. But are they simply due to the changing of the season, or is it something deeper and more personal that brings the Winds to us on this day?

Setting ceremony in the Wind is pretty amazing. It helps us to remember the power of our *own*. For there is no way you can open your ceremony bundle, no way you will lay out your blanket, no way you can light the smoke, or even hear the song you are singing…

… it is just you there… in the presence of Creator… calling out from that sacred place within… and using the power that is simply *you*… (your own inner-sacred)… and so it is from the purest, truest place within you… that you pray for all people… and it is from this most pure and true place within… that you receive the message you are to know at this time…

"… recover that which has been lost now, two-legged… for it is coming upon a time when you will need it more than ever… remember the power that is purely you… the power that is your *own*… and remember how to connect with all things… on your own… without the assistance of a stone, or plant, or animal, or even another…,

… remember that it is you who carries the power within you… and not the stone, the plant, the animal… and especially not another… remember what it is that you truly believe in… and hold it strong within you… for you are in a time when many will try to test your beliefs… as well as your trust and faith in your *own*… and these are powerful ones, two-legged… as strong and powerful as the *Winds of Change*…,

… but they are merely pests to those who stand strong and firm in their own… and they have no power when blowing against one who knows their own… and so know your own, two-legged… know it from the center of your being… know it in your heart… know it in your mind… know that it is the very essence of your truth, of your spirit… and it will be the strength and power that protects you in every way… that keeps you upright and balanced… even when faced with the most fierce Wind… or the strongest Storm…,

… know your *own*… and trust in your own… for it is by knowing and trusting your *own*… that you will remain steady against all or any *Winds of Change* that may ever come upon you…"

… a s qua di s di… and so it is good

I walk briskly on this cold and snowy morning. It is colder than I had prepared myself for, but my Star Relatives are close (and many), and so I call to them for warmth. I make my way to the barn, and begin to set ceremony within its warmth protection... when I feel the presence of an *Old Grey Horse*... an *Old One*... who has come to speak on this day.

"... know that you are wise, two-legged... then call upon your wisdom as you step forth into the new... for you are coming upon the ***ending of a season*** (a way of life, an experience or situation, a way of thinking, a way of being, a relationship, a time)... and there is always something ***new*** waiting at the ***end*** of each ***season's end***...,

... it is time for you to be fully present now, two-legged... and to be truthful with yourself about your feelings and emotions... for endings can open great emotional flow within you... and if you try to hide from that flow... you can cloud your own thinking and distort your own wisdom...,

... allow the emotion to flow, two-legged... and you will understand why it comes as a flow... for it is meant to pour in and move through... ***it is meant to move you***... and then to create an opening for thought and understanding... and this is where your wisdom is born, two-legged...,

... and it is time for you to acknowledge your wisdom, two-legged... and to bring it forth and use it... so that you can call upon it at will... and so let the emotions flow... and glean the lessons from them as they do... for each experience will become your wisdom then... and you will walk strong and ready as you go into each time of ***new***... and your own wisdom will be your guide...

... a s qua di s di... and so it is good

I walk beneath the Cloud People on this day. I feel the new life on the prairie as I walk, the new born calves, the new grass just sprouting... I even hear the birds at this early hour.

I set ceremony in the Grandfathers Prayer Circle, as my Star Relatives watch through a small opening the Cloud People have managed. I sing my gratitude song and I think of all the goodness and blessings in my life. I allow this feeling to expand and move out into the Universe now, and I pray gratitude to and for all people.

I look up to my Star Relative as I sing the prayer songs for all people, and I see even more of them are peeking through that small opening the Cloud People have provided. But something about this opening catches my eye, and as I trace the outline of this opening with my eyes, I see that it is the shape of a man… a shaman… and I quiet now… and listen for what this **great one** has to say…

"… from just the smallest expression of gratitude… you can create more… and when you give it out freely… and with the intention that others may receive (too)… you can bring about a shift that will cause the winds to stop and the tides to draw back… as if the Universe is taking in a deep breath…,

… and you should take a deep breath then too, (all people)… for when the Universe exhales from that joyous loving breath… it will pour forth upon you all… more abundance and reward than you can imagine…,

… it is a time of choice now (all people)… and it is a time of much confusion and great challenge as well… and when you feel there is nothing you can do… or that you have come to the end of your strength and hopefulness… stand in a quiet moment… and feel gratitude for everything you can…,

… for as you feel gratitude within your heart… it will expand through-out your entire body… and then throughout your entire being… and out into your life… and like a drop in still water… your gratitude will expand beyond you… out into the world around you… it will reach out and touch all people and all things… until it finally finds its way out into the Universe… and then it will go beyond…,

… and it will come back to you then… and you will feel it in your heart… and you will know that there is always something you can do when challenging times are upon you… for whenever you send goodness and blessings (gratitude, anything positive) out into the Universe... you help to transmute the negative and bring about more positive... and that will be for all people... and that is always good..."

... a s qua di s di... and so it is good

"**W**ho am I" seem to be the words in my head lately. And I have been pushing these words away with the excuse that *"I have much more important things to do right now"*. But as I walk the prairie today, this notion of "Who am I" becomes stronger than any pushing I can do, and so I settle down and listen... and I agree to seek...

... and Grandfather Wind comes up now... and he blows right through me... and I should have tied my hair up today... for it blows across my face... and I pull my blanket around me tight... and I listen for his words...

"... even though you take on many different characters throughout your Earth Walk... at your core... you remain the same unique being that you were created to be... and life is powerful... and it has the power to turn you and shift you and change you... especially during times of weakness, stress, and challenge...,

... and you can be so influenced by the voices of those around you... the ones who are near... as well as those who reach out from faraway places... and these are the voices of your brothers and sisters... and deep within, you know this... and so you are moved by the opinions and beliefs and personalities of these... and you begin to form and develop (evolve) into the person that you have become...,

... and this is just so, two-legged... this is just so...,

... and so the question *"who am I"* comes to you... not as dilemma that must be solved... but as reminder that you are unique... individual... valuable, important, and worthy... that there is a core within you... and that the *you* who stands here today... evolved from that very core...,

… and your core is your spirit… and it is important to never lose sight of your spirit… it is important to affirm each day that you are who you are… and that who you are is special and valuable and worthy and important…,

… and being your authentic-self… is paying attention when you feel certain reactions to what is being said or happening around you… and checking in with your core… your spirit… and taking your instructions from this place… rather than from the world around you…,

… for each has come with their own work to do… their own life path to walk… their own purpose for being… and when you live as your authentic-self… you honor that which you came to do and be… and you walk your path then… and you allow others to walk theirs… and there is balance then… upon your Star (within your world)… and you know who you are…"

… a s qua di s di… and so it is good

The Cloud People have come on this day, and the entire prairie feels like a Medicine Lodge. I sit on the old Pine stump in front of my altar singing the prayer songs for all people. I smoke the sacred pipe and sing prayers of gratitude for the rain, and for the Rain Keeper (*a ga s ga u (ga) se di*) who brought the rain that blesses the land.

I move into stillness as I hear the quiet mumbling of the Cloud People. I still myself as I breathe in the fragrant aroma of the prairie, and I hear Mother Earth speaking with the Cloud People…

… and I wait… quiet and still… as their conversation goes on… and I know that they have heard the prayers in my heart… for they speak to me now… and offer us their message for today…

"… and the people feel unsettled now… for there is much that is challenging them at this time… and there is fear and worry and even shades of panic it the hearts of the people… and many feel as though they have lost their center… and this just feeds their fear…,

… tell them now… that it is time to pull back… it is time to breathe in the fresh and clean air that comes to them after the rain… remind them that just as the rain washes everything clean again... they have the means within them (each) to wash clean anything that causes them pain or fear or worry or panic...,

... there are always at least two ways of approaching an experience... and when dealing with experiences that challenge... you can come forth as the victim... or you can rise up and let these times be the source of your strength... use them to bring out your courage and strength... so to become stronger, wiser, and more developed... and to inspire others to rise above as well...,

... you (each) have the power to create whatever it is you desire your life experience to be... and even when you feel there is no hope or no way... remember that all you have to do... is to begin... and you begin by remembering the power that lives within you... for that power is the same power that you call upon when you pray...,

... it is time for you (each) to take action now... to trust in your own inner-power... and to remember that your own inner-power... is the same power that created you... and as you do this... bring forth positive thoughts... a positive plan... and begin to break away from the notion that there is nothing you can do... for there is always something you can do... and trust that whatever it is that you do... will be powerful..."

... a s qua di s di... and so it is good

Our first baby-buffalo-calf of the year was born yesterday morning, announcing its arrival with a bang. No more than an hour or two old, it kept up with the herd as they ran straight toward me and then off to the East (startled by a suspected predator on the prairie I supposed). After taking a few hard tumbles and a few hits from its Father (our bull, O.B.), it settled quietly into life here on the ranch.

Crow met me this morning as I walked out, and sat with me in ceremony. We conversed about a lot of things during ceremony today, too many to write in just one message. So I asked Crow *"what is the message for today"*... and Crow graciously answered...

"… set your own code of ethics, two-legged… and live by your own integrity… but be sure that you go higher than that which your world has come to accept… for living by a higher standard will take your consciousness higher… and once you have raised your consciousness to a higher place… you will see there is an even higher place as well…,

… and do not fear this, two-legged… and do not hesitate… but run quickly… so to keep up with those that are running that way too… and then become new again… sweet and playful and friendly and curious… and learn from what that new life has to teach you… and then you will know your truth… and understand why you must set your standards so high…"

… a s qua di s di… and so it is good

I walk the prairie with caution on this day, as the doggies have been stirring around like there is something out here that doesn't belong. So I stay close to the ranch, traveling no farther than my ceremony area, and then I see the Old Coyote jump right in front of me. We stare each other down for several minutes, until I step back one step and he runs off into the North.

I walk the ceremony area (now) singing my gratitude song, and I continue to walk as I begin ceremony *in motion*. I sing the prayer songs for all people, and I feel the energy of ceremony rising up around me…

… and I sit now… in the place where that Old Coyote was… and as I move into stillness… that Old Coyote speaks…

"… ah, two-legged… you have seen me… I have been watching you for some time now… and wondering when you would find me… but you have been so consumed by the seriousness of life… that you have not noticed me lurking around the outer edge of your ranch…,

… listen now, two-legged… it is time to take a break from all that weighs on your mind… and release yourself from the cycle of lessons you have drawn upon yourself… for once you step back and breathe… all that you have learned and experienced will begin to settle in… and this is when the lessons become **wisdom**…,

... and remember... even though you are growing and changing... there is still a part of you who thinks it can fool you... and this time it is trying to convince you that you must buckle down and forge ahead and brave the storm... (keep moving through the lessons)... in order to make it to your next destination...,

... but that is wrong... for this time it is best for you to find a good cave... or a clearing deep within the trees... and rest for a while... and play for a while... and watch for a while... and just *"be"* for a while... for you have made many shifts and changes recently... and you must take time now... to let these become set within you... before you attempt to move on..."

... a s qua di s di... and so it is good

It is the Old Man who comes to me on this day... holding a shield and singing the blessing songs... I see him there... in the crystal clear vision of my inner-eye... and he is singing *blessings* for us all...

... and I see myself there with him now... and we are dancing the blessing dance together... and we sit when the blessing is done... and he tells me what he came to tell...

"... children, it is time to set your shield for what you intend to experience in the coming time... it is time to know your worth... and to set your boundaries... it is time to put within your shield that which you desire... and banish from your circle that which you do not...,

... make your circles now, children... and bless them with love and light... reach up into the High Place... and draw down all the goodness you desire... call forth what it is that you need at this time... and bless your circle in the spirit of your truth...,

... and trust now, children... any experience that is aligned with your journey... will find its way through... and that you will meet these experiences with your own inner strength, wisdom, courage, and guidance...,

... and ask for your shield to protect you as you journey forward... and stand in gratitude for the blessings that are yet to be... and know that as your shield protects you… it awakens your inner strength, wisdom, courage, and guidance… (it protects you from within)…,

… and so it is… as I dance the **blessing dance** for all of you here in the High Place… your spirits come to find me… and they carry your shields with them… and they join in this dance for you… and I know you by your shields… and I honor your lives and the journeys you have chosen…,

… and so I go now… to dance the **blessing dance** for you… and I continue to dance this dance… every day and everywhere… for you and for all people… and through this dance you are blessed… every day and everywhere… for now and for always…"

… a s qua di s di… and so it is good

It is the Black Bird who greets me on my first morning in Scotland… and I see the Raven who came not so long ago… and the Crow who watched over the birth of our newest Buffalo-calf… and I think of family… and of our relationship to one another… no matter the distance or circumstance…

… and Black Bird comes closer now… and speaks our message for today…

"… if you have been feeling out of sorts recently… it is because you are preparing for the birth of a "new"… and so… as it is during any birth process… there is always a time of discomfort… which can become more and more intense… the closer it gets to the time of birth…,

… this is true of rebirth, too… rebirth of the spiritual as well as mental… of the emotional or physical… as well as the birth of any new idea or way of being…,

… and so be sensitive to any need you feel for rest and/or comfort now… and tend to these needs as you would a mother preparing to birth a child… for that which is birthing through you (each) at this time… whether you are male or female… old or young… awake and aware… or still spiritually sleeping… is very big… and will create much spiritual growth and forward movement for all…"

… a s qua di s di… and so it is good

As I sit in the quiet of this morning, I feel the Medicine of the Old and Ancient Ones. The people of my Cherokee Clan from long ago have gathered in this place today, and remind me of the sacredness of all people… ***our sacred and holy essence that is perfect and unique to each of us as "our own"***… and they tell me that we have lost our connection with our deep and holy inner-sacred… for we hide it within…

"… begin to prepare now, two-legged of the Mother Earth… for there is an awakening upon you… and that which you have pushed deep within… is being called out…,

… your most sacred knowing is awakening… and the holiness that is at your very core… is beginning to find its voice again…,

… and your whole life will change and grow… from the awakening of this (your inner most sacred)… and your whole world will move and change (now) in good ways, too…,

… for that which you experience is always shaped around that which you know within… and when you have forgotten this pure and holy ***knowing*** that is ***your truth***… there is no center for you to build up from…,

… but permanence can only be attained from that which is true… and never from the illusion that is spun from the place of ignorance… especially when the ignorance comes in such an innocent way…,

… and when the spirit is strong and patient… the discovery of that which is truly sacred and holy… comes in such a way… that no explanation is required… and no denying could ever bring down…,

… so be patient, young ones… and keep your spirits strong… and do not be afraid of that which is sacred and holy within you… but rejoice when it begins to stir… for your awakening has begun…"

… a s qua di s di… and so it is good

Walking along the charming roads that took us to the park yesterday, we listened to the Sea Gulls as they flew close overhead. They seemed to be keeping close to us as we made our way home, and it is these interesting Winged that call out to me on this rainy Scottish morning…

"… as you move along your life journey… you are making your plans and reaching your goals… and it is important to keep looking up ahead as you do… for this will keep your journey smooth and flowing…,

… and you will find that you move through any difficulty or upset… with ease and grace then, too… for your sight is set on that which comes next… rather than fixed on (only) what is right in front of you at the time…"

… a s qua di s di… and so it is good

We spent the day yesterday, wandering the gardens at *Dean Village* in central *Edinburgh*. Grandfather Wind was cold and blustery, and the gardens were completely enchanting. I slept deep and still after such a day…

… and the *sweet mother earth* of this magical land… followed me into my sleep then… singing her song of gratitude for life… and reminding me of the importance of recognizing and honoring our connection to all things and to one another…

"… it is good to remember your connection with all things of nature… as you spend time in the quiet stillness of the gardens and parks and quaint sea side villages… but the most important relationship for you to recognize at this time… it the one you have to and with your own ancestry (family and loved ones)…,

… for there is much you can learn about yourself… once you begin to seek out the people and places of your beginning… (in this, your current physical life)… for woven deep within the lives and character of your ancestors… are glimpses of you…,

… and as you recognize and honor the people and places of your past… you will begin to see the shimmering thread of sameness that runs between all people… and you will begin to know, too… that these threads of sameness… have run through all people… from the very beginning…,

… and your understanding of one another becomes true and real, then… and you find ways to share your ideas and values and accounts of your experience of life… rather than through pushing and forcing and demanding (and such)… and this becomes the way you interact with one another… and you find there is tolerance within you, now… where impatience and judgment used to be…,

… and you move about with respect and honor for all things and people… and your world becomes the beautiful garden… and you make your way along, then… tending to the garden… with the intention that it be preserved for all future generations to enjoy…"

… a s qua di s di… and so it is good

Ceremony found me early this morning, and so I made my way out into the back garden. Singing the ceremony songs quietly within my head, I set ceremony for this day … and I felt the light as it came in from above…

… and my spirit reached up then… as the light reached down… and it was somewhere in the middle… that we met and became one…

"… set your aim high now, two-legged… and be inspired to go beyond your presumed (and self-set) boundaries… for there is no limit to what you can achieve…,

… and you feel the need to make great changes… and it is true that you must… but it is only in your own heart that change is needed… for all that is required now… is for you to awaken and secure deep within you… genuine and sincere trust and confidence in yourself…,

… and know this now, two-legged… once you make the change from believing that you are bound by circumstance and the acceptance of others… to truly knowing that you can achieve anything you desire… without restriction, limits, or boundaries… *you will*…"

… a s qua di s di… and so it is good

It is an Old One who sits with me in the back garden on this day, an old and wise one from a place I am not familiar. I *feel* the spirit of this one, though, and I know it to be good…

"… young one… remember now… remember back as far as you can… and then go back even further before that… to a place that is old and rich with wisdom… and then settle there in this place… to hear what it is your spirit longs to tell you…,

… for much is there… in the aged wisdom of your spirit… much that is your own wisdom and knowing… and it is not lost there, but only sleeping… and it is asking you to recall… to awaken it and bring it through… and you know how to retrieve it, young one… for it is only a memory away…,

… and so awaken (now) the old grandmother/grandfather within you… and feel the young one stir within, too… for it will be (then) as it has always been… that the kind and loving grandmother/grandfather… teaches the young grandchild… and then the young grandchild returns the teaching back again…,

… and as the young one within brings forth the wisdom… which is innocent and pure… the kind and loving grandmother/grandfather within… takes in this wisdom with clarity and grace… and the circle becomes stronger then… and there is fullness within as well… and a flow that cannot be broken… finds a new path to shape…,

… and this is a place of joy, young one… passed on to you from this Old One who has been watching you… and as you go on and on… you will pass this wisdom on as well… and the circle will become stronger then… and a fullness will become secure… and a flow that cannot be broken… will begin to shape a new path again…,

… and this is how it goes, young one… and it is a task for (all of) you…"

… a s qua di s di… and so it is good

I feel as though there is movement on this day… movement from all around… movement from within… and movement that is certain to be…,

… the morning is beautiful… and the kind (Scottish) Grandfather Wind whispers quietly… so to capture all of my attention… and I listen like a small child… captivated by the quietness of his voice…

"… listen, children… for there is much yet to be known… and yet there is very little room there within you… to store that which is offered to you now…,

… so tidy-up now, children… and gather up those things that have no use anymore… and set these out with a kiss and a wave… for the fine effort and good care they have given you… but with the knowing, too… that it is time to make room for that which you choose to discover… and let that which has been imposed upon you… to just go on its way…,

… and do this from your heart… regarding matters of the heart… and do this from your mind… regarding matters of the mind… and release from your physical body… any trauma, illness, toxins, or disease… and do this in every way you can… move and shake and jump and wiggle… dance and spin and tighten and release…,

… for every part of your being must be tidy and clean… and ready to receive that which is coming to you now… and have no regrets for that which you have kept there within for so long… but miss them not… for they will return in an instant if you do…,

… and notice as you look out into the night… that there is a light… and it is connected right to you… and it is within this light that you must seek… but as you seek you must be sure that you choose… only that which is right for you…"

… a s qua di s di… and so it is good

The Old Standing Ones have gathered around me on this day, and I feel as though I am on a high mountain. There is a feeling of urgency in the air, but there is a feeling of joy and sacredness as well…

"… listen to nature as it becomes more vocal now… and sit with the Old Grandfather Stones… stand as one with the Standing People… and the plants and herbs have much to tell you as well…,

… just as the animals and the movement of the earth and elements… have been speaking to you for many years… be open to all that is happening around you now (in nature)… and listen beyond what your physical ears can hear… for there is wisdom to be taken in now… and it will come from the oldest ones of this Star you know as Earth…,

… there are many two-legged who speak fear about the coming days… but it is the Old Ones you must listen to now… and it is time for you to take in the wisdom and teachings of these… and listen with your inner-sacred… and know that there is no end… only a shifting and a new beginning…,

… and **you** will write the future now, (all) two-legged… and those of you who can… must look out beyond what any other two-legged can foresee… to find truth and all possibility… in the quiet-nothingness **of the void of all potential…,**

… and begin now, (all) two-legged… reaching into **this High Place** for that which comes next… for if you begin from a place that is already bound by restriction and doubt… you will be restricted in what you can achieve… and never make it to the place you are to go next…"

… a s qua di s di… and so it is good

It is Owl who wakes me deep in the night, and she takes me for a journey into the shadows of my own reality. We fly through the darkness with only our sense of knowing, and then come to settle in a place that seems vaguely familiar…

"… there is more than one reality that you can experience here in this earth life of yours… in fact there are many… you do know by now that you can create any reality you desire… you must… for you have done much to create the reality that you are experiencing at this moment…,

… perspective is the issue for you now… and it is the issue for most who are working to expand… trust of that which is in the beyond comes next… and then comes the task of letting go of all those things that you think are your beliefs… but in fact are the beliefs of others (others who are content to trust and believe that which has been told to them)…,

… that is not to say that your entire existence is an illusion… but there are many misconceptions that you live by simply because "it is the way it is"… or is it?…,

… here in this place we have come on this day… you can look into these things you hold as truths… and find for yourself which of these are not truths for you…,

… and this is something you may need to spend some time with… for once you get these sorted out and settled… you will begin to reshape your own reality… and this, in turn, will assist others to reshape theirs…"

… a s qua di s di… and so it is good

I wake on this morning to fog, the heavy fog that rolls in off the North Sea and hovers over all of Edinburgh. I sit within it as I set ceremony for today. It is so thick and heavy that I feel as though I could actually pull it around me.

I was told yesterday about the heavy "Sea Haar" (which is what they call fog that occurs when a bit warm air passes over the cold North Sea air), and now I hear the voice of the Sea… from deep within the heavy *Sea Haar* that has come to sit upon this land today…

"… stay within for a time… and settle your mind to be still… for the voice of your higher spirit has come to speak with you now… and you have found your way to the place where you can understand the words spoken there…,

… you are aligning now… with a higher version of your being… and there is much to understand as you go through this transition… and so you begin by wrapping-up in the protection of the **Sea Haar**… while your spirit and your heart begin to align… and you set these within your physical body when it is time… and then call out for your mind to come in and complete the alignment…,

… and from deep within this place you have emerged… all illusion just fades away… and you look upon that which you can clearly see… and realize it had been there all along… you just hadn't grown tall enough to see it before… and you know now that there will be more… as you grow and expand (even) beyond this…"

… a s qua di s di… and so it is good

I sit among the herbs in the garden on this morning, and they teach me about the *Medicine* they carry. I listen closely as their wisdom pours out upon me, and I feel a knowing expand within me… as I sing the ceremony songs for all people…

"… as you seek to become more… know that it is your first priority to become wise… and so spend some time in quiet meditation… and seek from within yourself… that which has become wisdom…,

… for much of what you are to learn now… will come from your own wisdom… trust your intuitions… and the feelings that speak to you with a strong inner-voice… and remember that you have learned much in your life… and that you have become wise through the experiences of your life…,

… and seek (then)… within your own *self* for the wisdom that you need… and do not be too selfish in sharing your wisdom with others…"

… a s qua di s di… and so it is good

398

I hear the tiny voices of Scottish Fairies as I enter the garden on this day. I set ceremony quietly beside the place where I feel their movement. I whisper (softly) the prayer songs for all people now, and find my way into stillness as the Fairies begin to join me…

"… have you forgotten about reward… for we see only the working… and never the acceptance of reward…,

… and so we set you off with this task for today… to go on and work your good days work… and to settle in with a reward at the end… and look about you then, too… as you recount the events of your day… to notice the rewards that you hadn't before… for it is a fine time to recognize them now…,

… and begin to shape your life in this way… with a good day of work… and a reward a the end… for you must be practiced in recognizing the rewards that you have earned… so not to miss them when they come 'round…,

… and know there have been many rewards you have missed… in your hustling about as you do… but there are many more to be taken in… as you settle into a good and steady pace… and though you are about to receive a grand reward, indeed… mind you now, most are humble and small if you count them one at a time… but they gather-up to be quite grand, indeed…"

… a s qua di s di… and so it is good

The garden walk from my Son's house to the little village where we went yesterday is unexplainably beautiful. The charming cobblestone paths are lined with tall Standing Ones who reach across to touch one another. The age and wisdom of these Standing Ones speak clearly through the expression of the faces peering out from their trunks.

I set ceremony on this day in the back garden as usual, but it is the voices of the old and wise Standing People who speak as I ask for what it is we are to know on this day…

"… **be in the present moment**… it is a simple thing to say but a difficult thing to achieve… for the details of everyday living can pull you in more directions than should be physically possible…,

… but it is essential now… that all two-legged learn to devote some time daily to being in the present… *to truly spend time in the present*… by disconnecting from the details of your everyday life… take a walk in the park or sit in the garden… sit on the beach or hike on the mountain… find a park or even an Old Standing One in your own back yard…,

… the idea is not so much about what you do or where you go… as long as you are taking time to be in the present… to experience the life that exists around you… to not only feel the Wind… but to know him as your Grandfather…,

… for the healing that you are asking for now… for yourselves and for your world… requires you to be true Medicine People… and the first thing you will learn as a true *Medicine Person*… is that healing happens when you stand in the present moment… disconnected from all that came before… and from any expectation of the outcome…"

… a s qua di s di… and so it is good

Yesterday was a typical Scottish day in April, for it rained all day (and all night the night before), but I wake on this day to the promise of Sunshine and calm. The back garden is just overflowing with the fresh aroma of a morning after the rain, and it is the voice of our Mother the Earth who whispers the message we are to know on this day…

"… here now, children… on this day… understand the importance of setting a clear intention… for where your life goes from here… depends on the intentions you are setting now… and it is important where your life goes from here… and so the intentions you set now are important…,

… leave nothing to chance… (but know that there may be some unexpected moments to experience along the way)… and take your first real step forward… be clear and precise when you set your intention… and include even the smallest most personal details…,

… for it is time to stop wallowing around in the frustration of what you don't have or have not achieved… (as if it were the set course of your life)… and manifest the life you have every right to live… (and will be honored from above by achieving)… by setting a clear intention for it now…,

… and be sure to include every aspect of your life, now… from the emotional to the physical… from the spiritual to the workings of your mind… for you are a whole and complete being… and you must know this… that as you move forward to manifest the life you so desire… it will not form correctly or completely… if you do not include all the details in your intention…"

… a s qua di s di… and so it is good

It is an Old Woman who waits for me in the back garden on this morning. She is delicate and airy, and she smells of apple blossoms. But her voice carries wisdom, and she smiles as she tells of our message for today…

"… whatever joy you have come to know… is multiplied when it is shared… and whatever your sadness or pain… will reduce when you accept (or offer) compassion from (or to) another…,

… you walk in partnership with others in many ways throughout your life… and it is these partnerships that build the relationships which support and nourish you… and so honor each interaction with another… however brief or insignificant they may seem…,

… and examine your own perspective of how you live your life… and shift a bit if you must… but begin to move about with the knowing… that everything you so deeply cherish (the earth, your loved ones, your work, all of what assists you to live, any material things you have acquired, and such)… will multiply when shared…,

… and as you share the goodness of your life (and remember to accept that which is offered to you as well)… whether it be through a kind gesture, compassion, support, or the offering of something monetary or material… the sadness and pain of your world will reduce…,

… and you will begin, then… as a whole… as all people… as a world… to live in true partnership with one another… and good relationships will be born… and goodness will expand… and negativity will reduce… and this will become the "way"… and this "way" will live on and on…"

… a s qua di s di… and so it is good

I t is the Old Man Coyote who greets me on this day, and I am surprised to see him (even though I have been feeling his presence for several days). Old Man Coyote is a wise old Medicine Man who shows himself as coyote because he carries the medicine of Coyote, and he only comes when coyote medicine is urgently needed…

"… as you struggle with transition… consider the medicine of Coyote… and go beyond what you know about Coyote Medicine… to find the powerful gift it has to offer you… for Coyote Medicine can deceive and trick you… but Coyote Medicine can help you find your truth… and it is in that truth… that you will find peace, harmony, healing… trust, faith, honesty… (all the things you have been seeking)…,

… you have stepped out of a long and difficult **Winter Time** of your life… and you have been walking in a new **Spring Time** of your life for some time now… too much time to be only this far along… and there is fear and uncertainty within you… and there is the notion that you need more time… and that if you just stop… it will all come together soon enough…,

… but all of these notions are simply wrong… every new experience brings about some fear and uncertainty… and the issue is not that you need more time… or that you are not ready… the issue is that it is not only you who is making a transition at this time… but all people and the whole of your world… including the universe beyond your world… and the difference is… that you have no one to secure to… no one to hold you up (or to hold on to)… for everything and everyone is in motion now…,

… and so you cannot just stop and wait now… for the movement will just continue on… but you can call on Coyote… and Coyote will guide you through… for Coyote can see what is illusion and what is truth… and Coyote will help you reach into you past when it is time... for he knows the way... and Coyote will guide you into your future... for he has been there, too...,

... so, call to you old friend Coyote now... and when you need something to hold onto... for in this new place of constant motion... he is one who can remain still... and ask Coyote anything you need to know... and trust it will be truth... for all of the illusions that you have carried throughout your life... are falling away now... and you must let them go...,

... for in the place that you are heading... only truth can go...”

... a s qua di s di... and so it is good

One of the most stunning sights I have seen since arriving in Scotland during Spring is the beautiful Cherry Trees in full bloom. Many of the garden paths and small residential roads are lined with them, and these Old Standing Ones are so tall and mature that they reach across the paths and roads touching one and other, and creating a natural arbor that just goes on and on.

Today I am greeted by an Old Grandmother spirit who inhabits my favorite Cherry Tree (because I see this one every day), and it is she who offers us our message for today...

“... Spring symbolizes possibility (immeasurable possibility)... but with the knowing that anything is possible... one must also be aware... that this place of all possibility... (the Springtime of anything)... is accompanied by a certain vulnerability... for you are setting out to begin anew... and though you go with all good intentions... walking into the new... will inevitably bring about the unexpected...,

... Springtime also seems to awaken the emotional aspect of two-legged... and though it is good to follow your heart... following your emotions is not... and so it is essential now... to balance your emotions by using all of your senses, at all times... as well as to call upon the highest spiritual guidance you can access...,

... at this time, in real time... it is Spring... but you are also in the Springtime of a much larger kind... the Springtime of transition... and this transition is of a spiritual, emotional, physical, and mental kind… and so be aware of the vulnerable place that you are in… and ever more aware of the vulnerability of others… be patient and tolerant and understanding…,

… expect the unexpected now… and recognize the varying levels of difficulty each may be experiencing… for your emotions will certainly be out in front now… as you are guided by your heart… and emotions always rise up when the heart is involved… but you must use all of your senses now… and engage every aspect of your being… and call upon your highest spirit to awaken and guide you…,

… ah yes… and remember to breathe in the beauty of the new…"

… a s qua di s di… and so it is good

The Cowboy arrived yesterday, and with him came bits and pieces of the eastern plains of Colorado. I slept deeply and content, now that we are all here (all complete)… and I dreamed of home…

… and the Old Ones called to me in the Dreamtime… calling me back from my dreams of life on the prairie… and asking me to reach up now… into the High Place of Spirit… for they have much to show me there…

"… look, child… and see the beautiful people… see the light and perfection in each… and see that each has such a gift to share… and look now… see where they stand… some in front… some way in back… and some are just standing on the sideline waiting… while still more seem to be on the outside, looking in…,

… and there is a calling for all people now… to come in from the outside… to come up from behind… to come in off the sidelines… to stand up and step up… and to come out of their silence… so to speak with the voice from within… the voice that is only theirs… and offer to the world their **Medicine**… and not worry if **all** others agree or accept what they have to share… but to trust that many will…,

… for it is time for all people to move into **becoming**… and as each begins to birth their true spirit… all will begin to find their **kin in spiri**t… and as these families begin to form in spirit… all people will benefit and prosper… and the Star you know as Earth will benefit and prosper, too… and this is important to the healing of all things and all people… for this healing must take place… before the new can awaken and become so…"

… a s qua di s di… and so it is good

The back garden is singing with life as I walk out on this day, and the many Winged who inhabit this particular area of Scotland are already present and ready for ceremony. I listen to them as they fly overhead… and I recognize them one by one…

… but it is the Raven who wants to be heard on this day… and she comes from out of the shadow there… to offer us her message and to wish blessings upon all who have the courage to follow through with their choice to create the life they were born to live…

"… and so you know it is a choice… making changes and creating a new reality… and it can be done… but it will require your own will to keep you and your plan moving forward…,

… and so you must believe in what you have set out to create… and trust in your ability to create it… and you must believe that you are deserving of what you are creating… in order to begin the flow…,

… and you know this… for this is not a new task you take on… but one you have attempted may times before… but the piece you are missing… is in the acceptance of change… for there is this elusive fear hiding away within all two-legged… and it whispers to you deep in the night… and it brings up the questions that have the ability to sabotage even your best attempts… and it moves back into the shadow then… and sits comfortably upon its throne of *same*…,

… and change is difficult… and stressful, and even uncomfortable… and when you set out to make changes… *things change*… and no matter how much you desire to make changes and create a *new*… you fear the change… you fight it…,

… and so know this, two-legged… it will be the changing of the thoughts you think that will assist you best now… it will be reestablishing a relation-ship with your own will… and then letting *your own will* take the lead…,

… and it will require you to mind your thoughts closely… for the old thoughts will work very hard to make sure they are the ones you hear… but you must listen with your spirit now… and consciously write new thoughts to accompany the changes you have set out to make… so that the voice you hear deep in the night … is the one that assures you that you are moving in a good and positive direction…,

… and this will take time and effort and undivided attention… but it will be worth it… for after all… you *are* creating the life you were born to live…"

… a s qua di s di… and so it is good

I sit in the back garden on this day… I set ceremony and sing the prayer songs for all people… I quiet myself for a time of stillness… and it is one single Star-being who breaks through the heavy sleeping Cloud People above me… and moves in to sit with me in stillness, too…

"… you mustn't wait for something big and expansive… to allow yourself to celebrate… for it is through celebrating all things (small and large)… that expands the energy within you… and prepares you to receive more… to create more… to celebrate more…,

… and though there are times it is good to view your life as a whole… remember that in reality… your life is a collection of events and happen-ings… accomplishments and lessons both positive and negative … and each of these are to be celebrated by you…,

… and this is how you raise the vibration of appreciation within you… this is how you become aware of and appreciate everything within and around you… and this energy will soon become a solid part of who you are… and it will call into your life… even more for you to celebrate and enjoy…"

… a s qua di s di… and so it is good

MAY
2011

We spent yesterday exploring the ruins of Tantallon Castle, which is located on the North Sea. It marks the estuary where the North Sea comes into the harbor town there at the Firth of Forth, in Edinburgh... amazing!

Sleep was easy after such a day, and I was not surprised that I returned to Tantallon Castle in the Dreamtime... nor by the message I received just before I woke on this day...

"... close your eyes, children... and find your balance... feel the earth below you and the sky above you... feel the wind as it blows across the cold waters... and welcome in the sun... for it is close above you now...,

... and listen to the past... with honor and respect... and honor the present, too... as you live fully in each moment... and look ahead with hope... as you reach to grasp your future... and reach with confidence that you will know it...,

... and feel yourself become whole... here in this place... and feel yourself expand... as there is nothing to stand in your way... and call your spirit to you... as you feel yourself, *complete*...,

... and begin this new journey... of discovering all that has just awakened within you... for you are expanded now... and balanced in a new way... for from this moment forward... your balance will now include... the knowing of all that has come before... and all that is yet to be..."

... a s qua di s di... and so it is good

Owl came to me in the night, and sits out in the back garden with me as I set ceremony for today. His song is deep and low, and it resembles an ancient drum beat that is meant to guide us into our inner wisdom when we get lost in our life...

... and I find that I am back from a place deep within... and Owl is waiting to be sure I heard his message...

"… strength comes in the joining of your inner being… *your soul*… with your outer life… *all things of the flesh*… and once you bring these together… you will find that by following your own truth… you will discover important secrets of yourself… truths that are spiritual treasures…,

… and it will be, too… as you bring your soul and flesh together… that you find what is right for you… in all ways and at all times… for as long as you remain true to yourself… you own spirit will guide you forward… and keep you on your path of truth…"

… a s qua di s di… and so it is good

The Old One, who waits for me in the back garden on this day, is one I feel I have known through many lifetimes. We sit in ceremony together, and we sing the prayer songs for all people as if we were the same person… we are seamless… we are completely is sync… our hearts hold the same prayers for all people… and the power of our ceremony is intense…

"… come from within the shadows, people… and step into your new life… step up with bold and certain steps… and continue on with courage and grace… for it is your time to lay down those things that tether and weight you… it is your time to step into your rightful place and take charge of your life…,

… break through now… and sing out your own song… have confidence in your own vision… and allow all that you feel and know within… to pour out through your deeds and attitudes… for it is *your* time now… but you must rise up within it… and when you do… the restrictions of the past will fall away… and you will walk freely into your new life…"

… a s qua di s di… and so it is good

Here in this place of old stones and ancient places, I walk through the little village of Kenmore down to Loch Tay. I sit on the bank there and listen as old wisdom stirs around me, as old wisdom stirs within me…

… and I hear the whisper of my Grandfather the Wind… as he blows gently through the trees and across the land… and I feel my Mother the Earth sigh…

... I lay back now, and lose myself in all of this... and my heart begins to sing the prayer songs for all people...

"... and you feel more connected to all that is... as you sit in this place that is old and simple... and you hear the voice from deep within... and you wonder how you will ever hear it again...,

... but you did not have to come here to this place... to find the highest of your being... and you did not just become wise... as you sat down upon this ground... or when you walked among the old grandfather stones... or touched the ancient waters of this loch...,

... for all of what is there within you... was born within you... and it is not this faraway place... that has awakened your **highest being**... it is only that you have taken the time to find it... and that you have allowed a space so to invite it in...,

... and you have lived within the spin of physical life... and you have felt the stillness of your own spirit... and you have worked it all through your heart and mind... and you know the voice of God... for you can hear it...,

... and it is the highest of your being that guides you now... and the highest of your being has guided you always... and your whole life has been a journey... to become your true **Self**... and you worry that you will never know it... but you have always been just who you are... and you have just discovered how to show it..."

... a s qua di s di... and so it is good

The air is heavy with *Scotch* mist as I sit in the back garden, on this, my last day here in Scotland. I feel tears welling up within me, and my heart just cannot hold all the emotion I am feeling now... I wish it would rain...

I sit quietly as I sing the prayer songs for all people... and I release the water from my eyes... but I smile as I see the light from the sky... and I feel my spirit rise... and I smell the sacred smoke of ceremony... and I hear the drums calling... and I am sitting solid upon the ground... but I feel as though I am falling...

"... get your balance now (all people)... and reach out to one another... and join together in hand and heart... for you are growing stronger...,

... and follow your dreams... and reach as far as you can... and then look up... and reach even farther...,

... and gather together... and share what you have... and sing out your wishes... and listen with care...,

... and offer to others... what you would ask... and accept as openly as you receive... and do not stop, but continue on... for it is time for you to **BE**..."

... a s qua di s di... and so it is good

I sit in the back garden after a full day and night of rain. The fragrance of all the flowers and shrubs is intoxicating and completely delicious, and Mother Earth smells sweet and rich.

I feel the magical energy of tree and plant spirits all around me, and the high vibration of the Star People just above the gathering of Cloud People (who have moved in close to join in my ceremony)... and the sense that something new and exciting is about to emerge into our lives is overwhelmingly strong...

"... become receptive now, children... as there is much for you to receive just ahead... and if it is knowledge you call for... it is knowledge you will have... and if you call for happiness and joy... be ready to accept it... for happiness and joy will certainly be yours...,

... it is a time of receiving all of what you call out for... rather than just what you need... and if the two just happen to be the same... then that is what will be waiting for you... so be aware and be specific... as you call out for what you desire... for it is a time of receiving now... and these gifts will come for all..."

... a s qua di s di... and so it is good

After traveling for over twenty-four hours (including an eight-hour layover in London), The Cowboy and I returned home safe and sound (but missing our family in Scotland more than words can express).

I wake early on this day and make my way out to the prairie, where an unexpected and much appreciated surprise awaits…

… for I am greeted on this day by the Spirit Elders of my Cherokee Clan… and it is the wisdom and Medicine of these great (and holy) people from long ago… who speak our message for today…

"… as you set your intentions on providing only good for others to share… good is then provided to and for you… and the goodness that identify the gifts and talents of your very being… will become (then) what nourishes your life and future…,

… and so your life will begin to take shape around your true nature… and what has seemed to be difficult and regarded as the tests of your life… will serve as the greatest of your assets… providing strength, character, wisdom, and credibility… for the journey that is yet to be experienced…,

… a fresh start is upon you now… a new beginning… a second chance… a place of permanence… and you can look ahead now… with excitement and joy… for it is happiness that waits for you… upon this path that you have chosen…"

… a s qua di s di… and so it is good

The morning air is heavy on this day and I walk in a kind of cloudy haze. The prairie smells sweet like rain is coming, though I am told we are not expecting rain today.

I set ceremony quietly in my altar space, and enjoy the company of the Grandfather and Grandmother spirits who have made this their home. I sing the prayer songs for all people and feel my heart expand.

I feel a greater sense of all that surrounds me, as if I am reaching out farther or recognizing more… and I sit with this for a moment as I move into stillness… and it is the voice of the Old Grandfather from the North who speaks to me now… and tells me what it is I seek to know…

"… as you begin to align and harmonize your physical being with the highest of your spiritual being… you will become more sensitive to any inharmonious energy that affects you and your life path… (your intentions, your dreams, your goals, your desires, that which you are set on creating)…,

… it is essential now… to tend to these inharmonious energies promptly and thoroughly… whether they be emotion or thought… take each one to the highest of your spiritual perspective… for in that high place… you will naturally see and know the truth of each…,

… and all illusion will fall away then… and the inharmonious energy will automatically be transmuted…,

… and then… your physical reality will begin to align with your goals and dreams and desires and intentions… and you will feel true harmony… and you will be in charge of your own thoughts and emotions, too…,

… so remember that you can take charge of your thoughts and feelings at any time… and that it is essential for you to be in (conscious) charge of your thoughts and emotions… for in order to achieve the life experience that you desire… you must become permanently aligned with the powerful energy of your Higher Self…"

… a s qua di s di… and so it is good

It is the feeling of emerging from a cocoon that wakes me on this day, and I walk as though I am somewhere in-between the spirit and the body. The sound of wings fluttering all around me seems to lift me even higher, and as I walk into a lighted place, I see that Moths have guided me here…

"… quiet yourselves, children… and stop for a time… breathe with the slightest of breath… and make no sound… move into the innermost part of your being… and listen with the highest of all your senses… for you are awakening to an even higher aspect of your being… and your inner-sacred is rising to the surface now…,

... and this is transformation from the inside out... and your physical body is the symbolic cocoon... that your sacred spirit is emerging from within... and however old your spirit is... it comes new again now... and do not discount the importance of your body... for it has done its job well... and still has more to do...,

... and you will change now, children... for the journey that lies ahead for you... cannot be accomplished in the same old ways that once served you well... but the transformation has begun... and it will continue to pull you along and through... and if you avoid resistance... you will succeed with great reward..."

... a s qua di s di... and so it is good

As I stand on the open prairie... I smell rain... and I call out to all of the nature spirits... ***"yes rain"***...

... for there is fear upon this land these days... fear that is valid and strong... it originates deep within each and every farmer and rancher and home-owner who live on this prairie... for the danger of fire is great and becoming greater... as our thirsty prairie becomes more and more dry...

... I walk in the cool damp morning air now... and sing out prayers for nourishment to fall upon the land... and I listen as the voices of people who dwell in every other place upon our Great Mother Earth... call out for their fears to be eased as well... for if it is not fire that is feared... it is flooding... tornados... hurricanes... earthquakes... famine... poverty... disease... hate... war...

... and so I call out for nourishment to fall upon all people in all places... and for whatever it is that is needed... to become plentiful... and for whatever it is that destroys and hurts and takes and devastates... to be banished away...

... and I sit upon the top of the small knoll... and look out across the prairie... as Father Sun casts his first light of this day upon it... and I feel the fears that live deep within me begin to stir... and I sigh at how much (more) I have yet to conquer... from that place of uncertainty within me...

"… fear is a part of living in the physical… and it is as necessary as trust (and every other emotion)… for it creates a balance… it leads you to grow and learn and mature… to explore what lives deep within… and to find your strengths… as you face your fears… and to find your compassion… as you step up to assist another…,

… fear has come to symbolize weakness in the minds of many… but it is a strong and courageous person who will stand up and face their fears… and it is a wise and learned person who knows the value of lessons brought about by working through fear…,

… you have set upon a journey… by accepting this gift of life… and you have come to a place on your journey… where exploring when and where (in your past… in your life) your fears became fears, is essential… and with the greatest of compassion (and taking them one at a time)… it is time to conquer each…,

… for as you discover and work through the source of each fear… you will discover more about who you are… and the changes you desire to make, but just can't quite manage… will begin to manifest then… for deep at the root of everything you wish to change about your life and your *Self*… is a fear… and once exposed and conquered… each fear then creates a victory…"

… a s qua di s di… and so it is good

I stand in gratitude as I step out on this morning, for the Cloud People have brought us **rain**. Grandfather Wind blows strong and fierce today, too… and so I call upon the Wind and Rain to cleanse me as I turn to each direction and sing out my **gratitude.**

I wrap my blanket around me as I sit for ceremony here at my altar. I face the East, and I hear the Keeper of the West calling for me to hear his words on this day…

… and as I sing the prayer songs for all people… I feel myself move into the place of **sacred dreams**…

"… yes child… it is time to dream… to find your way into your own inner-sacred… and to sit by the fire of your own spirit… for the Universe is awake and open… and is calling you to move into alignment…,

... and once you align yourself with the Universe... from that purest fire that burns within... (and the whole of your being)... you will see the path that guides your way... for light will come from within it... and you will create your future then... from the place of your own inner-knowing..."

... a s qua di s di... and so it is good

Istand in gratitude as I look out my front door and see the snow. A full day of rain and a full night of snow, what a gift... a *li he li ge...*

I walk in the heavy wet snow as I pray **gratitude**, but I set ceremony at my altar inside. I sit wrapped in my blanket, and I sing the prayer songs for all people as Grandfather Wind whistles at the door. I light the sacred smoke and breathe in the spirit of all who came before... and I feel the presence of the "Little People" (*nun ne hi*) gather around me as I move into stillness...

"... we came in with the snow... and we announce a time of transformation... for the snow has come and it covers the land... and it brings the nourishment that has been too long coming... and when it has finished... the land will be renewed... transformed from brown to green... and it will be a time of growing, then...,

... and this is your time of transformation as well, two-legged... for you will find yourselves *within* for a (short) time... and when you emerge... you will have left some old things behind... and you will have welcomed in much that is new... and it will be your time for growing, too...,

... and you have experienced many times of transformation and growth... throughout the journey of your life... and it is true that any time can be a time to shift and change and grow... but do not take this time for granted, dear two-legged... for we have brought a special gift with us this time... and we give it to each of you now...,

... it is the ability to turn around completely... to change that which has been extreme... to the positive of its opposite..."

... a s qua di s di... and so it is good

I feel extremely high energy as I wake on this day. In fact it is the vibration of this energy that wakes me so early. I move with excitement and curiosity as I gather my ceremony bundle and make my way out onto the prairie… where Coyote, Wolf, Lion, Bear, and Owl await my arrival.

I stand for a moment to honor this beautiful *prairie song*, and then I make my way across the wet grass and muddy road to the Grandfather Prayer Circle. I hear the ancient voices of the Old Grandfathers as I settle myself upon the Old Grandfather Stone in the East… and I realize just before I begin ceremony… that it is *Friday the Thirteenth* … and a smile beams across my face as I realize why the energy is vibrating so high today…and maybe this is a good opportunity to explain…

…for *Friday the Thirteenth* energy has been so misunderstood for so long… I feel that it is important to offer some recognition (and explanation) to the positive energy everyone will feel on this day.

Extremely high energy can be disturbing to some folks, and adjusting to the higher vibration can bring about frustration as well as a sense of unrest. It can shake you up and throw you off balance if you are not used to riding the higher vibrations (kind of like the Full Moon phenomenon). But if one is prepared and open to receive, this energy will bring about amazing experiences and opportunities.

I settle into ceremony now, with the Grandfathers who sing their ancient songs and the prairie singing its morning song in the background… and it is the wisdom of the elders that flow into my circle now… and I listen as their wisdom speaks our message for today…

"… wisdom is your message for today, young one… for as the energy of this higher vibration awakens and expands you each… it is the perfect time to recognize the wisdom you have gained through your life experiences to now…,

… and so set out on this day as *wise ones*, children… be open to whatever experience comes your way… and allow yourselves to connect to and with the higher vibration that is so readily available for you now… for if you do… you will have gained a higher perspective… and you will experience life from that higher perspective… and your questions will become your wisdom… for you will see and know (now, and into the future)… the truths of what has frustrated and confounded you for so long…"

… a s qua di s di… and so it is good

I walked the prairie early this morning, my feet sinking into the soft damp earth. I felt the cold as it penetrated my skin and chilled me all the way down to my bones, and I breathed in the smoke of my ceremony fire…

… then I woke up… and found myself snug in my bed… Wow… What was that?…

… and then I noticed a feeling that came from deep within my heart… not words… not images… but a feeling… and that feeling spoke to me about the power (and danger) of illusion…

"… it is a time now… when each must be honest, accurate, credible, trustworthy, and impeccable in every way… especially with one's own *Self*… for the ability to discern truth… especially when so much change is happening within and around you each… is about to become more of a challenge than it has ever been…,

… for as your vibrations rise… you will become more and more aligned with the highest of your own spirit… as well as with (God, Creator), the Universe… and you will begin to rely more and more on your own inner guidance… and the question of truth verses illusion will become your greatest adversary… especially while you are adjusting to the higher vibrations and energy…,

… for illusion is strong and powerful… and it can seem so real… especially when spun by one who has mastered the art… (and each two-legged has spun illusion sometime in their life)… and no matter how innocent or justifiable that illusion was or is… it is time to make the shift from working in or with illusion… to working in and with truth…,

… for it is difficult (enough) to believe the visions and messages you receive from within (at first)… and it is easier to question whether you are making it all up…

or if it is true guidance (just as you always have)… until you have experienced enough truths to convince you… until you have stepped away from that thing called illusion in every way… (and this process will be different for each)…,

… truth knows truth… and illusion breeds illusion (deception)… and so as you move forward now… it is essential that you focus on your own impeccability… be honest, truthful, trustworthy, accurate, credible… especially with yourself… for it is the little lies that you tell yourself… that continue to feed the doubt within you… and there is no room for doubt now…,

… for change is upon you (all)… and as everything continues to change and shift around and within you… the ability to discern that which is truth and that which is illusion… will become more and more essential…"

… a s qua di s di… and so it is good

It is Grandmother Willow who greets me as I walk out into the early morning. She is fluid and flexible and supple, replenished by the rain and snow we have received here on the plains recently.

I stand for ceremony on this day and feel my heart connect with Grandmother Willow (as we stand facing one another), and it is through the connection of our hearts, that I receive the message for today…

"… it is a weaving that I show you on this day, grandchild… a weaving of all that has been your life… and as you look at this weaving… see that it is beginning to take shape… for you are beginning to consciously shape the spiritual aspect of yourself…,

… and as you look at this weaving… see the basket begin to form… see the support that you have woven into your being… and see the places where you are strong and sturdy… see the roundness of your basket… and see how flexible you have become (so to bend smoothly enough to become round)…,

… and they are wise and gracious hands that weave your basket… and they carry the gift of healing and vision and even an element of magic… and all of what is held within this being… lives within your basket…,

… so look now, dear grandchild… at the one who weaves your basket… and know that being is you…"

… a s qua di s di… and so it is good

I sit within my own sacred space as Grandfather Wind blows around me. I disconnect from all that occupies my mind and from every ache and pain. I release all feelings of emotion (positive or negative) as well as of being cold, and I call to my highest self (my true spirit) to come…

… I slip into stillness as I sit cocooned in the warmth and light my spirit brings… and I discover an entire new world exists here…

"… it is time for you (each) to take time now… to get to know the way of your true spirit… for life experienced from within this place… is rich with wisdom, guidance, happiness, joy… peace, balance, harmony… and the explanation of all of those things that continue to confound you…,

… and your entire being begins to blend… as you spend more and more time here in this place… your heart, mind, and emotions begin to blend together with the purity and perfection of your spirit… as you become more acquainted with the space of your highest/true spirit… and your vibrations rises (then) as your consciousness expands…,

… and you know this place… you have found many ways to reach it along the spiritual path of your journey… you come here often to be in this space… and this is good… and now it is time for you to explore this space as if it were a place of interest in the physical world… as if it were a place that you want to immerse yourself in and explore with great intent…,

… so come now… settle into the sacred place of your spirit… and expand yourself into it… let go of all the worries and woes of the physical world… let go of all obligations and concerns that bind you to another… (for this is the only place you have to be at this moment)… and give your full attention to this space… experience all that it has to offer… and be (then) ***fully in spirit***…,

… for the vibration of your Star (your earth) is trying to rise… and so the negative energy is doing its best to prevent that rise… and it is time now for all and any who have the notion, desire, ability, and generosity to raise their own vibration… to do so…,

… for as each **one** raises their own vibration… in whatever way they can… the vibration of your Star raises and expands… and others are inspired to raise their vibrations, too…,

… and this is good work, dear ones… this is very good work indeed…"

… a s qua di s di… and so it is good

It seems like a long time since I have seen our Grandmother the Moon, and for some reason I feel the need for her compassionate grace now more than ever. It must have been my heart that called out for her to come, sometime deep in the night. And being the kind and compassionate Grandmother she is, she was there waiting for me as I walked out onto the prairie this morning…

"… rain and moon, grandchild… that will stir emotion every time… you know this… and so move beyond the question **why**… to see the answers that are lighted for you now…,

… your heart is like the river, grandchild… fluid and flowing… and all things connected to and with your heart… must be able to bend and flow… like the river… but mind the current now… for it moves faster than it appears to be…,

… and your life is the structure that stands upon that river… and it has always been sturdy and strong… holding up to and weathering anything that has come its way… and there have been many times over the course of your life… that the structure of your life has been challenged and threatened… and you have done well to repair and strengthen that structure… (your life as it stands)… for you are the one who built it… through each and every experience from birth to now…,

… but look here, grandchild… for you are certainly aware of the rise in vibration and shifting of energy taking place upon your Star… and have you not noticed that these are significant changes emotionally and physically and mentally… as well as spiritually… and that the course of your river is changing… and that the structure of your life must change now, too… in order to remain strong and sturdy throughout…,

… so examine the structure of your life, now… and notice if it is strong and supporting… and if it is built to be flexible and able to bend with the flow if it must… is it open enough to allow the changing waters to flow through… or has it become a cage that holds you tight within it… and will it rise as your river rises… and remain sturdy all the way (holding onto its truth)… or will it let go and follow the flow… weaving and toppling along…,

… and you may feel that these are only more questions… added to the ones that caused you to call out for me, dear grandchild… and you may feel as though you are struck in the muddy waters, there on the bank of that river of yours… but pull yourself up now… and sit upon that bank… and watch as your river flows by… and listen to its song as it moves along before you…,

… and look for my light as it shines upon your river… and you will see the answers that you called out to know…"

… a s qua di s di… and so it is good

The Cloud People have come to sit in council with us and our Mother the Earth.

I walk slow and quiet as I make my way across the prairie this morning (by memory rather than sight), for I can see only one step ahead as I walk. I hear the animals and winged who have already joined in the council, and I feel the presence of the others who have come in spirit. The fragrance of the prairie tells me that all plant life has arrived as well, and I hear the ocean from deep in the south… ah… the swimming ones are here, too…

… and so it begins… the gathering for this day… lead by Grandmother Moon… whose light is so strong… that it cast a soft blue glow upon the prairie as it comes through the density of the Cloud People…

"… there is a sacred flame within you each… and that flame is supported and nourished by all that resides within the High Place… call them spirits, guides, angels, or ancestors… the support and nourishment they offer is pure and true… and it is infinite… never-ending…,

… become aware of that flame within you, now… and call upon your spirits, guides, angels, or ancestors to support and nourish you as your flame begins to expand within you… your mind will receive knowledge, then… and your heart, unconditional love… your body will be replenished, healed, and strengthened… and your spirit will speak to you in ways you have not known before…,

… for this is a time of birth for many… and of re-birth for others… of kindling the sacred flame… and of rekindling, too… and as this flame grows stronger within… so does the power of transformation… and in this time of renewal and change… you will move smoothly and swiftly… for you will have already begun… and you will have the power, support, and nourishment from within and from without…"

… a s qua di s di… and so it is good

Another good rain for us here on the eastern plains of Colorado, but the power of the cleansing brought about by these Rains, is available to and for all. For it is a symbolic Rain that comes to us each deep in the night, and washes away all of those layers of protection we have built up over the years… and awakens us to the purity of our true emotions…

"… and it is fear that causes you to layer protection around your heart (your emotions)… and where there is fear there is the need for trust… and it is the ability to communicate that will restore your trust now… and it is not only what you need to say that constitutes communication… but what you are willing to hear as well…,

… so look from within now… and examine the skin you have layered around you… is it thick and dense… or thin and strong… does its color speak of the kind of protection you require… or the kind of fear you have experienced… and where have you built these layers… around your heart, your mind, the whole of your physical being… or is it your eyes, your ears, your crown (spirit)…,

... stand in the rain now, children... and trust the sacred waters that fall from the High Place... and let your true-self (spirit) assure you... as you *will* yourself to trust... and open the channels of communication, then... so to speak your truth out to the Universe... and you will be given guidance then, children... for then you will be ready to hear it..."

... a s qua di s di... and so it is good

I feel the presence of two spirits as I walk out on this day. An old and ancient being who feels very wise, and a young spirit who gives me the sense of birth or rebirth. But it is just one being that I see there in the darkness, and this one appears to be neither infant nor old one...

"... it is your task now to create your future... and as you do... you will co-create the future for all people... and so it is that you must reach back... into your own past... (as well as the past of this Star you know as Earth)... for you will need to use the wisdom gained from reaching back... to help you create a future that is new and good and strong...,

... and it is a wise one, indeed... who takes on this task... who reaches back in order to go forward... and who can look far enough ahead to see what must be done now...,

... for the future is uncertain... and unstable if left to chance... and it is a solid foundation that is called for... from the hearts and souls of all who wait to be born into it..."

... a s qua di s di... and so it is good

I hear voices as I walk out on this day, a soft muttering of voices that come from all around me. I set ceremony quickly as I prepare for this day, and the voices come in closer. I sit for a time of stillness before singing the prayer songs for all people, and I feel the happiness and joy of the words they speak.

Voices of all people, in every language, seem to be speaking the same message… a prayer of gratitude for the blessings of their lives… a prayer of gratitude for life itself.

I sing the gratitude song now, and feel within my own being… gratitude for all I have been blessed with in my life… and as I sing the prayer songs for all people… the voices of all people rise up… and sing out loud and strong…

"… and heaven is coming closer to you now… and you are rising up to greet it… and as you step forward into this new day… know that a shift has occurred…,

… so let your spirit sing… and rise up within you… and honor your physical body… for it is the house of your spirit… and open your heart… to give as well as receive… and open your mind, too… for it has much to take in as well…,

… and as you bring all aspects of your being together as one… let it be your intention… to live as one people… to honor the path of each and every one… and that which each one has to offer… just as you have come to honor each and every aspect of your own *Self*…"

… a s qua di s di… and so it is good

It is a still morning here on the prairie and I stand in silence as I breathe in the quiet. I move slowly and with mindful, deliberate steps. I set ceremony and sit for a time in quiet contemplation before I begin…

… and the prayers for all people come now… low and soft at first… and then they rise up… in vibration as well as sound… I feel them before I hear them…

… and light comes now, too… not from any one place… but from all around me… as if I were suddenly held within a ball of light…

… I have no idea how long I was there… in the center of that brilliant sphere of light… and I cannot say how I came to be back on the prairie… surrounded by the ceremony I set this morning… but I do have a very clear knowing of the message I received during that time…

"... the time of building has begun... and it is a time of patience now... for that which you are building... will become the foundation for all future generations to build upon as well...,

... and this is a time to tend to every detail... and mind the order as you go... take no short cuts... do not skip ahead... and make good use of all the materials and tools you have acquired...,

... keep your thoughts positive... and focus on the outcome you desire... and when you get discouraged... return to the quiet place... so to see again your vision... stay above the shadows, now... and hold steady in the light... for the time of building has begun... and all are welcome to join in..."

... a s qua di s di... and so it is good

I sit in stillness this morning, and watch Father Sky awaken. I close my eyes then, to feel the presence of Creator around me. I *feel* the prayer songs for all people within my entire being, and then I feel all that stirs within me... begin to pour out...

"... into this sacred space... pour out all that you have stored within... do not distinguish positive or negative... right or wrong... good or bad... light or dark... for today is not about any of those... today is about becoming empty...,

... how long has it been since you have become empty... how long since your intention has been to open wide and welcome in... all the new that is to be known... how long since you have examined... the entire contents of your beliefs... how long since you have looked in on... who you have become...,

... but there is more to becoming empty... than just pouring out so to examine and purge... and there is more to becoming empty... than preparing a space within to receive... or to see the results of all the work you have done... or even to find a way to recognize who you have become...,

... for it is important to understand another *Medicine* of being empty now... for to spend time (from time to time) in the state of emptiness... is to feel how it is to be without burden, concern, worry, or woe... as well as without joy, achievement, belief, knowing, wisdom, and the like...,

… for spending time in emptiness… is how you find true appreciation for all that you have, all that you are, and for that which is your own unique gift… and when you rest for a time from all of everything that makes your life, your life… you encounter a clarity that is truly clear…

… and it is your spirit (then) that fills the empty space… and it is your spirit (then) that guides you to step forward with direction and grace… for you have glimpsed your own **Truth** in that place of emptiness… and it has shown you who you are…"

… a s qua di s di… and so it is good

It is my Grandmother who waits for me on this day. I see her there at my altar singing the morning song. I move quickly as I make my way across the road, though I walk with respect as I approach the place where she sits…

… Grandmother stands to greet me now… and our hearts touch as we reach to embrace one another… and everything begins to spin… *a spiral?… a circle?… the moving forward in time?…* I know I feel movement… but what is the circular motion of this movement that I feel…

"… granddaughter… it is the bringing together of wisdom and innocence… (the knowing of the past with the visions of the future)… that you feel… and as we connect… we stand at the most precious part of the circle… for we mark the end of one time and the beginning of another…,

… close your eyes as I sing the old songs to you, granddaughter… and I will beam with joy as I listen to the new songs you sing… and as we sing our songs together, granddaughter… you will feel a shift… as the songs that we sing come together and blend… as the past and the future unite to create a new vibration…,

… and many are working in this same way, granddaughter… and you must encourage others to take part as well… for it will be the wisdoms of the past… and the visions of the future… that come together and blend, so to create something new…,

... and this will calm the static that has brought about *disease*... and this will bring about the healing that all the people need..."

... a s qua di s di... and so it is good

The Grandfathers call me on this morning, and so I walk to the Grandfathers circle of stones. I slow as I near them, and I pause as I stand at the opening in the East...

"... come in, young grandmother... come and sit within our council... listen to our stories... and we will hear yours as well... for you have called out to know the wisdom that lives within you... and we have come to be sure you know it...,

... and this was a good council, young grandmother... your wisdom has been heard... but how can we say we have heard your voice... when you know you did not speak... and how can we hear you now as you ask this question... could it have been some other greater being that we heard, you wonder... and why did you not hear it, too...,

... it is your own wisdom that speaks from deep within, young grandmother... and it is your own voice that whispers in the silence between thoughts and words... and it is not a question of knowing that you are wise... it is a question of whether you have come to accept that you are...,

... for you are wise enough to know... that with the accepting that you carry wisdom... comes the responsibility to make your own choices... and then you must acknowledge... that those choices have been yours and yours alone...,

... so listen now, young grandmother... as you sit within this council... and hear these words we speak (from that wise place deep within)... and know our words are truth...,

... it is not that you must seek to know your own wisdom... but that you must release the fears that keep you from trusting it..."

... a s qua di s di... and so it is good

Grandfather Wind is doing his best to push me as I walk on this day, but I am warm and steady and peaceful as I make my way out to the prayer circles. I sit in silence as I watch Father Sun bring light upon the prairie, and I am spellbound by the rich colors that bring an even deeper sense of peace and harmony within me.

I sit wrapped in my blanket now, and Grandfather Wind blows around me. I sing the prayer songs for all people, and I offer this knowing of peace to **all** …

"… it is by your own vibration… that you can remain balanced, steady, peaceful, and in harmony with your highest spirit… even while there is turmoil, chaos, static, and disorder all around you…,

… and as you hold this higher vibration… even if only for a few moments at a time… you will naturally share the peace and harmony of it… with the environment around you… including any other two-legged who is near…,

… and the ability to remain in **high spirit** during times of chaos will become natural then… and without effort or thought… others will begin to strive to reach that place of peace and harmony as well…,

… and a higher vibration will become available and accessible to all beings then… and a shift will be made by the whole… and this will all begin again… as more people realize the raising of their vibration… and then even more will begin to feel and follow…,

… and this will become a circle… and the circle will move quick and steady… as more and more become the guides… for others to feel their spirits awaken within… and there will be no limit then… to how high and how far you can go…"

… a s qua di s di… and so it is good

Hawk calls me early on this day, and I emerge from deep within the Dreamtime. I walk out feeling low and heavy, knowing that I cannot fly with Hawk as long as I am weighted by whatever it is that creates this heaviness within me. Is it physical or emotional weight that calls out to be released? Is it something weighing on my mind, or is it a spiritual lifting I need at this time?...

... Hawk circles above me now and beckons me into the stillness... telling me the answer is there waiting...

"... look in on your present environment, two-legged... check the balance and alignment of all aspects of your being... do this daily... but do this consciously and consistently throughout each day as well...,

... for life will always bring about the unknown and the unexpected... and as a physical being... you will always be offered at least two ways to act or react in any situation... and when you are balanced and aligned... you will always choose the most appropriate way...,

... and you will find the path before you much easier to travel then... and when it is rough and difficult to travel... it is because there is something for you to experience... and if you look upon each experience as the gift it is... each experience will serve you throughout your journey of life... and offer you growth and self-awareness... and all of this will lead to self-discovery...,

... rise up now, two-legged... and fly high as you seek to follow your path... make your choice to find and follow the highest road, deliberate... and be conscious of this choice at all times... for once you choose to live by your own higher guidance (your spirit)... you will become a higher being... and you will fly above that bumpy road then... rather than stumble upon it..."

... a s qua di s di... and so it is good

I can see the impression of my foot (toes and all) in the soft earth as I walk (the soil here is mostly clay). Even though the earth is dry enough to walk on, it is soft enough to form the impression of my foot through the thin skin of my moccasins. I can even see the place where I sat in ceremony yesterday.

I find the place I am to set ceremony on this day now, and I wrap my blanket around me. Grandfather Wind has come again to the prairie, and I feel the need to be within while he does his work around me…

"… clay is your message on this day, Swan… for it is time to become serious about the material aspect of your life… and how you will shape it… and even though your spirit will be your guide… it will be your own hands that do the work… for your spirit will bring about the vision and truth that you seek… but it is you… in your physicality… that will make that vision a reality…,

… spend time in stillness now, (all people)… and call for your vision… then call for your creativity to rise up within you… and trust the inspiration that comes… and become like clay then, (all people)… and begin the shaping of you (of your life as you have seen it)… for it is time to become serious about the material aspect of your life… and it is your own hands that must step up to shape it…"

… a s qua di s di… and so it is good

Owl comes for me on this day, waking me early and taking me back into the Dreamtime…

… I fly with Owl now… through the gathering of Cloud People who have come as guides on this day… and then through the clear soft blue of the (lower) inner Sky… up and up… and into the deep blue of the (higher) outer Sky… and then through a space of black… that shifts our journey from going up… to going back… back through time…

… and I recognize this journey as I fly with Owl… and I recognize the young Mother Earth as we fly low and close across her… and she is rich and sweet and open and vast… and I smell the freshness of the air as we land to walk upon her… and all the animals have come to greet and welcome us… and we move quickly as we follow them into the cave where they are holding council…

"… be mindful of the rhythms of the earth now (all people)… and watch the animals closely… for they have been listening, watching, gathering, and collecting… and they are asking for you to hear what they have to say…,

… animals may appear to you in many ways… by actually crossing your path… or by showing up in other ways… and it is important now… that you open your minds to the subtle message each animal brings to you…,

… for the animals are speaking as guides now… and by allowing yourselves to awaken to the qualities of the animals who show up for you… you will realize a deeper connection to the rhythms of the earth… and this connection will show up in ways that are specific to and for your own path and journey… and your consciousness will expand then… to a more sensitive awareness of the rhythms of the earth… which will directly effect you and those around you…"

… a s qua di s di… and so it is good

I see the old village as I walk out on this day. In the dim light of dawn, I see the people building their village. The ancestors, who walked this land so long ago, come today in spirit, to show us the importance of working together to build something strong and safe, beautiful and kind, welcoming and supportive…

"… light the **sacred fire** that lives within you, young-ones… for it will be by your eagerness and passion to build something new… that something new will become…,

… and begin with the notion that many will be needed and many will assist… rather than the idea that this is solely your project and responsibility…,

… for to build something that will embrace and nurture all things and beings… all things and beings must be included in the creation…,

… and all will come then… to do their part… and each will share their gift and wisdom… as the building continues to expand…,

… and there will be unity and wholeness then… and respect and honor for that which has been created… for each will have done their part… and each will be equally welcome…"

… a s qua di s di… and so it is good

I walk up the road on this morning, and into the trees. The morning is still and yet I hear the elders of the Standing Ones calling me. Deep into their village I go now, quietly and respectfully… and I take my place in their circle as they begin their ceremony for today…

"… with attention to and for all people (all beings)… we stand rooted in our Mother the Earth… we stand steady and strong as life continues to move around us… and we watch as the changes tell us of the hearts and minds of the people…,

… and we stretch up throughout the days and nights of our lives… to draw down the light from the High Place… and we reach up in celebration and gratitude then… for the grace brought through by the light…,

… and we see from this highest place… all that we can… and we listen to the winged… who light on our branches… for they fly high and far… and they see what we can only sense… and our Mother speaks to us then… for she knows the hearts of all her children…,

… and so our knowing is clear and expanded… and our wisdom grows with each generations that comes… and we have kept this ground solid for yours to live upon… and we promise to keep this ground solid for many more to come…,

… and we call this to your attention now… and we place within your care… this seed… which is to be planted and nourished, cared for and tended to…

... so become still for a time... and breathe quiet and slow... let your feet take root and your arms take flight... and feel the life within you expand... as you are fed by the earth and nourished by the sky...,

... and do not think now... but let your senses speak... for here in this moment you have become a Standing One... and you must linger here for as long as you can... and wait... for the Old Ones will come to guide you... and you can go as far back as you need to go then... and as far forward as you are able...,

... and you will learn how to give and receive with balance and grace then... and you will know the importance of this... and you will understand how important it is to seek your own knowing... and how to trust it, too... and how valuable it is to hear the knowing of others... and to honor the teachings of their journey as well..."

... a s qua di s di... and so it is good

ABOUT THE AUTHOR

My *Spirit* name is Black Tail Swan, my birth name is Eva. I have been working as a *Medicine Elder* for many years. It is always difficult for me to figure out what information about myself people will want to know. I am a private person when it comes to who I am and what I do, but it is really the integrity of a *Medicine Person* that makes it difficult for me to write or speak about myself in this way.

Walking our *Medicine Path* (living our life purpose) is the true reason we are here. My tradition teaches that once we realize our life purpose, we are to go about living it with humility, truth, and grace. We put our energy and emphasis on the work we do rather than on talking about it. We simply walk our path.

That said, I can tell you that I have been teaching Native American Spirituality for many years. The Native American part of my ancestry is Cherokee and Salinan. Many Elders have called me "*a master of the Medicine Tools,*" for I have been making (and teaching others to make their own) *Medicine Tools* for many years. I walk an old and traditional path when it comes to *Medicine Work,* and I teach from tradition as well.

CLASSES BY EVA BLACKTAIL SWAN

My classes include making drums (medicine drum, shaman drum, pebble drum, and healing drum), rattles (snake rattle, dance rattle, medicine rattle, shaman rattle, turtle rattle, and others), medicine bags, shaman pouch, and medicine wheel. I also teach several personal empowerment classes such as:

"The Simplicity of Spirit"   "Living your Truth"

"Returning to the Truth"   "Awakening your Medicine".

CREATOR'S SONG DAILY MESSAGES

**If you are interested in subscribing to Creator's Song,
please email me at: weareonepeople@blacktailswan.net.**

As a Creator's Song subscriber, you will receive the current Creator's Song message daily via email, and your spirit will be present during my morning ceremony each day.

For more information about Eva Black Tail Swan or the work she does please visit: www. blacktailswan.net

www.ingramcontent.com/pod-product-compliance
Lightning Source LLC
Chambersburg PA
CBHW050955210726

48287CB00004B/1238